CULTURALLY SENSITIVE SUPERVISION AND TRAINING

Culturally Sensitive Supervision and Training is a comprehensive text that exposes readers to an array of culturally attuned approaches to supervision and training. The book consists of contributions from a culturally and professionally diverse group of scholars and clinicians who have been on the frontline of providing culturally sensitive supervision and training in a variety of settings. A major portion of the book provides the reader with an insider's view of clinical-teaching strategies as well as a plan for implementation, with one chapter devoted to experiential exercises that enhance cultural sensitivity in supervision and training. Part One examines the importance of the use of self in supervision and training, providing a framework for incorporating a multicultural relational perspective within supervision and training. Part Two explores how race, sexual orientation, class, and other dimensions of diversity affect supervision and training. Part Three focuses on specific strategies for integrating and promoting cultural sensitivity in supervision and training. Part Four addresses tactics for negotiating difficult dialogues and focuses on the specifics of executing diversity-related conversations. The text is intended for use in supervision courses, in classroom settings, and in any educational forum in which diversity-related issues are addressed.

Kenneth V. Hardy, PhD, is a professor at Drexel University in Philadelphia, Pennsylvania and is also director of the Eikenberg Institute for Relationships in New York, New York. He is the former director of clinical training and research at Syracuse University in New York as well as the former director of The Center for Children, Families, and Trauma at the Ackerman Institute for the Family in New York, New York. Dr. Hardy has had extensive experience training and supervising both beginning and seasoned therapists working in a variety of clinical settings.

Toby Bobes, PhD, is a licensed marriage and family therapist with experience in teaching graduate-level courses for 24 years and doing clinical supervision for 18 years. She currently teaches at Pacifica Graduate Institute and formerly taught at Antioch University. Her career includes 28 years in private practice. Dr. Bobes has taught many supervision courses for the California Division of the American Association for Marriage and Family Therapy, and she is an AAMFT Approved Supervisor and a CAMFT Certified Supervisor.

"This refreshingly honest book pushes the boundaries of supervision and training by challenging supervisors and trainees to explore how their cultural identities inform their clinical work. Hardy, Bobes, and colleagues masterfully demonstrate how to have difficult cross-racial conversations, including experiential exercises that move trainees from awareness to self-reflection. Given the increasing need to understand the vastly different lived experiences of our changing world, this book trains clinicians to be part of that moral imperative."

—**Laurie S. Kaplan, LCSW,** Co-Director, Diversity and Social Work
Training Program, Ackerman Institute for the Family, New York

"*Culturally Sensitive Supervision and Training* will not only become a must-read for supervision courses and classes in psychology, counseling, or other educational forums, but will be an invaluable resource for practitioners longstanding in the field as well as those newly in practice. The readings will not only validate some of current therapists' experiences, but will help guide them to take new, more effective paths in their work. This is an outstanding, most welcomed contribution to the field!"

—**Matthew R. Mock, PhD,** Professor of Counseling Psychology,
John F. Kennedy University

"The family therapy field finally has a supervision text of supreme quality that focuses our attention on self of the therapist work and dimensions of culture! Unlike other supervision texts, it doesn't just give a cursory nod to culture. It provides a clear theoretical framework for understanding dimensions of culture and the relationship to power, privilege and oppression. This book is a resource that should be a required text for all MFTs and AAMFT Approved supervisors."

—**Cadmona A. Hall, PhD, LMFT, FT,** AAMFT Approved Supervisor,
Associate Professor, Department of Couple & Family Therapy, Adler University

"*Culturally Sensitive Supervision and Training* takes a bold step in the right direction for those interested in integrating a culturally-sensitive and affirmative approach into their supervisory experience. Grounding the reader in both theory and practice-based examples in areas such as the use of the self-as-therapist, Hardy and Bobes provide deep insights into the effective practice of supervision intended to transform practice. A must-read for clinicians at all levels of experience in the field."

—**Tricia Stephens, LCSW-R, PhD,** Clinical Social Work
Practitioner and Supervisor, Hunter College

CULTURALLY SENSITIVE SUPERVISION AND TRAINING

Diverse perspectives and practical applications

Edited by
Kenneth V. Hardy
Toby Bobes

LONDON AND NEW YORK

First published 2016
by Routledge
711 Third Avenue, New York, NY 10017

and by Routledge
2 Park Square, Milton Park, Abingdon, Oxon, OX14 4RN

Routledge is an imprint of the Taylor & Francis Group, an informa business

Library of Congress Cataloging in Publication Data
Names: Hardy, Kenneth V., editor. | Bobes, Toby, 1940- editor.
Title: Culturally sensitive supervision and training : diverse perspectives and practical applications / [edited by] Kenneth V. Hardy and Toby Bobes.
Description: 1 Edition. | New York : Routledge, 2016. | Includes bibliographical references and index.
Identifiers: LCCN 2016004524 |
ISBN 9781138124585 (hardback : alk. paper) |
ISBN 9781138124608 (pbk. : alk. paper) |
ISBN 9781315648064 (ebook)
Subjects: LCSH: Cross-cultural counseling. |
Counseling—Study and teaching. |
Multiculturalism.
Classification: LCC BF636.7.C76 C86 2016 | DDC 658.3/02—dc23
LC record available at https://lccn.loc.gov/2016004524

ISBN: 978-1-138-12458-5 (hbk)
ISBN: 978-1-138-12460-8 (pbk)
ISBN: 978-1-315-64806-4 (ebk)

Typeset in Bembo
by diacriTech, Chennai

CONTENTS

PREFACE

The goal of this book is to provide educators, trainers, supervisors, and trainees with a comprehensive tool and road map for promoting and integrating cultural sensitivity into the core of their work. Thus, we are offering a more specialized version of supervision and training. We have made a conscious decision not to replicate the existing literature in which scholars already provide comprehensive coverage of supervision principles and practices. Instead, our focus is to address what is required to promote cultural awareness and sensitivity in the supervision and training process. In our view, training is designed for teaching specific skills and techniques and is time limited. Supervision facilitates the personal and professional growth of the therapist for an extended period of time.[1] Some of the chapters in this book are specifically focused on supervision while others highlight training, and, by extension, what happens in the classroom. Several chapters address both supervision and training.

From our experiences as educators, trainers, supervisors, and clinicians, we have found there is an insatiable thirst for more guidance about how to prepare clinicians to work with increasingly diverse populations. Many therapists struggle when working with clients whose cultural backgrounds are different from their own because their training has not adequately prepared them to do so. The gap that exists between what therapists need and what many receive from their respective trainings is not a consequence of a lack of *will* to incorporate issues of diversity into supervision and training but rather a lack of *skill*.

Our vision has been to better prepare supervisors and clinicians to increase their effectiveness with trainees and clients of diverse backgrounds and life experiences. Each of us has to be poised and prepared to work with those who are gender nonconforming and conforming, religiously devout and nonbelievers, racially and religiously oppressed and oppressive, as well as those who are refugees, immigrants, or any other identity or condition that is marginalized or devalued. In our view, devoting acute attention to preparing culturally sensitive clinicians is an ethical imperative. Becoming culturally sensitive and culturally competent requires educators to invite conversations with supervisees and students about similarities and differences in their key identities such as race, gender, class, sexual orientation, and how these intersecting identities influence therapy, supervision, and training.[2] We have found that trainers and supervisors who invite conversations about social location increase

---

1   The reader is referred to the following sources for further clarity about the definitions and distinctions between training and supervision: *Fundamentals of Clinical Supervision*, by J. M. Bernard and R. K. Goodyear (2014), 5th edition. Pearson Education, Inc.; *The Complete Systemic Supervisor: Context, Philosophy, and Pragmatics*, edited by T. C. Todd and C. L. Storm (2002), Authors Choice Press.

2   Dee Watts Jones writes in this volume and previously (2010) about location of self.

their sensitivities and attunement to supervisees' and students' lived experiences. Clients become the beneficiaries as this process translates isomorphically to therapy.

We believe that Experiential Teaching and Learning is the hallmark of supervision and training designed to promote cultural sensitivity. We have found that experiential approaches are particularly effective to enhance knowledge of one's cultural self, a necessary precursor to the effective "use of self." The reader will find experiential exercises and strategies that are powerful tools for preparing culturally sensitive therapists. All of the exercises share the common goal of encouraging self-reflection, which is requisite to providing sensitivity as well as promoting awareness.

The Multicultural Relational Perspective (MRP) is a worldview that provides a comprehensive framework for clinical supervision and is the conceptual framework of this book. The MRP highlights the significance of "self" work, culture, attention to the dynamics of powerlessness, privilege, oppression, and a worldview that values the ongoing examination of "Self" in relationship to other. The MRP is not only a way of looking at the world but also an invitation for each of us to be mindful of where we place ourselves in it because where we stand often dictates what we see. A central focus of our book is upon implementation and putting the principles of the MRP into actual practice.

The book is organized in to four interrelated sections:

Part I is devoted to an examination of the importance of the use of self in supervision and training. This part provides a framework for incorporating a Multicultural Relational Perspective within supervision and training.

Part II focuses on the various social identities that often emerge within the context of the supervisory and training relationships.

Part III focuses on specific strategies for integrating and promoting cultural sensitivity in supervision and training.

Part IV addresses tactics for negotiating difficult dialogues and focuses on the specifics of executing diversity-related conversations.

Reference

Watts Jones, D. (2010). Location of self: Opening the door to dialogue on intersectionality in the therapy process. *Family Process, 49*: 405–420.

ACKNOWLEDGMENTS

Projects of this magnitude virtually always require the steadfast and dedicated efforts of many, some who are very vocal and visible, as well as others who work quietly and tirelessly beyond the prism of the spotlight. This project has been no exception. I would like to thank the many varied and solid contributors for the task-oriented approach, hand-holding, guidance, and esprit de corps that made this endeavor possible. First I wish to extend my sincere gratitude to our very engaged and omnipresent editor, Elizabeth Graber, with whom it has been an extraordinary pleasure to collaborate with from day one. You have been chief among my ardent supporters, and this project would be nonexistent if not for your unrelenting support. Your vision and guidance have been inspirational throughout this process. Ours is a professional partnership that I look forward to extending well beyond this project.

The richness of the collection of chapters that comprise this book would have been woefully compromised if not for the substantive contributions made by each of the authors who gave generously of their time, expertise, and wisdom to transform what commenced as an abstract vision into a tangible reality. I thank each of you for the unselfish sharing of your personal stories and more importantly for your generosity of spirit. Fifi Klein and Dhara Desai: a special thanks to each of you for your gifts, talents, and expertise.

To my coeditor, long-term colleague, and, most importantly, friend Toby Bobes, thank you for your vision and passionate commitment to spearhead this important piece of work. I am grateful to you for inviting me to take this journey with you. Over the course this experience, what I have appreciated most about both our collaboration and our relationship is our common understanding that this book was never solely about clinical supervision and training, but also about providing some semblance of a blueprint for effectively negotiating and traversing cultural differences, a task that has never been more central to our survival as a field and society than now.

Finally I would like to extend my heartfelt gratitude to my family. There are not enough words in the English language or pages in this volume for me to convey how crucial your uncompromising support and unconditional love have been to sustaining me throughout this process. As always, it is my deepest desire that this piece of work will make all of you, as well as the next generation of Hardys and our ancestors, proud.

—KVH

I am deeply honored and grateful to my friend, trusted colleague, coauthor, and coeditor, Ken Hardy, for his compassion, dedication, and generosity in working on this book. I thank you, Ken, for our many spirited conversations that have been inspirational and have generated exciting new ideas for promoting cultural sensitivity. I appreciate your sense of humor and laughing together as we moved through the challenges of our work on the book. My deepest gratitude and thanks to you for all that I have learned through our collaboration. This has been the most significant learning experience of my life!

I am grateful to our contributing authors for their unwavering commitment to this book. Your stories are personally inspiring, and I have been deeply moved by your courage and willingness to share the depth of your experiences. My thanks to each of you for your infinite patience, diligence, and collaborative spirit as we worked together.

I thank Fifi Klein for her technical support and expertise in the organization of the book and for helping Ken and me to move through the myriad of details. Fifi, I will be forever grateful for your ongoing encouragement and for your guidance and suggestions. My thanks to Dhara Desai for your support and expertise. This has truly been a team effort!

I wish to acknowledge my colleague, Olivia Loewy, for her interest and enthusiasm in the early stages of the development of this project. Our conversations helped to shape my evolving ideas and vision for the book.

I thank our editor, Elizabeth Graber, for her enthusiastic support of this project. My deepest appreciation to you for your support and guidance.

My special thanks to my family for their interest and support, especially my husband, Norm, who has partnered with me throughout my career. Fifty-four years and counting! This book is written for all of my children, grandchildren, and for future generations so that their experiences of self and other are based upon dignity, curiosity, and respect.

—TB

CONTRIBUTORS

Argie Allen-Wilson, PhD, Drexel University, Philadelphia, Pennsylvania

Kiran Shahreen Kaur Arora, PhD, Long Island University, Brooklyn, New York

Deidre Ashton, MSSW, Private Practice, Philadelphia, Pennsylvania

Christiana Awosan, PhD, Seton Hall University, South Orange, New Jersey

Toby Bobes, PhD, Pacifica Graduate Institute, Santa Barbara, California

Benjamin E. Caldwell, PsyD, California School of Professional Psychology at Alliant International University, Los Angeles, California

Jessica L. ChenFeng, PhD, California State University, Northridge, California

J. Leonardo de la O, MA, Pacifica Graduate Institute, Santa Barbara, California

Diane R. Gehart, PhD, California State University, Northridge, California

Kenneth V. Hardy, PhD, Drexel University, Philadelphia, Pennsylvania

Ana M. Hernandez, PhD, Seton Hall University, South Orange, New Jersey

Ben K. Lim, PhD, Bethel University, San Diego, California

Soh-Leong Lim, PhD, San Diego State University, San Diego, California

Keith Mar, MA, Multicultural Specialist in Private Practice, Goleta, California

Mary M. Read, PhD, California State University, Fullerton, California

Thandiwe Dee Watts Jones, PhD, Health Plus Hospitals, Bronx Family Court, Bronx, New York

Marlene F. Watson, PhD, Drexel University, Philadelphia, Pennsylvania

Heidi A. Zetzer, PhD, Director, Hosford Counseling and Psychological Services Clinic, University of California, Santa Barbara, California

PART I

The Use of Self in Supervision and Training

1

TOWARD THE DEVELOPMENT OF A MULTICULTURAL RELATIONAL PERSPECTIVE IN TRAINING AND SUPERVISION

Kenneth V. Hardy, PhD

In the increasingly diverse world in which we live, it has become imperative for us to examine the myriad of contextual variables such as race, class, gender, religion, and sexual orientation (McGoldrick & Hardy, 2008; Schulz & Mullings, 2006; Frey, 2015) that give meaning to our lives and shape what we consider to constitute an undisputable truth. Nowhere are these struggles and sensitivities more critical to consider than in the process of supervision and training. The psychosocial and sociocultural landscapes upon which we, as clinicians, practice require each of us to engage in the process of rethinking and re-visioning the field of psychotherapy. The re-visioning of our field, for example, requires us to consider the ways in which both complex inter/intra-personal dynamics as well as the processes of training and supervision are profoundly shaped by the nuances of race, class, gender, and a host of other contextual variables. This re-visioning will assure that effective trainers and supervisors must not only understand and master the complex rudiments of psychotherapy, but must also possess a comprehensive understanding of how cultural factors shape the lives of those we train, treat, and supervise.

Possessing a comprehensive understanding of all of the nuances of every cultural group with whom we might possibly interact is often a desirable but unfortunately impossible and improbable feat to accomplish. The richness and complexity of diversity is such that it would be a daunting task to fully comprehend all of the subcultural variations that might exist within the same cultural group. For example, it is possible for two people to identify as Black and share many cultural commonalities, and yet also have vast and countless differences between them. I was born in the northeastern corridor of the United States to parents who were raised and socialized in the rural and racially segregated South. Their lives were permanently scarred by the insidious, inexplicable, and inhumane treatment that accompanied growing up Black in the racially segregated, Jim Crow, residuals of slavery–infested South. Growing up on a steady diet of stories saturated in racial suffering opened my young, innocent, and naïve eyes to the abject potential of humans' ability to treat others inhumanly solely on the basis of race. My conception of what it means to be Black, as well as the race-related values, mores, and perspectives that I subscribe to have been sharply influenced by where I grew up, my parents' experiences, and the racial climate of the country in the era in which I spent my formative years. On the other hand, I have a Black colleague who was born in Nigeria to Nigerian-born parents who migrated to the United States in their mid-forties and when she was thirteen. Her experience as a Black person has been markedly influenced by her experiences as an African, an African immigrant of immigrant parents, whose socialization and education have been split between two continents. Her experience of being Black, unlike mine, has been profoundly shaped by four devalued identities: Black, African, immigrant, and female.

Despite efforts to the contrary, it is virtually impossible to simplify culture or to employ reductionist thinking by neatly codifying it into discrete measurable entities. Unfortunately, many supervisors and trainers try to promote cultural sensitivity by attempting to simplify culture. In their efforts to do so there is a tendency to (over)focus on the central tendencies of discrete groups, followed by a "cultural prescription" for how they should be treated or supervised. A notable example is the propensity to mainly describe the characteristic of Latino males from the lens of *machismo* as a "cultural prescription," which often creates a narrow focus on hypermasculine relational interactions among Latino men in treatment and supervision (Sue & Sue, 2013; McGoldrick, Giordano & Garcia-Preto, 2005). While the intent and many efforts to prepare culturally sensitive clinicians and supervisors are laudable and timely, we believe the approach requires a more systematic, comprehensive, and ideologically driven approach. That is, rather than focusing heavily on the cultural proclivities of specific groups, we believe an approach that encourages and nurtures perpetual curiosity about the multifaceted role of culture is a more thoughtful and comprehensive path to explore. We believe that developing *a multicultural relational perspective* is a critical and necessary precursor to increasing sensitivity and inviting the type of perpetual cultural curiosity that we envision.

Toward the development of a Multicultural Relational Perspective (MRP) to training and supervision

A Multicultural Relational Perspective (MRP) is a metaframework that can be used to facilitate a shift in how supervisors and supervisees begin to think about clinical work and how it seamlessly interfaces "culture" in both the broadest and narrowest sense of the word. Hardy and Laszloffy (2002) describe the MCP (Multicultural Perspective), as referred to at that time, as "a worldview, an epistemology or way of thinking about the world and where we place ourselves in it" (p. 569). According to Hardy and Laszloffy (2002), "it is not a codified set of skills or tasks" that one performs with this type or that type of client or supervisee. Instead the MCP is a worldview that recognizes how the nuances of culture and all of its appendages are contaminants, informants, and meaning-makers throughout virtually all aspects of our lives. In this regard the MCP is predicated on the following assumptions:

1.   Culture is a broad-based multidimensional concept that is comprised of, but not limited to, race, class, religion, sexual oriental, gender, family of origin, ethnicity, age, regionality, and so forth;
2.   Culture is simultaneously dynamic, fluid, and static—because culture is broadly based and multidimensional, it is also multidirectional and fluid. Each dimension of culture potentially influences the other in a way that is active and ever changing. For example, my sexual orientation as a heterosexual informs how I think of and behave as a man. My gender identity as a male helps to shape and inform how I negotiate my heterosexuality. Both my gender and sexual orientation are influenced by my racial identity and the meanings I attach to being a Black, heterosexual male. Yet there are also aspects of culture that can be static. For instance, when I think of myself racially, how I think of myself now (racially speaking) is not different from how I have at any other points of my life. The specific meanings that I attach to being Black may have definitely changed throughout my life but not the fact that I think of myself as Black.
3.   Culture is a pervasive and potent organizing principle—culture is pervasive and influential. Everyone belongs to "a culture," whether it is recognized or ignored, claimed or disavowed. Furthermore, there is no aspect of our lives that is completely walled off from the influences of culture. For example, how we manage intimacy and conflict, express emotions (or fail to), as well as rituals that we embrace/reject, and/or how we think of ourselves are all experiences that are significantly shaped by culture. Although in contemporary parlance the terms "culture" and

"cultural" are often used to refer to those who are not a part of the "mainstream," the fact of the matter is that each of us is embedded in culture.

4. Culture is multifaceted and multipurpose—it serves many varied functions in our lives. It can provide a sense of rootedness, a source of identity development, a coping resource, "rules of engagement" dictating who is included/excluded, and be a marker of pride and/or shame, etc.

5. Culture is timeless—it transcends past, present, and future. In many ways culture can serve as a connective tissue to our past, situate us in the present, and provide a foundation for and/or give direction to how we envision our future.

Given our view about the omnipresence of culture and its concomitant influences, we believe that attempting to ignore or exorcise it from any aspect of our daily lives is myopic. We believe that making an effort to do so within the context of therapy is even more egregiously shortsighted. Thus it is our contention that preparing therapists to consider culture within the context of their clinical work is of paramount significance. The execution of this goal requires therapists, trainers, and supervisors to think differently about both their work and themselves. Supervision should minimally achieve two major objectives in this regard: 1) assist supervisees in seeing the ways in which human suffering and the appendages of culture are virtually inextricable; and 2) highlight the ways in which the supervisor-supervisee relationship is powerfully shaped by the intricacies of culture. This is a very significant and rudimentary step to help facilitate the development of a multicultural perspective.

Key foundational principles

Taking progressive steps toward the development of a multicultural relational perspective requires familiarity with and some degree of mastery of the following interrelated principles. While each principle is discussed individually, there is a rich synergistic interplay between and among them that defies separating them. Hence the segregated discussion of the principles during the ensuing pages is done solely for the sake of explanation and clarity.

1. **Promote relational thinking**. The essence of relational thinking is that it encourages us to think about how all *matter* is potentially connected, particularly *matter* that at first glance seems disparate. For instance, it helps us to consider the powerful relationship between the "haves" of the wealthy and the "have-nots" of the poor. It is through relational thinking that we are able to consider how past, present, and future are intertwined, for example. Or how human suffering can be the culmination of the delicate interweaving of many different domains of one's life. Relational thinking positions us to seek "connection" in the face of disconnection. When we develop some degree of mastery in relational thinking, we begin to realize that "disconnection," for example, is a symptom not of an independent condition; it is a consequence, not just a cause. Relational thinking frees us to see how our fates are interconnected. It helps us to shift our view from a polarizing and static either/or position of "self" *or* "other" to the relational position of *Self in Relationship to Other* (Hardy & Laszloffy, 2002). The visionary Martin Luther King (1963) spoke of the importance of Self in Relationship to Other over forty years ago when he famously noted that "the rich man can never be all that he hopes to be until the poor man is all that he wishes to be"—another powerful reminder that we all are interconnected and "entangled in a web of mutuality."

2. **Embrace Both/And Thinking**. Thinking Relationally and Embracing Both/And are interwoven concepts. In many ways one cannot exist without the other. However, this principle is so germane to the development of an MRP that it warrants special highlighting here. Embracing Both/And enables us to authentically hold seemingly offsetting, contradictory, and incongruous

positions. It is through the embrace of both/and thinking that we are able to not only see the potential relationship between one's behavior as a perpetrator and one's victimization, but also we can actually genuinely validate the existence of the coexistence of these two opposing aspects of self. We are able to comprehend with greater clarity how one can be simultaneously oppressed and oppressive, privileged and subjugated, or "good and evil." Hardy and Laszloffy (2002) explicate that "embracing both/and thinking not only invites us to think about the ways in which these phenomena may be connected; it also encourages us to respond in ways that place these interconnections at the forefront of what we *do*" (p. 571). In this case, "what we *do*" from the viewpoint of an MRP is authentically held by embracing both the oppressed and oppressive, or privileged and subjugated, aspects that coexist in a person.

3. **Advocate thinking culturally**. As human beings, we are cultural beings, and it is the various dimensions of culture (ethnicity, ability, nationality, etc.) that offer contextual meaning to our lives. When we begin to think culturally, it facilitates our ability to think of others and ourselves more broadly and complexly. We begin to think of others and ourselves in terms of the various cultural locations in which they/we are embedded. We believe that it is very difficult, if not impossible, to fully understand the essence of one's being without knowing something about one's cultural context. Thus thinking culturally ultimately means that we remain perpetually curious about the ways in which culture is a major organizing principle throughout our lives.

4. **Encourage the development of a multidimensional view of the self**. The process of thinking culturally should ideally start with thyself (which is generally true for all principles associated with the MRP). Developing a Multidimensional View of the Self is the first crucial step toward beginning to see others more complexly, that is, culturally. Developing a deeper and more complex understanding of the self paves the way to understanding others similarly. The development of a Multidimensional View of the Self challenges the notion that what is typically thought of as *the self* is actually comprised of many *selves*. For example, each of us has a gendered self, a racial self, a religious self, an ethnic self, a sexual orientation self, and Family of Origin (FOO) self, as well as a host of others. Since many of our selves are socially constructed, they are imbued with varying degrees of power, powerlessness, privilege, and subjugation as they are reified in the larger culture. Many of us are equipped with both privileged and subjugated selves. As a Black, heterosexual, middle-class male, I possess several privileged selves—gender, sexual orientation, and class—while also possessing a subjugated self, which is my racial self. As each of us begins to see ourselves through the prism of our multiple selves, including those that are privileged and subjugated, we are much better equipped to see others similarly. The more comprehensively we can see ourselves and others, the greater the degree of compassion, under-standing, and humility we can have for each other.

5. **Encourage an intense focus on the "Self."** One of the major hallmarks of the MRP centers on the development and understanding of the self. There are three interrelated com-ponents of "Self"-oriented work that warrant highlighting: Knowledge; Interrogation; and Location or Use of Selves. These are critical and essential components of the MRP. "Self" knowledge refers to the developing sense of awareness that one has and remains committed to exploring with regards to one's multiple selves. Self-interrogation, on the other hand, refers to the process of actively questioning one's developing sense of self-awareness. This process may involve unpacking and critiquing unexamined internalized messages that may be harmful or beneficial to the self and others. The Location or Use of "Self" refers to the facility with which one can draw from the knowledge one has of one's self that can be accessed as a potential interpersonal resource to promote connections. The Location or Use of "Self" is predicated on the effective use of "Self" disclosure, which is an important component of a Multicultural Relational Perspective.

The term "self" is used here for the ease of reading; however, it is done so with the understanding that the Self is conceptualized as a multidimensional concept. Thus the use of "self" in quotes throughout the remainder of this chapter is to remind the reader of this distinction.

6. **Focus on social justice by promoting awareness of and sensitivity to the dynamics of power and powerlessness, privilege and subjugation.** Social Justice and Diversity are often thought of interchangeably. While the two concepts share a powerful connection, we maintain that there are discernible noteworthy differences between the two. Diversity attends to issues of inclusion and focuses on WHO is included. Social Justice, on the other hand, while also attentive to WHO is included, is also concerned about HOW one is included. In other words, Social Justice is concerned about issues of equity, especially the equitable distribution of power. It is possible to succeed at achieving high levels of diversity and fail the social justice goal of ensuring that power is shared equitably. When social justice is a focal point, it places the issues of power, powerlessness, privilege, and subjugation under careful scrutiny. Power and powerlessness have a profound effect on how relationships are transacted. Despite the widespread influences of power and privilege within relationships, the impact and effects of it are seldom, if ever, recognized and/or acknowledged. When either the existence of power or its unequal distribution in relationships is denied or unacknowledged, the potential for misuse and/or abuse increases substantially. It is difficult to examine the dynamics of power and powerlessness without also lending consideration to the two closely related phenomena of privilege and subjugation. Power and powerlessness as well as privilege and subjugation are intricately fused and seamlessly coexist. Whereas privilege refers to the status that an individual or group possesses that confers power upon them, subjugation is an assignment to a position or status that is devalued and systematically stripped of power, influence, and privilege. Promoting a greater understanding of the dynamics of power, powerlessness, privilege, and subjugation is essential to the development of a multicultural relational perspective.

7. **Promote awareness of and sensitivity to the anatomy of socio-cultural oppression.** When power, powerlessness, privilege, and subjugation become calcified in relationships, it invariably contributes to the creation of oppressive conditions. Oppression is a pervasive and debilitating condition that systematically "suppresses" the emotional, psychological, spiritual, and interpersonal life experiences of those who are affected. It is unnamed, often unacknowledged, but insidious and infectious in the lives of the marginalized, the vulnerable, and the powerless. In many ways, oppression and trauma are interchangeable—two different terms essentially describing the same experience. In describing African Americans' experiences with the legacy of trauma from slavery to present-day encounters with racial oppressions, DeGruy Leary (2005) emphasizes the interconnection between oppression and trauma as well as the ways in which the legacy of trauma negatively affects the lives of marginalized communities. She states, "While the direct relationship between the slave experience of African American and the current major social problems facing them is difficult to empirically substantiate, we know from research conducted on other groups who experienced oppression and trauma that survivor syndrome is pervasive in the development of the second and third generations. The characteristics of the survivor syndrome include stress, self-doubt, problems with aggression, and a number of psychological and interpersonal relationship problems with family members and others" (p.124). Thus, she further defines the circumstances that produce Post Traumatic Slave Syndrome (PTSS), specifically in the lives of African Americans and by extension other oppressed groups as "multigenerational trauma and continued oppression plus a real or imagined lack of access...to the benefits of the society we live in" (p. 125). Virtually all experiences involving oppression are traumatic, although not all traumatic experiences involve oppression. An oppression-sensitive approach to

understanding the intricacies of human interaction is endemic to an MRP. Understanding the world through an Oppression Sensitive Lens (OSL) heightens conscientiousness of the critical interplay of power, powerlessness, privilege, subjugation, and trauma.

8. **Highlight, deconstruct, and make visible the invisible trauma wounds of sociocultural oppression**. Perpetual experiences with oppression often leave those who have been affected by it with an array of invisible wounds. These wounds are often invisible to both the Self and Other and are relegated to invisibility because they are unnamed and therefore unacknowledged. Since many of these wounds have not been incorporated into the classical mainstream psychological nosology, they essentially don't exist. Chronic and debilitating conditions that routinely affected those who are non-white, non-Christian, non–middle class, gender non-onforming, non-abled body, etc. remained unnamed and invalidated. For example, the hampering effects of devaluation, psychological homelessness, assaulted sense of self, and internalized oppression, just to cite a few, are not a part of current mental health lexicon (Hardy & Laszloffy, 2002). It is possible, however, for a phenomenon to exist even when it is not named.

9. **Enhance cultural awareness and sensitivity and promote the distinctions between the two**. Both awareness and sensitivity are much needed and essential properties of the MRP. Awareness is important because it is a metric to determine how much and "what" we know about another culturally, while sensitivity gauges "how" we interact with or actually treat another culturally. The concepts are intertwined; however, some distinction between the two is warranted. According to Hardy and Laszloffy (1992, 1995), cultural awareness is a cognitive process. It is akin to having an intellectual knowledge of culture. Its counterpart, sensitivity, on the other hand, is an affective experience. Sensitivity is an affective, or intuitive sense, of knowing where an acute "feeling" of conscientiousness exists with regard to self in relationship to other. As Hardy and Laszloffy (1992, 1995) noted, cultural awareness can exist void of sensitivity; however, the reverse is not true. We believe that the knowledge that is inclusive of "others" is most effective when it translates into how "others" are actually treated. This is both the beauty and the effectiveness of demonstrating both awareness and sensitivity.

10. **Promote the recognition of the co-existence of multiple realities**. The Multicultural Relational Perspective espouses the notion that reality is relative and context is significant. Thus when our contexts are different, oftentimes so are the realities that govern our lives. Context is a major marker of reality. The subjective and contextual nature of reality is what makes it possible for two people to gaze at the very same phenomenon and yet affix very different meanings to the observed. As we prepare this chapter there is an intense debate unfolding in the United States regarding what it means for States to fly the Confederate flag from government buildings. Many southern Whites argue that the Confederate flag is a symbol of history and legacy, while many Blacks and other people of color view it as a symbol of hatred and racism. This is a potent, highly emotionally charged, contemporary illustration of two groups observing the same phenomenon and extracting diametrically opposed meanings. Unfortunately, when our conflicting realities cannot occupy a place of peaceful co-existence, neither can we as a people.

Implications for supervision

These principles provide a conceptual foundation for the types of changes that are necessary to operationalize supervision within an MRP framework. In the spirit of the MRP, the following is a list of some sample "self"-directed questions that we believe are important for supervisors to ask themselves:

1.   What are the dimensions of the "self" that significantly inform how I think about myself? What is my dominant privileged self? How does it shape what I look for and what I tend to see?

2. What are the Selves of the Supervisor that inform my approach to supervision? What is my dominant subjugated self, and how does it contribute to my role as a supervisor and the supervisory process?
3. What role does power and privilege play in my approach to supervision? What role does power and privilege play in the Supervisory relationships in which I participate? To what extent, if any, do I encourage supervisees to explore the impact of power, privilege, and oppression within the auspices of their clients' lives and their relationships with clients?
4. How often and under what clinical circumstances do I initiate conversations about the dimensions of culture? What dimensions are most difficult to talk about? What dimension is the easiest to discuss?
5. How often and under what circumstances do I encourage supervisees to explore cultural dynamics within the context of their clinical work?
6. What is my current philosophy of supervision, and what role does "self"-disclosure play? To what extent, if any, might I explore the multiple selves of the supervisee? How often do I encourage supervisees to consider how their multiples selves may impact their participation in supervision and their therapy with clients?
7. How would I describe my supervisory style?
8. To what extent do I explore or encourage exploration of the signs and symptoms of sociocultural trauma within the context of my work as a supervisor?
9. What strategies do I routinely employ to assist supervisees in sharpening their skill in thinking relationally? Culturally?
10. What specific strategies do I employ to enhance cultural sensitivity in both my supervisory relationship as well as within the clinical work of my supervisees?

Implications for training

Similarly, we believe that it is also important for clinical educators and trainers to engage in a process of "self"-interrogation with regard to their efforts to move toward the development of a Multicultural Relational Perspective within training. As a preliminary litmus test, we think it would be important for educators and trainers to ponder the following sample questions:

1. What is the philosophy of our training program? Are we advocates for diversity, social justice, both, or neither? How is our training philosophy operationalized in terms of what we say and what we do?
2. Are issues of social justice and diversity integrated throughout our curriculum, or are these issues relegated to a specific course or seminar?
3. Whose responsibility is it to carry the mantle for diversity and social justice? Is the responsibility for teaching from a social justice and diversity informed lens shared by all faculty, or does it rest solely with specific faculty?
4. Do our curriculum and pedagogical styles allow for experiential teaching and learning as well as traditional didactic approaches?
5. Does our curricular design enhance trainees' sense of cultural awareness and sensitivity? If so, how? If not, why not?
6. Does our curricular design afford the trainee the opportunity to develop a Multidimensional View of the "Self"?
7. What are the principle teaching and training strategies we use to enhance our trainees' ability to think relationally?
8. What are the principle teaching and training strategies we use to enhance our trainees' ability to think culturally?

9. Do our training philosophy and practice support trainers engaging in a process of "self"-interrogation?

10. As a trainer, what are my privileged and subjugated selves? What are the ways in which these selves inform my relationship with trainees, what I teach, and how I teach?

Summary

The *one size fits all* approach to therapy, supervision, and training is no longer a viable approach to practicing effectively in our world of rapidly shifting demographics. Each of us to has to be poised and prepared to work effectively with clients and trainees representing a variety of backgrounds, demographics, and life experiences, including those who represent the so-called mainstream as well as those who are gender nonconforming, religiously devout, racially and religiously oppressed, and those who are refugees and immigrants. In our view, devoting acute attention to preparing culturally sensitive clinicians is an ethical imperative. However, the pathway to doing so has to be more comprehensive than simply offering an isolated course or two in training programs or by having a supervisor discuss "culture" only when a person of color is involved. Instead, we believe that adopting an MRP in training and supervision holds a far greater promise for preparing culturally sensitive clinicians. The development of an MRP forges a paradigm shift that highlights the significance of "self" work, culture, attention to the dynamics of power, powerlessness, privilege, and oppression, and a worldview that values the incessant examination of "Self" in Relationship to Other. The MRP is not only a way of looking at the world but also an invitation for each of us to be mindful of where we place ourselves in it, because where we stand often dictates what we see.

References

DeGruy Leary, J. D. (2005). *Post-traumatic slave syndrome: America's legacy of enduring injury and healing.* Milwaukie, OR: Uptone.

Frey, W. H. (2015). *Diversity explosion: How new racial demographics are remaking America.* Washington, DC: Brookings Institution Press.

Hardy, K. V., & Laszloffy, A. (2002). Couple therapy using a multicultural perspective. In A. Gurman (Ed.), Clinical handbook of couple therapy (pp. 569–593). New York: Guilford Press.

Hardy, K. V., & Laslozffy, A. (1995). The cultural genogram: Key to training culturally competent family therapists. *Journal of Marital and Family Therapy, 21*(3), 227–237.

Hardy, K. V., & Laszloffy, A. T. (1992). Training racially sensitive family therapists: Context, content, and contact. Families in Society: *The Journal of Contemporary Human Services,* June 73, 364–370.

King, M. L. (1963). Letter from a Birmingham jail. www.theatlantic.com (accessed March 24, 2016).

McGoldrick, M., & Hardy, K.V. (Eds.). (2008). *Re-visioning family therapy: Race, culture and gender in clinical practice.* New York, NY: Guilford Press.

McGoldrick, M., Giordano, J., & Garcia-Preto, N. (2005). *Ethnicity and family therapy.* New York, NY: Guilford Press.

Schulz, A. J., & Mullings, L. (Eds.). (2006). *Gender, race, class and health: Intersectional approaches.* San Francisco, CA: Jossey-Bass: A Wiley Imprint.

Sue, G. W., & Sue, D. (2013). *Counseling the culturally diverse: Theory and practice.* Hoboken, NJ: Wiley.

2

CORE COMPETENCIES FOR EXECUTING CULTURALLY SENSITIVE SUPERVISION AND TRAINING

Kenneth V. Hardy, PhD, and Toby Bobes, PhD

We have drawn from our authors' work a list of core competencies that we believe contribute significantly to the promotion of culturally sensitive supervision and training. The following core competencies are built upon the key foundational principles set forth in Chapter 1. Our primary focus is upon implementation and putting the principles into action.

1. **Be a "broker of permission" to give voice to previously silenced topics**. Supervisors and trainers have the power and privilege and therefore the responsibility to deliberately initiate conversations about cultural diversity. The trainer grants permission to trainees to "speak the unspeakable" and "find the safety and comfort necessary to risk saying things they have been unable to say." Some topics such as those involving issues of race and sexual orientation are especially difficult issues to discuss openly and directly. It is thus incumbent upon supervisors and trainers to invite these types of difficult dialogues (Hardy & Laszloffy, 2002, p. 580, 581).

2. **Introduce dimensions of diversity early on in the training process, preferably no later than the second session, to set the tone to explicitly acknowledge and validate the lived experiences of group members of diverse backgrounds**. The trainer invites a conversation with trainees to discuss similarities and differences in their key identities such as race, gender, class, sexual orientation, and how these intersecting identities influence therapy, supervision, and training (Watts Jones, 2010, 2016). The trainer models identification of social location and promotes a climate of safety, risk-taking, and transparency in conversations about dimensions of diversity.

3. **Turn missteps into steady steps**. Making mistakes should be viewed as part of the learning process and an opportunity for personal and professional growth. The supervisor or trainer turns missteps into steady steps by self-disclosure and empathic understanding, thus modeling transparency and risk-taking. Turning missteps into steady steps involves relational risk-taking and is a two-step process. The person demonstrates a willingness to make mistakes and a corresponding willingness to be vulnerable, stay connected to talk about what happened, and turn missteps into steady steps (Zetzer, 2016).

4. **Explicitly name and address the impact of power relations and privilege upon relationships**. The trainer discloses his or her social location and invites thoughtfulness and dialogue about the explicit and implicit ways that power, privilege, and subjugation operate in therapy, supervision, and training contexts (Watts Jones, 2010). Power and privilege are often unacknowledged but influential properties of virtually all relationships. Power is relational,

contextual, and inequitably distributed. Differentials in possession of power are common in relationships. Those who possess greater degrees of power must also assume greater responsibility in relationships. Hence, supervisors and trainers have the power, privilege, and the responsibility to purposefully and deliberately initiate conversations about power differentials in supervision and training.

5. **Engage in critical self reflection and self interrogation.** The Critical Self Reflection/Self Interrogation (CSR/SI) process is one that each of us should ideally undergo before attempting to engage in meaningful conversations about race, gender, sexual orientation, class, and other dimensions of diversity. The CSR/SI process enables us to get more intimately acquainted with ourselves as cultural beings. It is a "looking within process" designed to help us to *begin* identifying our realities, biases, assumptions, and wounds. Once these various parts of our cultural selves have been identified, the next step involves "self-interrogation." This process involves demonstrating a willingness to critically examine one's deeply held internalized views about race, gender, ethnicity, and sexual differences (Hardy, 2016).

6. **Expand on knowledge of self and deepen understanding of "Self in Relationship to Other."** Once a new and/or refined sense of self has been chiseled out through the Critical Self Reflection/Self Interrogation process, it is important to move from an individually oriented focus of self-examination to one that is more relationally sensitive. As the term "Self in Relationship to Other" (SIRO) implies, the process is a relationship concept that acknowledges that the Self is fluid and malleable—it affects and is affected by others' selves. Through this process the individual expands on the knowledge of self that is gained from the Critical Self Reflective/Self Interrogation process to include a deeper understanding of what happens to/with one's cultural self as it interacts with the cultural selves of others. Deepening one's understanding of SIRO enables individuals to *self-reflect during intense conversations*, to *have an unrelenting commitment to remain curious—not just about "the other" but also about one's own perceptions, feelings, and reactions*. Engaging in the SIRO process makes it possible for one to remain intimately committed to an intense diversity charged conversation while both acknowledging and embracing that changing "the other" is beyond the scope of the conversation. Ultimately, the CSR/SI process works in concert with the SIRO process and helps to eliminate blaming, fault-finding, and self-exoneration during diversity charged conversations (Hardy, 2016).

7. **Promote awareness of and sensitivity to the anatomy of socio–cultural oppression.** Understanding the world through an Oppression Sensitive Lens (OSL) heightens conscientiousness of the critical interplay of power, powerlessness, privilege, subjugation, and trauma (Hardy, 2016).

8. **Highlight, deconstruct, and make visible the invisible trauma wounds of sociocultural oppression.** Perpetual experiences with oppression often leaves those who have been affected by it with an array of invisible wounds. These wounds are often invisible to both the Self and Other and are relegated to invisibility because they are unnamed and therefore unacknowledged (Hardy, 2016).

9. **Be alert to discomforts and emotional responses when diversity/multicultural issues arise.** Monitoring responses and making sense of one's feelings and those of trainees are important to facilitate learning (Sue, 2010). Supervisors and trainers bear the primary responsibility for working through emotional discomfort when it inevitably arises during conversations about multicultural differences (Christiansen et al. 2011, p. 109).

10. **Effectively manage culturally based hot buttons or emotional triggers.** It is essential that trainers and trainees have the ability to encourage and tolerate discomfort and intensity. Staying with the intensity is essential and is a critical attribute for supervisors and trainers (Hardy & McGoldrick, 2008).

11. **Deepen difficult conversations**. Facilitate difficult dialogues during emotionally charged conversations that inevitably arise during discussions about multicultural differences in supervision and training. Staying with the intensity is essential. Be sensitive to the vulnerabilities that often emerge during emotionally charged conversations, such as shame, humiliation, anger, and sadness. Be prepared to convey understanding and empathy at these moments (Ring, et al., 2008). Having the ability to encourage and tolerate discomfort and intensity is a critical attribute for supervisors and trainers (Hardy & Laszloffy, 2002).

12. **Utilize the "Validate, Challenge, and Request Approach,"** a requisite skill for engaging in difficult dialogues. "The VCR approach allows us to demonstrate a respect for another's position on a matter, while also allowing us to present our own view. Essentially, we are employing both-and thinking by attempting to create enough space for the coexistence of two contrasting views. Although we never deny the passion with which we believe in our views, never at any point does this passion result in a need to destroy or defile differing points of view" (Hardy & Laszloffy, 2002, p. 592). Having the capacity to recognize the redeemable qualities in others is essential to addressing racial, ethnic, and sexual differences. "We must recognize that all people, no matter how flawed, have redeemable capacities in their being. It's our responsibility to find their virtues and connect with them" (Hardy, 2009, p. 51). If we fail to find a person's redeemable qualities, this is tantamount to accepting the inevitability of hopelessness about change.

    "V" Always "validate" first. It is important to find something to validate in every person. It is possible to validate an issue or point of view without agreeing with it. The ultimate goal is to introduce a different viewpoint for a person to consider, and validation is only the first step. When used effectively, generously, and sufficiently, it facilitates our efforts in moving on to the next step: to challenge/confront. The person being validated determines when our validation is sufficient. We pay close attention to our intuition and to nuances and subtleties of communication to determine when our validation is enough before moving on to the next step.

    "C" The "challenge/confront" message means that we take the validating part of our message and use it as a springboard for presenting our challenge. The challenge/confront message is always the other side of the validating message. Through this process a person is asked to consider how a behavior pattern can have two different sides.

    "R" The "request" message entails making a request that presents the person with a concrete way of responding to our challenge. It is unhelpful to challenge without offering a corresponding suggestion for what a person might do differently (2002, pp. 583, 584).

13. **Embrace "Both-And Thinking," a critical dimension of the VCR (Validate, Challenge, and Request) approach**. Conversations are deepened when people are challenged "to face and embrace their different positions while staying in relationship" (Fish, 2008. p. 199). Supervisors and trainers model cultural sensitivity when they demonstrate the ability to respectfully hold and embrace the other's differences while staying connected and engaged. Embracing "Both-And Thinking" is one of the 10 Key Foundational Principles discussed in the Introduction to our book. Multiple viewpoints are embraced as all aspects of human struggles are recognized, even when contradictory and opposing ideas exist (Hardy & Laszloffy, 2002). "What we all hunger for is a new world of choices without those poles of either/or pulling us away from the complexities of our everyday experiences" (Hardy, 1995, p. 57).

14. **Recognize that all relationships are cross-cultural**. It is essential that trainers recognize and understand the similarities and differences that exist between themselves and their trainees.

This is a basic building block in facilitating dialogues about cultural differences and validating the lived experiences of those with whom we work. All human relationships are characterized by sameness and difference. The differences form the basis for the cross-cultural nature of our interactions (Hardy & Laszloffy, 2002, p. 572).

15. **Master "context-talk."** Develop the fluency and comfort to speak openly, non-defensively, and routinely about culture and context. Mastering "context talk" means that trainers should have the comfort and facility to talk about dimensions of diversity with trainees. Context talk is facilitated by attending to issues relevant to the cultural context of the supervisee, the supervisor, and their relationship (Hardy, 2016).

16. **Distinguish between awareness and sensitivity**. "The term *cultural competence* is defined as the presence of both cultural awareness and sensitivity whereby awareness refers to a state of cognizance of, insight into, and knowledge about diversity issues, and *cultural sensitivity* refers to a state of attunement to, emotional resonance with, and meaningful responsiveness to the needs and feelings of others" (Hardy & Laszloffy, 1995). [In Laszloffy & Habekost, 2010, p. 334].

17. **Be curious and sensitive about how language informs trainees' experiences**. Understand how language differences inform supervision and training contexts. When the dominant language is used, it is important to understand how words and phrases, and tone and pitch, impact the conversation. We may all speak English and still have a hard time understanding each other. We need to continually ask ourselves, "What role is language playing in our process here?" Alertness and sensitivity to language practices will promote *a culture of curiosity* and contribute to a greater sense of humility, connection, and meaningful engagement in our conversations with supervisees and students (Smith, 2011, p. 61).

18. **Embrace a stance of compassion, humility, and curiosity**. By embracing a stance of compassion, humility, and curiosity, trainers demonstrate authenticity and a genuine desire to expand understanding of their trainees. Cultural competence is not just about acquiring knowledge. It is also about having the humility to say what we do not know. This means having a lifelong commitment to self-reflection and self-critique as well as to redressing power imbalances (Tervalon & Murray-Garcia, 1998; Gehart, 2016).

19. **Create culturally informed questions**. The use of questions is a powerful skill utilized by supervisors and trainers. Often the questions we ask are more important than the answers. Supervisors and trainers should be less concerned about specific answers and remain focused upon provoking critical thinking and self-reflection through the process of questioning.

20. **Embrace cultural diversity and social justice**. Location of self is the first step in the process of embracing cultural diversity and social justice. Our authors model identification of their social location and chronicle how their personal cultural narratives promote and integrate cultural sensitivity into the core of their work.[1] Use of self is the vehicle for translating location of self into meaningful action. Supervisors and trainers who identify their social location increase their capacity for cultural sensitivity and attunement to supervisees and students.

Demonstrating cultural sensitivity is central to the work of supervisors and trainers. It is not a quality that is easily acquired. Instead, cultural sensitivity is developed to varying degrees over a period of time depending on one's life experiences and commitment to diversity. In most cases, one has to be deliberate in one's desire, intention, and effort to develop and enhance cultural sensitivity. It is rare that this process occurs passively or serendipitously. Enhancing cultural sensitivity requires us to expand our thinking with a greater appreciation and focus for what we do. Supervision and training should be a "deliberate educational process" with teaching and learning strategies that are proactive, purposeful, and intentional (Borders, 2002, pp. 417–418). The core competencies are based upon these premises.

Note

1   Monica MoGoldrick describes a *Social Location Exercise* in which "Trainers model identification of their social location............to encourage trainees to discuss their own social locations" (Hardy & McGoldrick, 2008, p. 455).

References

Bernard, J. M., & Goodyear, R. K. (2014). *Fundamentals of clinical supervision* (5th ed.). Upper Saddle River, NJ: Pearson Education.

Borders, L. D. (2002). Counseling supervision: A deliberate educational process. In D. C. Locke, J. E. Meyers & E. L. Herr (Eds.), *The handbook of counseling* (pp. 417–432). Thousand Oaks, CA: SAGE Publications.

Christiansen, A. T., Thomas, V., Kafescioglu, N. et al. (2011). Multicultural supervision: Lessons learned about an ongoing struggle. *Journal of Marital and Family Therapy, 37*(1), 109–119.

Fish, L. S. (2008). The Semitism schism: Jewish-Palestinian legacies in a family therapy training context. In M. McGoldrick & K. Hardy (Eds.), *Re-Visioning family therapy: Race, culture, and gender in clinical practice* (pp. 197–203). New York, NY: Guilford Press.

Hardy, K. V. (1995). Embracing both/and. *Psychotherapy Networker, 19*(6), 42–57.

Hardy, K. V. (2009). When "them" becomes "us." *Psychotherapy Networker, 33*(1), 47–57.

Hardy, K. V. (2016). Anti-racist approaches for shaping theoretical and practice paradigms. In M. Pender-Greene & A. Siskin (Eds.), *Anti-racist strategies for the health and human services*. Oxford, UK: Oxford University Press.

Hardy, K. V., & Laszloffy, T. A. (1995). The cultural genogram: Key to training culturally competent family therapists. *Journal of Marital and Family Therapy, 21*(3), 227–237.

Hardy, K. V., & Laszloffy, T. A. (2002). Couple therapy using a multicultural perspective. In A. S. Gurman & N. S. Jacobson (Eds.), *Clinical handbook of couple therapy* (pp. 569–593). New York, NY: Guilford Press.

Hardy, K. V., & McGoldrick, M. (2008). Re-visioning training. In M. McGoldrick & K. Hardy (Eds.), *Re-visioning family therapy: Race, culture, and gender in clinical practice* (2nd ed.) (pp. 442–460). New York, NY: Guilford Press.

Laszloffy, T., & Habekost, J. (2010). Using experiential tasks to enhance cultural sensitivity among MFT trainees. *Journal of Marital and Family Therapy, 36*(3), 333–346.

Ring, J. M., Nyquist, J. G., Mitchell, S. et al. (2008). *Curriculum for culturally responsive health care: The step-by-step guide for cultural competence training*. United Kingdom: Radcliffe Publishing Ltd.

Smith, G. (2011). Cut the crap: Language—Risks and relationships in systemic therapy and supervision. *The Australian and New Zealand Journal of Family Therapy, 32*(1), 58–69.

Sue, D. W. (2010). *Microaggressions in everyday life: Race, gender, and sexual orientation*. Hoboken, NJ: Wiley.

Tervalon, M., & Murray-Garcia, J. (1998). Cultural humility versus cultural competence: A critical distinction in defining physician training outcomes in multicultural education. In *Journal of Health Care for the Poor and Underserved, 9*(2), 117–123.

Watts Jones, D. (2010). Location of self: Opening the door to dialogue on intersectionality in the therapy process. *Family Process, 49*, 405–420.

3

LOCATION OF SELF IN TRAINING AND SUPERVISION

Thandiwe Dee Watts Jones, PhD

Introduction

Location of self (LOS) falls under the umbrella term "self of the therapist." It emerged out of a framework of therapists committed to being collaborators in healing from oppression. Most often, the therapist initiates LOS in the form of a conversation in which s/he identifies to her clients a conglomeration of her/his identities—racial, ethnic, marital, parental, class, sexual orientation, religious/spiritual status, and perhaps more. It opens the door to thinking and talking about the mix of social locations in the room, the therapist's and the client(s), and how they might impact the work. It announces the therapist's awareness and interest in social locations, in the differences and similarities in the room, and in race, class, gender, and others as significant influences in life. While LOS emerged as a concept within the context of therapy, it can also be utilized in the supervisor-supervisee relationship. Initiated by a supervisor, LOS can similarly announce the supervisor's interest in social locations and her/his influence in supervision. I encourage supervisors to stop waiting for supervisees to bring up these locations and their concomitant and relative degrees of power. Supervisors signal to their trainees, through their silence and by their reactions when these issues are brought up, whether such perspectives are welcome or unwelcome (Garcia et al., 2009).

I have written previously (Watts Jones, 2010) about the specifics of a particular model of location of self that I use in my own clinical work and in the supervision of family therapy trainees. In that article, I also cited the work of scholars from various marginalized groups that cleared a conceptual path leading to the idea of disclosing and discussing social location in therapy. I do believe that trainees and clinicians need to be exposed to LOS and the social justice lens of therapy to which it is linked. In this chapter, my intent is to expand the discussion of location of self, based on subsequent observations and experiences about its use in the years following the original article. In so doing, I hope to further the usefulness of LOS in training and clinical work.

Self of therapist umbrella

For purposes of clarity, it is useful to locate LOS as one of several forms of self of therapist work. A second self of the therapist process consists of the therapist's self-disclosure of a personal experience with client(s), an expression of feeling the therapist experiences in the room or a past experience that seems pertinent to the present therapy work. A third form involves the process of identifying themes and vulnerabilities of the therapist, via family-of-origin genogram work, alerting the therapist to issues that may be trigger points in working with clients/families, and to their own self-care needs. In doing this work, therapists increase their ability to be fully present and congruent, a la Satir (Lum, 2002) and decrease their reactivity (Kerr & Bowen, 1988; Aponte, 2014). A fourth dimension of self of the therapist work has been proposed by Simon (2006), and refers to the therapist's worldview and its fit with the family therapy model used by the therapist.

As a form of self-of-the-therapist disclosure, LOS is most similar to the feminist perspective on therapist disclosure in attempting to give clients access to therapists' values to make it possible for clients to examine and discuss their impact in the therapy (Cheon & Murphy, 2007).

My vision in this work is shaped by all the identities I occupy, and thus I will locate myself in regard to some of the primary ones I have had or currently have. I believe it is useful for me to remain mindful of this context and for the reader to know it as informing the information I present. I am a Black, African American, African Caribbean, divorced woman with two grown children and a grandson. I am heterosexual, second-generation middle-class, and my spirituality draws on indigenous African, Native American Indian, and Asian beliefs and practices. I am originally from the South and lived through "Colored" and "White" water fountains. In the late '60s, the fire of Black Power ignited in me and I emerged as a political activist, which continued side by side with my training as a social worker and later a psychologist and family therapist. I have recently been able to wrap my mind and voice around the claim of being an elder, though not elderly. Finally, in my view, the nest is never empty and fertility is beyond the ovaries.

Teaching and supervising location of self

LOS is one element in the process of addressing issues of oppression and social location in therapy, and doing so from a position aligned with social justice. Trainees or clinicians cannot engage in LOS absent an understanding of social location's centrality in the everyday lives of all human beings. It is a thread to be followed in therapy from beginning to end, as much as beliefs or family-of-origin patterns or structural hierarchy are tracked and explicated. The array of social locations that any one of us occupies is linked to our experiences of relational comfort and feelings of worth as well as our relational wounding and distress. This is true of interactions within the family as well as those between the family and people and institutions outside the family. Even the quality of the boundary between the family and the outside world is influenced by social location. Class and racial privilege, for example, insulate certain families against the intrusion of various public sector agencies, and buffer even the most negative of circumstances. For example, following Dylan Roof's arrest for killing the nine church members in Charleston, police officers bought him a Burger King lunch on his way to jail (Raymond, 6/22/2015). Freddie Gray of Baltimore, on the other hand, whose crime was running from a police officer, incurred a nearly severed spine on his ride to jail, and later died (Graham, 2015).

Trainees and clinicians cannot engage meaningfully in LOS with families if they have had little here-and-now talk of its components in training. Thus, from start to finish, the didactic and supervisory teaching needs to identify social location and oppression, including colonialism, as basic factors that influence family functioning, theories of family functioning, and the therapist who appears in the therapy room. If not, LOS will likely be a perfunctory exercise or one relegated to the "if we have time" category.

Near the beginning of the first class of live supervision, I asked trainees (all of whom were post-graduates with master's or higher degrees) to locate themselves per Almeida's pyramid of hierarchy, and to reflect on the potential influence of the particular privileged and subjugated identities they held. As in the LOS process, I believe that the empowered person, the supervisor in this case, should lead such vulnerability. Therefore, I presented first. This process could be taken further. That is, after the trainees and I had all identified the intersection of various locations that we occupied, we could have gone on to consider what concerns we might have or potential benefits we envisioned in our mix of subjugated and privileged identities. This could also have been extended to include thoughts about the influence of the LOS of supervisor, therapist, and family. The purpose would not be to entertain the full complexity of such layers of interaction but simply to allow any readily occurring concerns or possible benefits to be raised. So, for example, a Japanese therapist working with a Japanese or other Asian family might have some concerns about being encouraged in supervision by a White supervisor to take a direct approach or one that encourages excavation of conflict, in the event that the family values a more traditional form of their culture that eschews conflict. In the beginning of training, each trainee may not know what kind of cases s/he will have but even one such discussion lays the groundwork for more as cases are assigned. In addition, it provides an additional opportunity for engaging in LOS prior to doing so in therapy.

Prior to trainees (who worked as co-therapists) engaging in LOS with their family, class members discussed which identities they felt most and least comfortable sharing with the family and why. At a minimum, they were asked to locate themselves in terms of race, ethnicity, class, parental status, and, if heterosexual, in terms of sexual orientation. When it came to invisible, subjugated identities that trainees held but did not feel comfortable sharing in LOS, I felt it important to honor that. Nonetheless, such trainees were asked to discuss their concerns and to consider under what conditions might they locate that aspect of themselves. The prep for doing LOS with a family also included a team discussion of possible advantages and disadvantages of the family-therapist mix of social locations, to the extent that the client(s)' locations were known. The particular trainee up for doing LOS at a given time took the lead in a dry run practice followed by other team members "trying on" how they would language such LOS. Thus, there were multiple rounds of practice. These included the rationale for doing LOS, a critical precursor to LOS that provides a context for families. Thus, from the outset of case formulation the foundation for LOS was present.

With some exceptions, most trainees on their first time out with LOS appeared somewhat ill at ease, and offered minimal thoughts about race and class. This was true even though many appeared genuinely open and understanding of the potential value of such a process. They most elaborated on their thoughts about the possible disadvantage of not being parents, if working with parents, and at the same time offered some counterbalance to that based on their experience of working with children or families. Watching them through the one-way mirror, they often appeared like anyone facing a new, anxiety-evoking task, eager to get through it as quickly as possible. Nonetheless, they took the leap. They acknowledged these omnipresent social locations aloud and for consideration, and I found it important to validate and applaud their effort in stepping out on unfamiliar terrain.

Some trainees felt able to extend their process by sharing more thoughts about the social locations. They appeared more relaxed and tended to have fuller discussions. In the routine post-session team discussion, LOS was included in the routine feedback, structured around what seemed to go well in the session, what one might have wanted more or less of, or what one might have done differently. I always positioned myself last in these rounds.

Sharing such personal information, that is, the invisible social locations, had generally not been part of the trainees' graduate school training. Despite the growing literature on self-disclosure in general (Roberts, 2012; Quillman, 2012; Gibson, 2012, Roberts, 2005, Cheon & Murphy, 2007), it seems that teaching self-disclosure as a potentially therapeutic tool is far from the norm in academic programs that credential therapists. While a rigid boundary between the therapist's personal self and the client(s) is part of the traditional therapy frame, we are well into the postmodern era that ushered in the paradigm that the personal is always present in our observations, knowledge, and even in paradigm shifts in science (Kuhn, 1962).

Racial permutations of location of self

In the discussion below, some of the complexity of various racial locations is explored, as well as how other locations may interact with race.

LOS with clients/families of European descent or Caucasians presents a different interface than LOS with families of color. Naming whiteness is itself a novelty for many Whites who know they are White but live as though their whiteness requires no thought, examination, or comment, as though their racial identity is above that. For some, perhaps many, to have it named in LOS or elsewhere is to violate the un-named expectation they often hold. The therapist thus steps past a bar of privilege and risks that the client/family will be annoyed, anxious, challenge the therapist, or discontinue therapy. But such discomfort does not necessarily discredit the effort, any more than it does with any clinical question or exploration. These dynamics can be applicable in supervision with White supervisees as well. While probability favors the likelihood of the above risk, it is nonetheless possible that a White client or supervisee will be open to such attention given to race, including their own, along with other social locations, and/or have some social justice consciousness.

LOS with people of African, Asian, Latino, Native Indian, and Pacific Islander descent are most often keenly aware of their racial status and the associated subjugation, even when buffered to some degree by being privileged in other identities. For many, having a therapist who recognizes their experiences with oppression can be relieving and assuring. For supervisees of color, it can be encouraging that the supervision can mirror their experience of how race/racism impacts them as therapists as well as the clients. But it is also possible to encounter people of color who for various reasons have adopted a position of minimizing their race and racism, or who construe the mention of these realities as oppressive. They may seek relief from being seen in terms of their race, or because of the devaluation of their race, they experience the mention of it as another occasion of being treated differently (apart from Whites). In the latter instance, it could be helpful to inform them that LOS includes discussion of race with White clients as well. It is a reaction worth bookmarking for further exploration down the road.

White therapist–White client(s)

Some faculty members have shared their experiences with some White trainees who have questioned the point of bringing up race with White families. I've yet to meet that question from trainees of color faced with LOS with families of color. The question seems to emerge from the misconception that race is relevant to only people of color. It is as important for a White therapist to consider how similarity of race might handicap or support therapy as for therapists of color working with clients of color. Similarities can be limiting and enhancing factors.

A White therapist might reasonably wonder how racial similarity might constrain her/his ability to carry through on challenging oppression, particularly if the White client occupies more privileged locations than the therapist: for example, in class, gender or sexual orientation. The therapist might reasonably wonder if the client(s) might find her/his efforts to explore the possible impact of social location in the therapeutic relationship and therapy a drawback. Or the therapist might be in touch with her/his anxiety about raising such issues, and be concerned that this will lead to her/him avoiding them.

If a White therapist is undertaking a therapy that addresses oppression, there is another reason to consider how racial similarity may impact that. It is not uncommon for people to share racist or sexist or heterosexist beliefs and practices with those who occupy similar locations with them, on the assumption that the other feels similarly, or at least won't ignite in response to them. While there may be no people of color in the therapy room, the racism expressed is not confined within those walls. It affects people in the community and the world in which clients and we all live. Whites are fellow subway riders, colleagues, employers, supervisors, customers, and occasionally employees and supervisees of people of color.

What does it mean for a White therapist to be silent when present for racist words or the recounting of racially subjugating actions? If one takes the position that private therapy means caring about the hurt of only those in the room, then silence is the mandate. But akin to the way feminists challenged the notion of the privacy of a man's home, I've come to challenge the notion of private therapy. Both notions of privacy support the status quo in regard to oppression, via nonintervention.

For the therapist of any race to challenge the presence of an ism in the room is a matter of inquiry about the client(s)' perspective, how s/he came to that, what experiences, what messages from society taught it, and how does that impact his/her relationship with those targeted by the ism. It is also a matter of the therapist sharing her/his experience of that comment or information s/he might have.

In the context of the supervisor being White, the issues addressed above may parallel each other in the supervisor-therapist and therapist-client(s) relationships.

Black/person of color therapist–White clients

Inherent in this permutation of the racial identities in LOS is the same issue of de-privileging the experience of whiteness as an unmentionable. However, in this instance the therapist doing so is a member of the racially subjugated. The therapist is empowered professionally but less empowered racially. Given that racial superiority and inferiority are the hallmarks of racism, the question that can arise in the therapist's mind is whether s/he will be viewed as an inferior or diminished therapist. To what extent will the doubt that shadows people of color in regard to their goodness, their competence, hang over the relationship? How may it limit the therapeutic alliance? This question can arise off the top, so to speak, before any of the other locations in the room are considered.

In my view, Blacks and other people of color have every reason to wonder this. The history and present of racism is not delusional or fantasy. I think it is critical for therapists of color to internalize how reasonable it is, and to normalize it. Holding that sense is particularly helpful if and when the response is one of being miffed or accusatory. It is important that supervisors be able to hold this understanding as well; otherwise, they may be unable to support this kind of exchange around race, out of their own anxiety.

The concern I have is not about whether someone is racist, which goes far beyond a conscious sense or explicit act of superiority. As I have noted, I don't believe any of us, privileged and subjugated, are fully cleared of generations of oppression. My question is whether at a conscious level, a White family may have anxiety or doubt about their getting help from me, as a therapist of color of similar or dissimilar class, parent, and marital status. My interest is not in accusing, but rather in acknowledging that this is a possibility, and if so, how might we deal with that?

To say that this is a possibility is reasonable. I repeat this because of the invisible yet powerful injunction that exists in society against having such thoughts expressed to Whites, and the history of people of color carrying the burden of keeping Whites comfortable, of wearing the mask, as Paul Lawrence Dunbar (1994) put it, in order to survive. I underscore it also because the therapist of color may be vulnerable to feeling the need to defend this practice or to equivocate about it when faced with a White person's anxiety or devaluation of LOS. My supposition is that the clearer the therapist is on the normalcy of her/his concern or question, the less s/he may get hooked into an emotional press of defending the framework or obscuring her/his therapeutic vision. That is, s/he can take her/his "I" position as a therapist.

Adding on the other locations will not eliminate the effect of race. Rather, it becomes part of a stew that is unique for every therapist and client in this variation, but will also have some similarities. If the clients are further elevated in class and parental status, there may be more concern on the therapist's part about how open clients will be to his/her input. If the clients are LGBTQ and the therapist is heterosexual, the racial difference may be moderated by the shared marginal locations of race and sexual orientation, depending on how the therapist communicates her/his awareness of possible limitations in their sexual orientation differences.

What all of this complexity means is that there is no script, only a conversation to explore thoughts about how the mix of similarities and differences may work for the therapy or hinder it at times. It is a conversation that initiates the therapist's and client(s)' ability to be mindful of and talk through such influences in the course of therapy. The same is true for the supervisory relationship.

But how can this concern of devaluation be put into words with the White client(s)? I have not yet found a way to language this directly, and the reason is that I find it hard to imagine a constructive conversation about race and racism with a White client going well with a lead-off akin to saying, "I'm wondering if your racism may be an obstacle for us." And so I have continued with my approach of owning some concern about whether this is a new experience for them, given that the majority of professionals in nearly all careers are White.

If they indicate that they have worked with people of color before, I will ask in what capacity and whether it is one in which they were seeking/receiving help with a problem or collaborating with professionals of color. If they have, I will ask how that went. If not, I will note that since this is a new experience for them, I wonder if they have any thoughts or concerns about how it might go. Rarely has anyone voiced a concern. Occasionally, I've been asked a question or two related to my experience. From there, I will note that our racial differences are likely connected to different experiences and understanding of race, and that I hope that if it comes up for either of us, we can share it and figure out together how to work with it.

Therapists of color bring into the room a litany of personal and professional experiences of racism and denial of racism by Whites. There is baggage of anger and frustration. At the same time, as therapists, our interest is in facilitating transformation, and thus our challenge is to be well centered in that role and desire. So, for example, if a therapist of color notes the surprise of the White client(s) upon meeting her/him (not uncommon), and the client denies that s/he was anticipating a therapist who looked different, the therapist of color harnesses her therapeutic voice in going further into the reality that even though there are more therapists of color now, most remain White. In effect, if the clients had been surprised, it wouldn't be surprising. In some sense, this normalizes it, and at the same time, the therapist of color can suggest that such a difference may be or is (depending on how adamant the dismissal) worth thinking about as part of the therapy relationship. Even in a minimal exchange, the therapist has bookmarked the issue for a future time, and through use of self, has initiated an authentic exchange of her/his experience of the initial racial intersection.

This approach does not require the therapist to deny thoughts or feelings of frustration, annoyance, or anger about the client being untruthful or unwilling to engage or own the racial issue. The challenge is not to allow those feelings to lead the response or to defer the response until that can be the case. In our role as healers of color, we need to honor, that is, accept whatever anger, frustration, or hurt we may feel in the moment, as well as the opportunity to open a new space of being, thinking, and doing in our clients by the way we respond. It may not be enough to create transformation, but I've come to believe that in life, whether in therapy, supervision, or elsewhere, our job is to show up as well as we can. Beyond that, we cannot ensure or insure.

White therapist–Black/person of color clients

It is the prevalence of this combination that motivated my interest in LOS. In my experience working with people of color, they almost always bring up race and racism. Marginalized people are well aware of what is palatable and understood by the empowered. We know with whom we can bring up our belief in Santeria or Vodou, our feelings of anger about discrimination and devaluation by Whites, or the visions we may have of our ancestors. We know all too well the dominant narrative and its limited scope. We will typically not bring into therapy experiences that fall outside that scope, unless we have a sense that there is a non-pejorative, malleable framework, an openness to receive our experience, an awareness of the realities of oppression, and a caring about it. We will often seek out therapists of color, if we have that privilege.

These are the concerns that I wish Whites to have as they embark on therapy with people of color: Not whether people of color will trust them or feel free to share issues of racism, but whether they, as therapists, can provide people of color the assurance that they have some understanding that racism impacts people of color, that they are aligned with defeating and healing from oppression, and that they know that because of their whiteness, there are limits to their experience of that oppression and other ways of knowing. I wish White therapists to say they will try to be accountable for not perpetuating racism and at the same time invite clients of color to share when they feel they may be encountering blind spots of their therapists. I wish White therapists to want to know.

As with all therapists representing various social locations, I wish for the modicum of courage, awareness, and confidence to open the therapy door for witnessing all forms of oppression.

Black/person of color therapist–Black/person of color client(s)

While many, if not most, people of African descent will also identify as people of color, those of Asian, Latino, or Native American Indian ancestry may not. The same can be said of biracial client(s). Thus, how members of this group locate themselves becomes part of LOS. As with other locations of race, there is greater complexity than may appear on the surface. There are variations among people of African descent and between Africans who've immigrated and others of African descent. There is a history of tensions between various groups, and the same may be said in regard to different Asian and Latino identities. As a Black, or person of color, therapist, there are reasons to wonder about how racial and cultural differences may impact the work. For example, how might the understanding and point of view on women's roles in couple relationships and families of a middle-class Latino therapist intersect with that of a working-class or poor Latina or Asian Indian woman?

It is important to note that therapists of color can be triggered in working with people of color of similar or different ethnic backgrounds as well as with Whites. It can be related to issues of internalized racism and racial identity or other locations. Further, it is likely that on occasion, any therapist may not be successful in managing her/his affective response to oppressive actions or non-actions in the room. I have certainly had that experience. When I have realized this, usually after the session, I return the following week with an apology and acknowledgment that I went "over the top" in my response in the previous session. I do this as an act of transparency, providing some context for my reaction, but I am clear with clients that the responsibility to manage such strong reactions belongs to me and that I failed in that instance.

White supervisors who supervise therapists of color working with clients of color need to be open to learning about nuances of racial meaning and experience to which the therapist may be privy. When therapist and clients are of different cultures, it can be helpful for both supervisor and therapist to share readings about the legacies of culture and historical oppression of the clients. This does not take the place of exploring the clients' location in regard to such traditions or oppression, but it demonstrates a commitment to not showing up empty-handed in this respect. Clients may be able to suggest a particular reading, though it should not be left to them.

If and when good clinical work comes to include openly addressing manifestations of oppression in therapy, all the relational processes in therapy and supervision have the opportunity to deepen. This becomes possible with the willingness to see and enter more fully the places of injury and injuring that we as therapists, supervisors, and trainees, and our clients have experienced or are experiencing from oppression. Such a space offers the potential of us all connecting more with the wholeness of our being.

In conclusion, LOS is a part of a process of therapy that includes the examination of oppression's manifestations across multiple intersections and its deleterious relational impact. It is also a process that can be engaged by supervisors and supervisees to strengthen their ability to recognize and negotiate places in supervision and in therapy where their intersection of locations is creating some discord or therapeutic constraint. LOS makes no demand of perfection, only a willingness to stand in the heat of ugly, painful legacies in us and others, to persist into skillfulness and its variations, and to take heart in authentic showing-up. It is my hope that over time greater refinement and variations in method will emerge through the written contributions of others using LOS.

References

Almeida, R. (1998). The cultural context model: An overview. In M. McGoldrick (Ed.), *Revisioning family therapy: Race, culture and gender in clinical practice* (pp. 414–431). New York, NY: Guilford Press.

Almeida, R., Woods, R., Messineo, T., Font, R., & Heer, C. (1994). Violence in the lives of the racially and sexually different: A public and private dilemma. In R. Almeida (Ed.), *Expansions of feminist family theory through diversity* (pp. 99–126). New York, NY: Harrington Park Press.

Aponte, H., & Kissil, K. (2014). "If I can grapple with this I can truly be of use in the therapy room": Using the therapist's own emotional struggles to facilitate effective therapy. *Journal of Marital and Family Therapy, 40*(2), 152–164.

Carter, B., & Peters, J. (1996). *Love, honor and negotiate: Making your marriage work*. New York, NY: Pocket Books.

Carter, B., & McGoldrick, M. (1999). *The expanded family life cycle: Individual, family and social perspectives* (3rd ed.) (p. 6). Needham Heights: Allyn & Bacon.

Cheon, H-S., & Murphy, M. (2007). The self of the therapist awakened: Postmodern approaches to the use of self in marriage and family therapy. *Journal of Feminist Family Therapy, 19*(1), 1–16.

Coates, T-N. (2015). *Between the world and me* (pp. 91–92). New York, NY: Spiegel & Grau.

Crenshaw, K. (1991). Mapping the margins: Intersectionality, identity politics, and violence against women of color. *Stanford Law Review, 43*(6), 1241–1299.

Dunbar, P. (1994). We wear the mask. In E. Ethelbert Miller & T. Cummings (Eds.), *In search of color everywhere: A collection of African-American poetry*. New York, NY: Stewart, Tabori & Chang.

Frost, D., & Meyer, I. (2009). Internalized homophobia and relationship quality among lesbians, gay men and bisexuals. *Journal of Counseling Psychology, 56*(1), 97–109.

Garcia, M., Kosutic, I., McDowell, T., & Anderson, S. (2009). Raising critical consciousness in family therapy supervision. *Journal of Feminist Family Therapy, 21*, 18–38.

Gibson, M. (2012). Opening up: Therapist self-disclosure in theory, research and practice. *Clinical Social Work Journal, 40*, 287–296.

Goodwin, A., Kaestle, C., & Piercy, F. (2013). An exploration of feminist family therapists' resistance to and collusion with oppression. *Journal of Feminist Family Therapy, 25*, 233–256.

Graham, D. (2015). The mysterious death of Freddie Gray. *theatlantic.com*, http://www.theatlantic.com/politics/archive/2015/04/the-mysterious-death-of-freddie-gray/391119/ (accessed March 24, 2016).

Halevy, J. (2007). Shame as a barrier to cultural sensitivity and competent practice. *Journal of Feminist Family Therapy, 19*(1), 17–38.

Hardy, K., & Laszloffy, T. (2005). *Teens who hurt: Clinical interventions to break the cycle of adolescent violence*. New York, NY: Guilford Press.

Johnson, D., Cabral, A., Mueller, B., Trub, L., Phil, M., Kruk, J., Upshur, E. et al. (2010). Training in intersectionality sensitivity: A community-based collaborative approach (pp. 4–15). *AFTA Monograph Series, Expanding Our Social Justice Practices: Advances in Theory and Training*. Washington, DC: American Family Therapy Academy, Inc.

Kelly, S. (2013). Morrison speaks on evil, language and "the white gaze." *Cornell Chronicle*, (accessed 9/3/2013).

Kerr, M. & Bowen, M. (1988). *Family evaluation* (pp. 285–286). New York, NY: Norton.

Kuhn, T. (1962). *The structure of scientific revolutions*. Chicago, IL: University of Chicago Press.

Lum, W. (2002). The use of self of the therapist. *Contemporary Family Therapy, 24*(1), 181–197.

McDougall, S., & McGeorge, C. (2014). Utilizing women's feminist identities in family therapy: A phenom- enological exploration of the meaning women assign to their feminist identities. *Journal of Feminist Family Therapy, 26*(2), 73–98.

Orsi, R. (1992). The religious boundaries of an InBetween people: Street feste and the problem of the dark- skinned other in Italian Harlem, 1920–1990. *American Quarterly, 44*(3), 315.

Raymond, A. (2015). Arresting officers bought Dylann Roof some Burger King. http://nymag.com/daily/ intelligencer/2015/06/arresting-officers-bought-dylann-roof-a-burger.html (accessed March 24, 2016).

Roberts, J. (2005). Transparency and self-disclosure in family therapy: Dangers and possibilities. *Family Process, 44*(1), 45–63.

Roberts, J. (2012). Therapist self-disclosure: Think before you get personal. *Psychotherapy Networker, 36*(4), 3-58.

Simon, G. (2006). The heart of the matter: A proposal for placing the self of the therapist at the center of family therapy research and training. *Family Process, 45*(3), 331–344.

Waldegrave, C., & Tamasese, K. (1993). Some central ideas in the "just therapy" approach. *Australian & New Zealand Journal of Family Therapy, 14*(1), 1–8.

Watts Jones, T. D. (2010). Location of self: Opening the door to dialogue on intersectionality in the therapy process. *Family Process, 49*(3), 405–420.

Weingarten, K. (2003). *Common shock: Witnessing violence every day: How we are harmed, how we can heal.* New York, NY: Dutton.

PART II

Issues of Identity and Social Location in Supervision and Training

4

POWER AND PRIVILEGE IN SUPERVISION

Multicultural feminist reflections on practice

Heidi A. Zetzer, PhD

Malcolm Gladwell (2008) popularized the report that it takes 10,000 hours to become an expert (Ericsson, Krampe, & Tesch-Romer, 1993). I believe that I am halfway to the 10,000 hours needed to become an expert at multicultural missteps. You might think that this means that I have gotten pretty good at making mistakes (and I have). However, what I really mean is that I have gotten much better at being human. I am more accepting, forgiving, and have a better sense of humor. How did I do this? With practice!

The key ingredients for becoming a culturally sensitive expert in counseling, psychotherapy, and supervision are compassion, integrity, and 10,000 hours of practice. This is a lifelong journey (Sue & Sue, 1999) that has no end, which is why acceptance of self and others as living, learning beings is so crucial. As Gertrude Stein (1937, p. 289) said, "There is no *there* there." As soon as you feel culturally competent, conditions will change. New clients, trainees, contexts, and identities will emerge as the culture shifts. Hence, it is essential that we treat our selves and our trainees with the loving-kindness we afford our clients.

As has been aptly pointed out by critics of Gladwell (Popova, 2014), part of the formula for developing expertise is *deliberate* practice, often guided by proper coaching. Otherwise, practice results in the repetition of mistakes. In the fields of counseling and psychotherapy, clinical supervisors are the coaches. However, unlike in other disciplines, supervisors are charged with promoting and protecting client welfare in addition to fostering the professional growth of trainees. Supervisors not only provide valuable feedback to trainees on their performance, they also teach supervisees how to engage in "reflection on practice" and "reflection in action" (Schön, 1984). Such reflection is a "meta-competency" (Hatcher & Lassiter, 2007). This ability cannot be taught didactically. It grows out of the dynamic circular flow between action and reflection (Freire, Ramos, & Macedo, 2000) in therapeutic and supervisory relationships.

Client-centered multicultural feminist supervisors provide opportunities for trainees to learn about what it means to be in a deeply personal yet wholly professional multicultural relationship. Client-centered supervisors (Patterson, 1997) enter the relationship with a commitment to the core conditions (Rogers, 1957). Feminist supervisors ground their approach in the principles of feminist therapy (Enns, 2004), which encourages helpers to be explicit about their values, transparent in their approach, and appreciative of the mutuality of the helping relationship. Feminist supervision is uniquely characterized by explicit attention to the supervisor's use of power in the supervisory relationship (Burnes, Wood, Inman, & Welikson, 2013).

As a multicultural feminist and client-centered supervisor, I use counseling, consulting, and teaching skills (Bernard, 1997) to build the trainees' cultural competencies. However, the deeper learning takes place within the context of multicultural supervisory relationships. Cultural sensitivity is learned *in situ* through the beauty of "parallel process" (Ekstein & Wallerstein, 1958; Inman & Kreider, 2013; Zetzer, 2014). The supervisory relationship is the place where trainees and I work out what it takes to turn missteps into steady steps. This approach requires integrity, compassion, and reflection on practice. It also requires that I attend to the role of power and privilege in supervision.

The purpose of this chapter is to describe how parallel process may be used to foster cultural sensitivity among trainees and within oneself as a supervisor. I will illustrate the relevance of power and privilege in multicultural supervision through a case example that is yet another *mea culpa*, which increases my misstep tally to 5012 hours!

Sociopolitical location and privilege

Years ago, I was fortunate to participate in a one-day training with Kenneth V. Hardy (2002), who advised participants to begin multicultural dialogues with clear statements about their sociopolitical locations. Situating oneself in a broader historical, political, and cultural context serves as a reminder of what each of us brings to these interactions. I typically begin supervision with a reflection on the multiplicity of my identities.

I am a fifty-something, well-meaning, white (Wolfe, 1995), second-wave feminist woman. I benefit from white (Kendall, 2006), thin (Loewy & Pyle, 2104), heterosexual (Croteau, Lark, Lidderdale, & Chung, 2004), and cisgender privilege (Walls & Costello, 2011). I have high standards. I am intolerant of my own missteps. I aim to be an A+ person who has a reputation for being helpful and kind. I strive for empathy, equity, and equanimity in all that I do.

Can you spot the irony in what I just said? It's in the *striving*. It is my attachment to a "good" *conceptualized* self (Hayes, Luoma, Masuda, & Lilles, 2006) that makes it challenging for me to embody the noble "e" words when I make a misstep. In those moments, I am hindered from expressing multicultural empathy, acknowledging inequitable treatment, or responding with equanimity because I am defensively holding on tightly to an ideal self that is unrealistic and "unworkable" (Hayes, et al., 2006). Five thousand hours of missteps have taught me that letting go (as best I can) of my highly conceptualized good-white-person self allows me to *respond rather than react* when I am in the midst of a cultural misunderstanding. Over time, I have gotten better at recognizing when I am *grasping onto* my ideal self rather than *living in* my real self (Rogers, 1961) and engaging with trainees authentically.

Parallel process

Despite controversies over the definition and arguments about its roots, there is consensus that parallel process in supervision is real (Raichelson, Herron, Primavera, & Ramirez, 1997). Bernard and Goodyear (2014) proclaimed, "This now has become the best-known phenomenon in supervision: perhaps even the signature phenomenon" (p. 65).

In its original definition (Ekstein & Wallerstein, 1958; Searles, 1955), parallel process occurs when the therapist unconsciously "enacts the patient's dynamic with the supervisor" (Frawley-O'Dea & Sarnat, 2000, p. 171), which gives the supervisor insight into the therapeutic relationship and guides supervisory interventions. In its modern form, parallel process occurs when "the dynamics of the therapeutic relationship stimulate and are reflected in the supervisory relationship" (Falender & Shafranske, 2004, p. 111). The reverse dynamic is also considered to be true

(Doehrman, 1976), whereby the dynamics of the supervisory relationship get played out in the therapeutic relationship.

Parallel process is a key ingredient in multicultural supervision. Inman and Kreider (2013) used a case example to show how parallel process, and Ladany, Friedlander, and Nelson's (2005) *Critical Events Model* (CEM) and Ancis and Ladany's (2010) *Heuristic Model of Nonoppressive Interpersonal Development* (HMNID) may be used to foster multicultural competence in a trainee. "By recognizing trainee behavior as parallel to behavior of the client, supervisors may model multiculturally competent behavior in supervision in order to influence interactions within the therapy setting" (p. 349).

Two features of these approaches stand out. First, trainee growth and development is promoted when the supervisors successfully identify and resolve critical events in psychotherapy and/or supervision, primarily by attending to their own use of power in the supervisory relationship (Ladany et al., 2005). Second, resolution of such events is influenced by a complex interplay of intersecting identities expressed by the client, trainee, and supervisor. According to Ancis and Ladany (2010), these identities stem from membership in "socially oppressed groups" (SOG) or "socially privileged groups" (SPG).

Any one person may have multiple memberships in these groups. For example, I am white and therefore benefit from white privilege, but I am also female and denied certain freedoms because of sexism (e.g., cannot walk alone at night because of risk of sexual assault, will not earn as much as a male counterpart because of inequitable salaries, and fewer reproductive choices because of differential health care coverage). In addition, identities develop through broad phases, from adaptation (i.e., conformity) to incongruence (i.e., dissonance) through exploration and into integration. These stages resemble Helm's statuses of racial/cultural identity development (Helms, 1995). As a supervisor, I will achieve the best outcomes with trainees if I attend to the multiplicity and developmental phase of the multicultural identities within the supervisory triad (i.e., client, trainee, and me) as well as how each identity holds and expresses power in our society.

Power and privilege in the supervisory relationship

The dynamics of power and privilege are an inevitable part of supervision (Nelson et al., 2006) because at a minimum, supervision involves a relationship between a more senior professional supervising and evaluating a less experienced trainee (Bernard & Goodyear, 2004; Falendar & Shafranske, 2004). However, there are a myriad of other types of power differentials, which derive from differences in participants' sociopolitical locations related to characteristics like race, gender, age, and prominence in the field. Ignoring such differences contributes to ruptures in the supervisory alliance and via parallel process, the therapeutic alliance too. Trainees who feel unsafe in the supervisory relationship are unlikely to raise questions about cultural differences between themselves and their clients or supervisors, let alone invite dialogue about differences. Supervisors who presume that trainees will speak up or that the salience of cultural differences will become obvious during supervision of the case miss opportunities to discuss and resolve critical events (Dressel, Consoli, Kim & Atkinson, 2007).

I prepare for ruptures in the supervisory alliance by framing it with an awareness of my sociopolitical location, a clear definition of my role, and a statement of values. Then, when missteps occur and/or parallel process comes into play, I do my best to demonstrate authenticity, humility, and transparency. I aim to provide the trainee with an experience of me that fosters their personal and professional growth as a whole person with intersecting personal and professional identities, which they then translate into therapeutic behaviors that affirm and support the integration of their clients' intersecting identities and therapeutic goals.

Basic principles and practices that promote cultural aensitivity in supervision

I begin supervision with a values statement and a confession that I am imperfect. I tell trainees that I prize integrity and express the hope that I will behave in a manner that is consistent with my stated values. I apply the multicultural feminist approach to psychotherapy described by Goodman et al. (2004) to supervision, which is characterized by six basic principles and practices:

- *Ongoing self-examination*: I am obligated to think about my own cultural identity and its impact on my working relationships.
- *Sharing power*: I share my knowledge and skills and recognize that trainees have valuable knowledge and skills to share with me.
- *Giving voice*: I want to hear what trainees have to say, and I aim to support them in having a "voice" in supervision, especially in domains where they feel silenced.
- *Consciousness-raising*: I share an intention to talk about the impact of oppression and privilege on our lives.
- *Build on strengths*: I reinforce trainee strengths and draw upon those strengths when addressing areas for growth (e.g., when trainee sensitivity, which is a strength, makes it difficult to set boundaries, which would be therapeutic for the client).
- *Develop tools for social change*: We work together to explore the full range of roles that a trainee may take when providing psychotherapy (e.g., advocating for clients in educational settings or promoting social justice in the community).

A client-centered approach to supervision hinges on my commitment to the core conditions (Rogers, 1957): empathy, unconditional positive regard, and authenticity. In addition, knowledge of the Integrated Developmental Model (IDM) (Stoltenberg & McNeill, 2010) has been invaluable as a source of empathy for and understanding of trainee needs. Despite trainee missteps, I unconditionally prize their humanity. Lastly, authenticity is essential in the development of trusting therapeutic and supervisory relationships. Trainees, like clients, can tell when we are faking it. They hunger for experiences that will help them develop their cultural competencies with clients (Fetherson, Anderson, & Duncan, 2013) and are appreciative when opportunities for learning are embraced and not avoided (Wong, Wong, & Ishiyama, 2013).

Misstep to steady step: Case example of reflection on practice in supervision

I am supervising Tim[1], a 35-year-old heterosexual Chinese American man. (See Zetzer, 2015, for a discussion of this same case with a different emphasis.) He was born in the United States to immigrant parents and is the eldest son of a university professor. Tim is an advanced practicum student, has excellent clinical skills, and makes good use of supervision. He was recently assigned a new client named Annie. Annie is a 40-year-old heterosexual biracial woman (Asian and white). She is seeking services after her partner, a 45-year-old second generation Eastern European man, ended a 5-year relationship in which he was physically and emotionally abusive. He repeatedly lied to her about important matters, especially money. The two were cohabiting and had comingled their assets. The ex-partner emptied the bank account before terminating the relationship. Annie is currently living with her sister, who is supporting her financially.

Annie reports to Tim that she feels lonely and depressed. She misses her ex terribly. She also reports feeling some relief because he was "manipulative and controlling." Annie said that she spent most of the relationship feeling "confused." Despite these feelings she tells Tim that she is trying to contact her ex so that she can see him to find out "what happened to the money." He has not returned her calls or replied to her e-mails, and she hopes to locate him through his family. It seems likely that Annie simply wants to see him and hopes to rekindle the relationship. She claims that he was her ideal partner in many ways. Annie's lack of resentment toward her ex is notable. It is almost as though she disappeared while in the relationship: no voice at all. It was only after the relationship ended and she could look at it from a distance that she could discern his impact on her.

Mutually determined short-term therapy goals include reducing depressive symptoms and getting a job. Long-term goals include fostering hope, resilience, and self-efficacy, and helping her find her "voice" in relationships.

Upon hearing about Annie's plan to meet with her ex, I developed a concern about her safety and advised Tim to learn more about Annie's experiences of domestic violence. I also directed Tim to work with her to form a safety plan in case her ex-partner became abusive during their meeting. I insisted that Tim talk to her about this even after he informed me, "She won't like it." I advised him to "proceed with finesse," which he did.

Annie did not respond positively to the emphasis upon risk and safety. A measure of the strength of the therapeutic alliance (Duncan, 2011) showed an unexpected decrease. In session, Annie reported feeling confused, which prompted Tim to justify his concern for her welfare. Tim said that Annie appeared increasingly distant and disconnected in response to his explanations. Tim said he felt confused and uncertain of the approach. Then I felt confused! I did not expect attention to Annie's personal welfare to be a contentious issue.

Initially, I held my ground in supervision. In my opinion, it seemed wise to prompt the client to prepare for an altercation with her ex-partner. But then I asked myself a question that I frequently ask trainees: "Who's it for?" Who is benefiting from the intervention and in what way? Annie? Tim? Me? How essential is it to force this issue? What is motivating my behavior? What part of this dynamic is indicative of a multicultural parallel process in the relationship between Annie and Tim and Tim and me?

As I reflected on the feminist multicultural aspects of the case and considered the potential bi-directionality of parallel process, I wondered if I had instructed Tim to enact power dynamics that resembled Annie's former relationship. My concern for her welfare had taken on a protective, perhaps even patriarchal quality! Annie responded to Tim's direct guidance with confusion, which prompted Tim to try to be more instructive, which further disempowered the client.

What were the cultural and clinical factors at play here? What aspects of the therapeutic relationship were appearing in the supervisory relationship? The client seemed to lack trepidation about seeing her ex-partner. This same lack of wariness was noticeable in Tim's report to me of her plans to see her ex, but Tim also appeared adamant in his appraisal of her resistance to thinking about protecting herself. Was the "client's less-adaptive" response being brought into supervision, or was I simply missing something?

Tim's persistence in raising doubts about our approach led me to wonder what assumptions had I been making about the benevolence of my own actions. Was I being triggered? Had I misapplied my authority as a supervisor? How had my own ethnocentrism and sense of privilege affected my approach in supervision? Here is a client who needed to build her own sense of competence, a trainee with good judgment and multicultural attunement, and me with the "pull" to protect Annie from harm. How was the way I located myself as "knowing better" than Tim or Annie herself different from presumptions white feminists have made about promoting social justice in multicultural contexts (hooks, 1984/2000)?

There were effectively four markers (Ladany et al., 2005) of a multicultural misstep in this case. First, Tim's prediction, "She won't like it." Hearing this should have signaled a deeper discussion, but I missed it. Second, Annie and Tim's experience of "confusion," which may have been a culturally consonant way of saying, "I don't understand," or "I disagree," and maybe a little of, "Can we please ignore that part of the story?" The third marker was a reduction in the strength of the therapeutic alliance. Finally, the fourth marker was my own feeling of discordance. Something was awry.

As I took time to reflect on my actions in supervision, I realized that my recommendations were insufficiently attuned to the cultural dynamics of the three people involved. The two most closely connected people, and the two who possessed some cultural similarity, were not sufficiently heard. Not very feminist! While imagining the exchange between Annie and her ex, whose cultural identity and behavioral history suggested a patriarchal approach to relationships, I predicted that there would be enough risk of violence to warrant preparation for it. While this judgment may have been accurate, the approach was disempowering for the trainee and the client. Luckily, I started to listen to Tim, and we were able to change the misstep into a steady step.

I hypothesized that raising the issue of safety had the effect of discounting Annie's desire to reconnect with her partner. There were real risks, in that she intended to confront him about his dishonesty. Safeguards were missing, but it was the manner in which the intervention was delivered that replicated the client's interpersonal and sociopolitical dynamics. I directed Tim, who then directed Annie. A more oblique, collaborative approach like Motivational Interviewing (Miller & Rollnick, 2013) would probably have been more effective.

Once I realized my mistake, I apologized to Tim for my insistence and took responsibility for the misstep. I owned that I had pressured him into addressing the potential for domestic violence without accounting for the cultural and clinical aspects of the client's hope for a reunion. I encouraged Tim to repair the rent in the alliance by honoring the client's wisdom and reinforcing her for having a voice in relationships, including the psychotherapeutic one! He in turn took a step back and adopted more of a one-down position with her, which led to immediate improvements in the therapeutic alliance and psychotherapy outcome.

Commentary

Where's the humor in this? The humor is in the irony and the familiarity. I have been here before! Sometimes I think that my job is to help students learn how to make mistakes and correct them. I have observed that my willingness to be transparent increases trust and increases the likelihood that trainees will tell me when they see indicators of their own missteps. In this way, we are able to use parallel process to inform supervision and psychotherapy.

The use of power in multicultural feminist supervision is a complicated matter. Supervisors have the authority to define the narrative of the client *and* the trainee. Action without reflection can lead to unintentional misuse of that authority (Zetzer, 2011). It is essential that supervisors avoid making one-way interpretations of parallel process that locate the problem in the client or the trainee (Miehls, 2010). There is great value in recognizing the bidirectional nature of the phenomenon and using it to invite self-reflection. As a supervisor, I have the honor of recovering from missteps in the presence of trainees who wait patiently for a resolution that makes sense to them. Practicing in their presence, and reflecting on that practice together, makes for 10,000 hours of good work.

Questions for further reflection

1. What is your conceptualization of the case presented?
2. What would you have done differently?
3. What role does integrity, compassion, and reflection on practice play in your approach to supervision?
4. What is your latest misstep? How did you resolve it?

Note

1 Client, trainee, and ex-partner described in this chapter are de-identified and disguised. Names are pseudonyms.

References

Ancis, J. R., & Ladany, N. (2010). A multicultural framework for counselor supervision. In N. Ladany & L. J. Bradley (Eds.), *Counselor supervision* (4th ed.) (pp. 53–94). New York, NY: Routledge.

Bernard, J. M. (1997). The discrimination model. In C. E. Watkins (Ed.), *Handbook of psychotherapy supervision* (pp. 310–327). New York, NY: Wiley.

Bernard, J. M., & Goodyear, R. K. (2014). *Fundamentals of clinical supervision* (5th ed.). Upper Saddle River, NJ: Pearson Education.

Burnes, T. R., Wood, J. M., Inman, J. L., & Welikson, G. A. (2013). An investigation of process variables in feminist clinical group supervision. *The Counseling Psychologist, 41*, 86–109. doi: 10.1177/0011000012442653.

Croteau, J. M., Lark, J. S., Lidderdale, M. A., & Chung, Y. B. (Eds.). (2004). *Deconstructing heterosexism in counseling professions: A narrative approach.* In P. B. Pedersen (Series Ed.), *Multicultural aspects of counseling series,* Volume 20. Thousand Oaks, CA: SAGE Publications.

Doehrman, M. J. (1976). Parallel process in supervision and psychotherapy. *Bulletin of the Menninger Clinic, 40,* 9–104.

Dressel, J. L., Consoli, A. J., Kim, B. S. K., & Atkinson, D. R. (2007). Successful and unsuccessful multicultural supervisory behaviors: A Delphi poll. *Journal of Multicultural Counseling & Development, 35,* 51–64. http://dx.doi.org/10.1002/j.2161-1912.2007.tb00049.x (accessed March 24, 2016).

Duncan, B. (2011). *The Partners for Change Outcome Management System (PCOMS): Administration, scoring, interpreting update for the Outcome and Session Ratings scale.* Jenson Beach, FL: Author.

Ekstein, R., & Wallerstein, R. S. (1972). *The teaching and learning of psychotherapy* (2nd ed.). New York, NY: International Universities Press.

Enns, C. Z. (2004). *Feminist theories and feminist psychotherapies: Origins, themes, and diversity* (2nd ed.). Binghamton, NY: Haworth Press.

Ericsson, K. A., Krampe, R. Th., & Tesch-Romer, C. (1993). The role of deliberate practice in the acquisition of expert performance. *Psychological Review, 100,* 363–406. http://dx.doi.org/10.1037/0033-295X. 100.3.363 (accessed March 24, 2016).

Falender, C. A., & Shafranske, E. P. (2004). *Clinical supervision: A competency-based approach.* Washington, DC: American Psychological Association.

Fetherson, B. T. L., Anderson, M. Z., & Duncan, L. E. (2013, August). *What about me? Using grounded theory to understand how African-American counseling professionals become multiculturally competent.* Poster session presented at the Annual Meeting of the American Psychological Association, Honolulu, HI.

Frawley-O'Dea, M. G., & Sarnat, J. E. (2000). *The supervisory relationship: A contemporary psychodynamic approach.* New York, NY: Guilford Press.

Freire, P., Ramos, M. B., & Macedo, D. (2000). *Pedagogy of the oppressed: 30th anniversary edition.* New York, NY: Bloomsbury Academic.

Gladwell, M. (2008). *Outliers: The story of success.* New York, NY: Little, Brown & Co.

Goodman, L. A., Liang, B., Helms, J. E., Latta, R. E., Sparks, E., & Weintraub, S. R. (2004). Training counseling psychologists as social justice agents: Feminist and multicultural perspectives in action. *The Counseling Psychologist, 32,* 793–837. doi: 10.1177/0011000004268802. http://dx.doi.org/10.1177/0011000004268802 (accessed March 24, 2016).

Hardy, K. V. (November 2, 2002). *The invisible wounds of oppression.* One-day workshop presented at Antioch University, Santa Barbara, CA.

Hatcher, R. L., & Lassiter, K. D. (2007). Initial training in professional psychology: The practicum competencies outline. *Training and Education in Professional Psychology, 1,* 49–63. http://dx.doi.org/10.1037/1931-3918.1.1.49 (accessed March 24, 2016).

Hayes, S. C., Luoma, J. B., Bond, F. W., Masuda, A., & Lilles, J. (2006). Acceptance and commitment therapy: Model, processes, and outcomes. *Behaviour Research and Therapy, 44,* 1–25. doi: 10.1016/j.brat.2005.06.006 http://dx.doi.org/10.1016/j.brat.2005.06.006 (accessed March 24, 2016).

Helms, J. E. (1995). An update on Helms' white and people of color racial identity models. In J. G. Ponterotto, J. M. Casas, L. A. Suzuki, & C. M. Alexander (Eds.), *Handbook of multicultural counseling* (pp. 181–198). Thousand Oaks, CA: SAGE Publications.

hooks, b. (1984, 2000). *Feminist theory: From margin to center.* Cambridge, MA: South End Press.

Inman, A. G., & Kreider, E. D. (2013). Multicultural competence: Psychotherapy practice and supervision. *Psychotherapy, 50,* 346–350. doi: 10.1037/a0032029. http://dx.doi.org/10.1037/a0032029 (accessed March 24, 2016).

Kendall, F. E. (2006). *Understanding white privilege: Creating pathways to authentic relationships across race.* New York, NY: Routledge.

Ladany, N., Friedlander, M. L., & Nelsen, M. L. (2005). *Critical events in psychotherapy supervision: An interpersonal approach.* Washington, DC: APA. http://dx.doi.org/10.1037/10958-000 (accessed March 24, 2016).

Loewy, M. I., & Pyle, N. C. (May 16, 2014). *Body size diversity: Prejudice and privilege.* Invited presentation at the University of California, Santa Barbara.

Miehls, D. (2010). Contemporary trends in supervision theory: A shift from parallel process to relational and trauma theory. *Clinical Social Work, 38,* 370–378. doi: 10.1007/s10615-009-0247-8. http://dx.doi.org/10.1007/s10615-009-0247-8 (accessed March 24, 2016).

Miller, W. R., & Rollnick, S. (2013). *Motivational interviewing: Helping people change.* New York, NY: Guilford Press.

Nelson, M. L., Gizara, S., Cronbach, A. Phelps, H. R., Steward. R., & Weitzman, L. (2006). A feminist multicultural perspective on supervision. *Journal of Multicultural Counseling & Development, 34,* 105–115. http://dx.doi.org/10.1002/j.2161-1912.2006.tb00031.x (accessed March 24, 2016).

Owen, J. J., & Reese, R. J. (2014, March). Overview of client feedback research: Where we are and where we need to go. In R. J. Reese (Chair), *Client feedback and Counseling Psychology: A match made in evidence-based practice heaven?* Symposium conducted at The Counseling Psychology in Action Conference, Atlanta, GA.

Patterson, C. H. (1997). Client-centered supervision. In E. Watkins (Ed.), *Handbook of psychotherapy supervision* (pp. 134–146). New York, NY: Wiley.

Popova, M. (January 22, 2014). Debunking the myth of the 10,000 hours rule: What it actually takes to reach genius level excellence. https://www.brainpickings.org/2014/01/22/daniel-goleman-focus-10000-hours-myth/ (accessed March 24, 2016).

Raichelson, S. H., Herron, W. G., Primavera, L. H., & Ramirez, S. M. (1997). Incidence and effects of parallel process in psychotherapy supervision. *The Clinical Supervisor, 15,* 37–48. doi:10.1300/J001v15n02_03. http://dx.doi.org/10.1300/J001v15n02_03

Rogers, C. R. (1957). The necessary and sufficient conditions of therapeutic personality change. *Journal of Consulting Psychology, 21,* 95–103.

Rogers, C. R. (1961). *On becoming a person: A therapist's view of psychotherapy.* New York, NY: Houghton-Mifflin.

Schön, D. (1984). *The reflective practitioner: How professionals think in action.* New York, NY: Basic Books.

Searles, H. (1955). The informational value of the supervisor's emotional experiences. *Psychiatry, 18,* 135–146.

Sparks, J. A., Kisler, T. J., Adams, J. F., & Blumen, D. G. (2011). Teaching accountability: Using client feedback to train effective family therapists. *Journal of Marital and Family Therapy, 37,* 452–467. doi:10.1111/j.1752-0606.2011.00224.x

Stein, G. (1937). *Everybody's autobiography.* New York, NY: Random House.

Stoltenberg, C. D., & McNeill, B. W. (2010). *IDM: An integrative developmental model for supervising counselors and therapists* (3rd ed.). New York, NY: Routledge.

Sue, D. W., & Sue, D. (1999). *Counseling the culturally different: Theory and practice* (3rd ed.). New York, NY: Wiley.

Walls, N. E., & Costello, K. (2011). "Head ladies center for teacup chain": Exploring cisgender privilege in a predominantly gay male context. In S. K. Anderson & V. A. Middleton (Eds.), *Explorations in diversity: Examining privilege and oppression in a multicultural society* (2nd ed.) (pp. 81–94). Belmont, CA: Thompson/Wadsworth.

Wolfe, N. (1995). The racism of well-meaning white people. In M. Golden & S. R. Shreve (Eds.), *Skin deep: Black and white women write about race* (pp. 37–46). New York, NY: Doubleday.

Wong, L. C. J., Wong, P. T. P., & Ishiyama, F. I. (2013). What helps and what hinders in cross-cultural clinical supervision: A critical incident study. *The Counseling Psychologist, 41,* 66–85. doi:10.1177/0011000012442652. http://dx.doi.org/10.1177/0011000012442652

Zetzer, H. A. (2015). Parallel process in multicultural supervision. *Psychotherapy Bulletin, 50,* 19–23.

Zetzer, H. A. (August, 2014). *The beauty of parallel process in multicultural supervision: Cultivating cultural competence in context.* Roundtable discussion, Annual Meeting of the American Psychological Association, Washington, DC.

Zetzer, H. A. (2011). White out: Privilege and its problems. In S. K. Anderson & V. A. Middleton (Eds.), *Explorations in diversity: Examining privilege and oppression in a multicultural society* (2nd ed.) (pp. 11–24). Belmont, CA: Thompson/Wadsworth.

5

MAKING THE INVISIBLE VISIBLE

A closer look at social class in supervision and training

Kenneth V. Hardy, PhD, Ana M. Hernandez, PhD, and Christiana Awosan, PhD

Social Class is a powerful but often unacknowledged dimension of culture. Like race, gender, and the myriad of other dimensions of culture, it is a powerful organizing principle that significantly shapes all spheres of our lives. It dictates where we are born, critical circumstances surrounding our birth such as access to healthcare, where and how we live, and how/when we die. It also can be easily concealed, denied, and/or obfuscated in many ways that make it easy to ignore. Social class is omnipresent and represents an ideology, system of classification, and a potent organizing principle that is also often unacknowledged. Understanding the critical intersection of these three entities is crucial to enhancing awareness of the potent impact that class has on our lives.

Social class as ideology

Social class is not just about finances and financial stability; it is also a significant and underlying belief system. Class as an ideology promulgates the following assumptions: 1) the world is comprised of "the Haves and the have-nots," whereby the former is valued while the latter is devalued; 2) class is a system with permeable boundaries that facilitates progressive movement within and across class lines; 3) class movement is solely determined by the "expenditure of effort," which asserts that anyone who works hard enough can traverse the boundaries of class. Thus in a very sophisticated way, social class encompasses a set of values, assumptions, and prescriptions for living that is weaved into our perceptions of who we are, who we aspire to be, how we see others, and how we believe we are seen by others. It imparts subtle and hidden messages about our worth and value. Unfortunately, we all, to some extent, subscribe to the principles of the underlying ideology of social class.

Social class as a classification system

Social class is also a classification system that informs the ways in which the ideology of "the Haves and the have-nots" is created and supported in our society. Social class division is a reality throughout the United States despite the perception that we live in a classless society with exceedingly permeable boundaries (Laszloffy, 2008). Hence we live within the context of a class-based classification system that is hierarchically arranged, where those on the top are greatly valued, those on the bottom devalued, and the those in the middle are valued more than some and not as much as others. This classification system is largely reinforced and solidified by social inequality and the inequitable distribution of resources such as access to quality health care, adequate education, job opportunities, and living environments. Consequently this arrangement places some people at a disadvantage, creating deprivation, while simultaneously affording advantages, privileges, and excess to others (Rothenberg, 2012). These inequities often lead to feelings of shame, denial, fear, rage, and guilt, all connected to one's social class location.

Social class as an organizing principle

Social class as an organizing principle is present in our everyday lives. The common narrative often used to justify the ideology of a classless society while simultaneously highlighting social class divisions is the notion that "anyone who works hard enough can achieve upwardly mobile class success." This notion of rugged individualism and hard work translating into class-based wealth and success is embedded within the concept of "the American Dream." This class-coded term refers to "the successful, self-reliant, independent, and high achieving, self-made individual" who allegedly pulls *oneself* up by the bootstrap. The belief in this class-driven notion that "simply working hard" is sufficient to achieve the American Dream, regardless of family of origin, social and economic status, race, gender, sexual orientation, education, nationality, or ability is a deathtrap. It denies the harsh reality of the structural dimensions of class that ensure that some can work as hard as they wish, and their "class assignments" will remain unaltered. The view that everyone is afforded similar opportunities in our society to transcend their social class status through hard work perpetuates the class classification of the Haves and the have-nots. Furthermore, it leads to and perpetuates judgments with regards to who is "working hard" and who is not. It contributes to a divided society in which some are revered for working hard to achieve the American Dream, and others are shamed and accused of not working hard enough to attain the "Dream." The latter, therefore, is responsible for their lack of class mobility and success. For instance, individuals in middle or higher social classes are not just perceived by others as stable, hardworking, and respectable, they perceive themselves as such and believe that with effort they have achieved at least a piece of the American Dream. Not only do they view themselves as hardworking and take pride in their efforts in achieving the American Dream, they may also internalize a sense of superiority due to their access to resources—while oftentimes, low-income individuals and those living in poverty are seen as lazy, unreliable, unworthy, and deserving of social blame for their lack of class mobility. Sadly, many within the lower class and those who live in poverty internalize the negative views that they are aware that society has of them. Society's view of them essentially becomes their view of themselves. Consequently, many low-income families and families in poverty are not only aspiring for financial stability to sustain themselves, but they are also striving to have material access, respect, positive regard, and other "luxuries" that are often afforded to those in higher social classes.

Making the invisible visible in supervision and training

We all come from an array of class locations that affect how we experience the world and those around us. As supervisors and trainers, it is imperative that we remain cognizant of class and its impact on the clinical process. The following vignette illustrates how class can be an unidentified dynamic in therapy and supervision.

> Maria, a lower-income mother in an intake session with a middle-income Family Therapy Intern, instantly noticed her therapist's gold watch. It seemed to stand out like a diamond. She disgustingly commented to her daughter, "She's not from around here with her fancy watch glittering like gold." The watch, in the eyes of Maria and perhaps with Jessica, her therapist, as well, was a symbol of class. For Maria the nice expensive watch contributed to an internalized

belief that she had about both expensive jewelry and "rich people." Her assumption was that rich people could afford luxuries, and that they probably also looked down on people like her who couldn't. As a supervisor, and one whose life experiences with class have been dangerously close to those of Maria's, I (AMH) encouraged Jessica to talk with Maria about "the watch" and what it symbolized for her.

From an early age, I (AMH) felt a strong sense of shame and rage connected to my lower-income class status and not having nice things. My family was sustained through the Welfare system, Women, Infant, and Children (WIC) subsidies, and other government assistance programs. My most debilitating emotions were often triggered by encounters with people who enjoyed expensive material possessions and who I believed saw me as inferior to them. I was never directly told I was inferior but I knew others felt this way, and at times I did as well. This is the nature of class: even when its significance is vociferously denied, its potency can be felt nonetheless. As a child of working-class immigrant parents, I often helplessly observed the disrespect and inhumane treatment my mother received because she was among the "have-nots" of our society. She wanted me to have a better life and consistently encouraged me to *work hard* and get an education to advance my social class status in the USA. As a newcomer to the United States, she quickly understood the ideological tenets of class and that our worth would be measured by it.

   Given my personal experiences with class, a major portion of my supervision with Jessica entailed encouraging her to explore her class location and the ways in which, even during the beginning stages of the therapy, it was already a powerful organizing principle. As is often the case with attempts to address issues of diversity in clinical work, Jessica was reticent to the idea of talking about class or addressing Maria's comment and ultimately talking about the watch. Her view was familiar. She argued that her watch was not the issue. She went on to assert: "It seems odd that I have to be made to feel guilty about wearing a watch that I worked hard to purchase…it is not clear to me what my watch has to do with Maria's problems with her children." Jessica's response was both predictable and understandable. Class, class privilege, and the value judgments attached to it are sometimes difficult to see. As a well-intentioned middle-class therapist, Jessica perceived herself as "just a person." She, like so many of us, especially when we occupy a position of privilege, was oblivious to the ways in which her life was embedded within a context of class (and other dimensions of culture as well). She was also unaware of the ways in which class was also an informant for her as well. She passionately and convincingly assured me that Maria's socioeconomic status was not an issue for her, a perception with which I concurred. However, her humanistic embrace of Maria was not sufficient to cleanse her of the class-based biases and blind spots that would be reasonable for her to inevitably have. After all, a part of my interest in having her slow the process down to discuss "the watch" and ultimately "class" was directly connected to my experiences as someone who knows intimately what it means to live under the armpits of the middle class and the wealthy, where I have felt inferior while they appeared embracing and oblivious. Interestingly, each of us, Maria, Jessica, and I, was subjectively influenced by our class locations and experiences.

   Jessica reluctantly explored Maria's reaction to "the watch." She talked openly and painfully about her unfulfilled dreams of owning "nice, expensive things" when she arrived to the United States. Instead of being dismissive, Jessica invited a deeper conversation with Maria by asking her about the impact of living life where she has to work so hard to survive. I encouraged and coached Jessica to engage with Maria rather than to minimize her experience or express indifference. I did this with the keen understanding that engaging in conversations across social class barriers can be a challenge. Jessica felt judged and initially had difficulty connecting with Maria's comment, which created an impasse in the therapeutic relationship between the therapist and the client. At the time Jessica was unaware how class was a divisive dynamic and a barrier to her engaging with Maria. After many extensive and painful conversations about Social Class in our supervision sessions, Jessica had an epiphany. She realized that every time she was encouraged to talk about "the watch" and ultimately Social Class, she felt tremendous guilt and embarrassment about how much she "had" (in terms of material possessions) and how little Maria had. Jessica admitted that she often felt anger and frustration toward me for "harping on the issue." Fortunately, she eventually acknowledged that it was a difficult but unquestionably beneficial process for all parties involved.

I (CIA) had a similarly difficult time in a graduate level Diversity Course I teach when attempting to encourage a student to identify and connect with the pain of his upper-middle-class status. During a lecture and class discussion devoted to a critique of Social Class, he uttered:

> I own a business…I've worked hard to keep the business, but people think my family and I are well-off, but the business is struggling. We're struggling! But, I'm working hard and I am happy and proud to say that we don't need any handouts.

In order to make explicit the several implicit messages about social class that this student unconsciously verbalized, I gently pursued him by asking him to identify the emotions attached to his social class experiences. My goal in engaging the student around his social class experiences was to aid him in recognizing and naming the emotions (pride/shame?) attached to belonging to a social class in society that is perceived as "hardworking" and, at the same time, to a family who found themselves struggling financially. Additionally, I hoped to assist him in noticing the implicit messages of stigma connected to needing and receiving social assistance in our society and that such a need was reserved for only working-class and poor families. In this trainee's social class narrative, he expressed emotions of shame on the one hand, coupled with an intense feeling of superiority on the other. He felt his social class status and experiences placed him above those in society who needed and received social assistance. Similarly, making visible the invisible messages about class was to assist the trainee in staying connected to his emotions and to recognize and potentially relate to clients' emotions around their social class experiences, even when expressed implicitly. It was during this critical teaching exchange that my dual experience of being born into class privilege but also having to struggle enabled me to respectfully stay in the conversation with this student. In fact, I felt a genuine sense of compassion for him and his struggle. I understood at a deeply experiential level that his struggle was a personally recognizable one for me. In fact, it was a struggle that I hoped he would embrace and be able to draw upon in his clinical work with clients, just as I was doing in my interaction with him.

I (CIA) was born and raised in a middle-class Nigerian family where both my parents were employed by one of the most prestigious universities in Nigeria. My family was among the "Haves" of that society. In my country of origin, my family lived in an affluent middle- to upper-class neighborhood in a large house with a massive backyard and front yard. When we moved to the United States, we could not escape the discriminatory realities of being black immigrants from Africa, and our lives changed dramatically. Upon moving to the United States, we became part of the "have-nots." We now lived in a tiny one-bedroom apartment. Despite the fact that my father had a PhD, he worked as an adjunct professor for several years, and my mother worked two jobs. We were considered a lower working-class family in terms of our economic achievement in the USA. The experience of moving from a middle to lower class status allowed me to live and experience life in two very different worlds. The pain and shame of moving from middle- to lower-class status have often stayed with me through adulthood. As a career woman, the feelings of shame and devaluation that I experienced as a result of the social economic status my family and I were in still haunts me to this day. I often feel like an imposter in my current middle-class status. Even though I am proud of the ways in which my family and I have navigated the challenges of moving from an affluent social class status to one in which we found ourselves living in an impoverished neighborhood, I still struggle with the difficulty of embracing this experience as a part of my social class narrative. It has been extremely difficult to include it in this chapter, even though I recognize why it is important for me to do so. In spite of my parents' hard work and all the efforts that my siblings and I put into attaining college degrees, achieving the "American Dream" seemed to require much more than us "working hard." No matter how hard we all worked, it was not enough to offset other forms of oppression that we experienced as black immigrants from Africa. I have often felt the shame and sadness of watching my parents "work hard" and still run into difficulties of progressing into the middle class. It was my personal experience and my keen awareness of it that was informing me now as a professor.

The interaction I (CIA) referred to earlier with the student also created an additional opportunity for me to model what it meant and looked like to engage in a constructive conversation about a difficult topic such as social class. Another student in the class, Yolanda, who had previously identified her social class status as poor, expressed with indignation and resentment that she didn't understand why Michael, the male student from the upper middle class, was complaining. She stated, "I didn't want to say anything, but sitting here and hearing you say you and your family are struggling financially when you own a business, does not make any sense to me." As the professor witnessing this interaction between the students, it was apparent to me that creating a space within the classroom for a deeper cross-class dialogue was necessary. I invited Yolanda to expand on what she meant and how she felt. She further expressed tearfully that "coming home on several occasions to find all of our belongings on the street, not knowing where you're going to lay your head at night, or where your next meal is coming from, day after day, night after night…that's struggling financially! Owning a business that is struggling is NOT ONE!" This intense exchange between the students around the different experiences and emotions that their social class statuses and narratives evoked exemplified the types of interaction that can and often do occur in both therapy and supervision when there are divisive cross–social class dynamics present. The difference is that the sentiments and corresponding dynamics remain unspoken, unacknowledged, and unaddressed.

From my personal experiences, I (CIA) could relate to Yolanda's disclosure and emotions. I understood that standing in her poor-working-class experience, she had a difficult time understanding Michael's experiences and emotions because of his upper-middle-class status. Given her life-altering experiences with class, she could neither fathom nor emotionally embrace what Michael meant by the statement that he and his "family were struggling financially even though they owned a business." Yet, from Michael's perspective and his class experiences, his struggle was legitimate and was as troubling for him within his context as Yolanda's was within her context. On the other hand, their respective struggles were not the same, nor were they equal. My (CIA) immediate goal was to validate the vulnerable and painful disclosure made by Yolanda, and to encourage her to have openness to hearing and holding Michael's feelings and experiences as well. I verbally validated Michael for his patience and ability to listen to Yolanda's point of view attentively non-defensively, and while in the midst of experiencing a kind of *social-class-induced* pain and anxiety. I then respectfully and patiently challenged some of the implicit assumptions buried in Yolanda's heartfelt words. I used the heated exchange as a teaching moment about the hidden dimensions of class. I expanded our difficult cross–social class dialogue by helping all the students understand that the class-based feelings and assumptions that they had were embedded in broader societal messages that we internalize. Messages that allow us to not see or hold regard for the poor or messages that reinforce that those who are economically privileged are immune to life's struggles and challenges. I underscored such implicit bias because it has the potential to prevent and disrupt the relational connection and therapeutic process between a therapist/client and supervisor/supervisee.

For example, I (KVH) have had clinicians from working- and middle-class backgrounds who were working with wealthy clients report in supervision that they had a difficult time relating to these clients. The supervisees often found it hard to have empathy for rich clients, who they felt were whining about suffering, yet they had so much financially. They often expressed that the problems upper-class clients reported seem to be superficial compared to clients who seem to have so much less. Indeed, the danger in not attending to the emotional and relational difficulties that trainees and supervisees from poor and lower-class status may experience in their clinical work with middle- and upper-class clients is that the relational empathy needed for effective therapeutic engagement and treatment will be lost. Such interactions then have the potential to shut down the emotional struggles that wealthy clients bring to therapy while at the same time heightening the pain and shame that clinicians might feel toward them and their social class experiences. Conversely, it may also be difficult for therapists from upper-class backgrounds to genuinely relate to the gravity of suffering encountered by poor and working-class clients seeking treatment as well. The host of variable and complicated class dynamics that is often threaded within the therapeutic relationship virtually demand that trainers spend considerable time assisting trainees to see and understand the many faces of social class. This process entails promoting the visibility of social class as an ideology, classification system, and a major organizing principle. The Social Class Symbolic Engagement Activity (SCSEA) is one of several experiential exercises we use to highlight and expose the many faces of social class.

The Social Class Symbolic Engagement Activity: An experiential strategy for focusing on social class in training and supervision

Within the context of training and supervision, social class is often invisible and thus unaddressed. However, there are symbols of social class all around us that emit messages (some accurate, some not) about our standard of living. The Social Class Symbolic Engagement Activity (SCSEA) is a self-reflective interrogative exercise designed to facilitate explicit conversations about class and to tap into the array of unacknowledged, intense emotions associated with it. Expressions of rage, sadness, and shame are some of the deep emotions that often emerge when trainees engage in conversations that explore and expose their respective experiences with social class. It is crucial that facilitators of this activity are prepared to respond appropriately to the overt expressions of emotions that may arise for trainees. The goal of the activity is to assist trainees in explicitly examining how social class is an organizing principle in their daily lives regardless of their class status. The desired outcome of the exercise is to increase awareness of and sensitivity to the prevalence of class-based issues in society and as a result help clinicians to be better prepared to recognize and effectively address them in therapy and supervision.

As a precursor to starting the Social Class Symbolic Engagement Activity, all participants are encouraged to write a statement describing their respective social class narrative. In preparing the Narrative, participants are invited to examine both implicit and explicit messages they received about their class location in and outside of their family of origins. As Trainers we stress that the Social Class Narrative must speak to the internalized messages that participants received about their class location and the meanings they attach to them. To start the SCSEA, participants are encouraged to select an object or symbol that represents an aspect of their social class location that is associated with pride or shame. The participants may bring as many objects they wish, provided there is a willingness to answer the following questions for each object introduced:

1. What social class generalizations are associated with the object/symbol? What are the emotional, interpersonal, and psychological consequences of these generalizations?
2. What social class values are associated with the object/symbol?
3. What is the impact of the object/symbol on your social class?
4. In what way is the object/symbol a source of pride? A source of shame?

5.   How does the object/symbol fit into a narrative about your social class location?
6.   How does the object/symbol not fit into a narrative about your social class location?

When the exercise is used in a didactic course or group supervision, the facilitator is encouraged to engage other participants in the discussion to reflect and comment on their respective perceptions about the objects/symbols that are being shared. This is done primarily to help participants express their thoughts and feelings with each other and to possibly demonstrate how one object/symbol can generate a range of class-based thoughts and emotions. Participation in the exercise helps to foster empathy and human connection by promoting self-interrogation and constructive conversations about class. When used properly and effectively, our use of the exercise has dramatically altered our training and supervisory experiences by enabling trainees to engage in difficult, sometimes painful, class-related conversations while also remaining genuinely connected with each other.

The proper execution of the SCSEA exercise demands that the Facilitator pay careful attention to his/her internalized class narrative. In doing so, there are several guidelines that we recommend to Facilitators to assist in this process:

1.   **Be cognizant of the potential premature alignment and/ or over-identification with trainees who share a similar class experience**. For example, a Facilitator from a working-class background may prematurely align with working-class supervisees.
2.   **Be aware of the potential unacknowledged aversion to trainees who share a similar class experiences**. Facilitators may have unexplored class-based shame that gets projected onto a trainee from a similar class background.
3.   **Be proactive in establishing a safe and nurturing milieu where trainees from stigmatized class backgrounds are not further shamed, stigmatized, or humiliated**. Facilitators must be mindful of and intentional in creating a learning environment where students from poor and working-class backgrounds are not further shamed or stigmatized.
4.   **Be proactive in ensuring that trainees from privileged class backgrounds are actively included in the self-exploratory process and not tacitly supported in distancing or disengaging from the process**. Facilitators must pay attention to the ways that trainees from privileged class backgrounds may minimize their class status or avoid engagement. These actions maybe prompted by feelings of guilt, pain, or embarrassment.
5.   **Be aware of and self-monitor one's class-based emotional triggers associated with shame, pride, or internalized inferiority/superiority**. Unrecognized or disavowed pride/ shame issues associated with social class location can ignite emotional triggers and hinder awareness and sensitivity. This type of blockage can contribute to supervisory blind spots, thus making it difficult for supervisors to identify the shame, pride, and internalized superiority or inferiority of their supervisees and students.

Ultimately, the goal of SCSEA exercise is to make Social Class visible by promoting class-based self-exploration and facilitating subsequent conversations. Through these processes participants are able to reach a deeper understanding about the role social class plays in their lives and in the lives of others. It is our belief that naming social class is an important step forward in the healing process that is generated when telling one's story. We also believe that the role of the Facilitator is central to the overall effectiveness of the exercise.

To deconstruct and make visible the invisibility of social class in supervision and training is critical because class permeates our being. As we have indicated throughout this chapter, class is a very powerful organizing principle that leaves no aspect of our lived experience untouched and perhaps, in some cases, untarnished by it. Identifying the social class status of clients is not merely enough in making class visible in our training programs and supervision; we also have to explicitly highlight and help trainees understand both cognitively and affectively the ways in which class and the invisibility attached to it often create barriers for authentic and healing connections within ourselves and with others in our work.

References

Laszloffy. T. (2008). Social class: Implications for family therapy. In M. McGoldrick & K. V. Hardy (Eds.), *Re-Visioning Family Therapy: Race, Culture, and Gender in Clinical Practice* (pp. 48–60). New York, NY: Guilford Press.

Rothenberg, P. S. (2012). *White privilege: Essential readings on the other side of racism.* New York, NY: Worth.

6

SUPERVISION IN BLACK AND WHITE

Navigating cross-racial interactions in the supervisory process

Marlene F. Watson, PhD

The enduring legacy of slavery has passed easily from one generation of Americans to another through racism. Most especially, the myths of white superiority and black inferiority that were constructed in slavery are entrenched deeply in our minds, whether conscious or unconscious (Watson, 2013). As Americans whose cultural pride lies in democracy, justice, and equality, we have difficulty remembering, naming, and making meaning of the painful events of slavery. Therefore we tend to have difficulty acknowledging racism or healing from slavery's damaging and divisive effects. Supervisors and therapists are members of the American community and also are affected by the contentious experiences and accounts of the past, despite our notions of objectivity and neutrality. Objectivity frequently stands for supervisors and therapists taking an expert position, causing us to look outside ourselves instead of inside. Similarly, neutrality often means being a bystander, silently witnessing without challenging self or other.

Supervisors and therapists should see race. Color, even more so than gender, is likely the first observable physical characteristic of a person, particularly in a race-based society such as the United States of America. Hence, race is probably the most visible and prominent marker of a person's identity, arousing assumptions and judgments about that person. Race tells its own constructed story about a person before we ever get to know that individual. Race is a predetermined, albeit a skewed, story of who's worthy and who's not, based on assigned characteristics of each racial group by the dominant white group. Though we hide behind American ideals such as meritocracy, we secretly harbor beliefs rooted in white supremacy. It's not just ignorant people who have encoded in their psyches that white is good and black is bad, we all do to varying degrees and, sadly, many of us avoid facing up to this reality. It's not enough to say you don't see color, or blacks can't be racist. We have to become alert—conscious—to the shadows of racism that are present in cross-racial and same-racial interactions. To do so requires deep, meaningful self-reflection.

The myth of white superiority and black inferiority has a far reach, also touching multiracial, Asian, Hispanic/Latino, and Native peoples. In reality, white is the consummate racial group, with all others lining up behind them from lightest to darkest. Depending on skin color, multiracial, Asian, Hispanic/Latino, and Natives peoples may be perceived or perceive themselves to be inferior to whites and superior to blacks, likely resulting in social and psychological consequences. Also, darker-skinned members of the same group (e.g., Puerto Ricans) may be regarded as black, while lighter-skinned members are regarded as white, possibly causing internal conflicts and friction within the family and group.

Self of the supervisor

I am an unmarried, black, African American "other mother," a term used in the black community to honor women who have a nurturing role in the lives of non-biological or adopted children (Watson, 2008). Born in the segregated South, I experienced and witnessed racism during my formative years. I attended a segregated black elementary school and stood at the counter of Paul's Drugstore in my hometown of Cheriton, Virginia, to buy an ice-cream cone while white children sat enjoying their ice cream. I watched my grandfather pay for my ice cream cone while subserviently and painstakingly avoiding direct eye contact with the white waitress. At age 9, I moved to the integrated North, where racism was more subtle.

My identity as an "other mother" is significant to my "being" as a supervisor. I'm not looking only to help supervisees understand theory and apply techniques. I'm seeking to nurture and engage with supervisees toward the broader goal of helping to ameliorate suffering and oppression and to promote healing.

Gazing at the seated white patrons while waiting for an ice cream cone, I wondered why they couldn't see me when I could see them. Thus began my developing sense of the need to be connected to one's humanity as critical to seeing the other. Being connected to one's own humanity then becomes the bridge to seeing the other's humanity. Since "therapists bring more to the therapeutic process than theory and technique" (Aponte & Kissil, 2012, p. 1), therapists need self-awareness to connect to their own humanity.

The supervisory context

I supervise master's and post-master's students. The Drexel University Couple and Family Therapy Department's model of supervision is three-tiered: on-site, off-site, and group. On-site supervision occurs at the student intern's practicum. Off-site supervision occurs in the field and/or program with the American Association for Marriage and Family Therapy (AAMFT) approved or equivalent supervisors. Group supervision occurs in the program with core or adjunct faculty with AAMFT approved or equivalent supervisor status. As core faculty, I provide off-site and/or group supervision. Off-site supervision comprises two students, and group supervision comprises six students.

Philosophy of supervision

Self of the therapist and social justice are the cornerstones of my philosophy of supervision. According to Aponte and Kissil (2012), person of the therapist (POTT) core issues referred to as the therapist's signature themes (e.g., fear of rejection, low self-esteem) develop and occur over an individual's lifetime, influencing and organizing that individual's relationships with self and other. Thus the self of the therapist is essential to the therapeutic process. In the same way, supervisors and therapists likely have signature themes (e.g., internalized superiority or internalized inferiority) from living in a race-based society.

People of color in general and blacks in particular have endured a long history of oppression alongside whites' privilege, resulting in different experiences of race. For instance, racism is real to blacks and not as real to whites. Blacks are seen as a group and whites are seen as individuals. Thus blacks and whites approach cross-racial interactions from polar positions, which may explain the common tendency to avoid talking about race. Therefore, it is my responsibility as supervisor to facilitate the engagement of supervisees in conversations about race, particularly since I strongly believe that therapists have crucial roles in social justice and should not miss the opportunity to help oppressed clients.

As a supervisor, I believe I am obligated to help prepare therapists to fully understand themselves as personal beings in the professional arena. I accept that I must help supervisees to understand their multiple contexts and identities in order that they recognize and appreciate clients' multiple contexts and identities. Since race is still one of society's biggest social issues, it is a critical context for inquiry, necessitating supervisors and therapists to grapple with our racial selves and that of our clients. Therefore, it is crucial for supervisors and supervisees to gain awareness of our conscious and unconscious racial perceptions, attitudes, and biases that influence the therapeutic encounter.

From a systems view, an active force between the supervisor's personal self and the supervisee's personal self, or the therapist's personal self and the client's personal self, is stirred from the moment of contact in the supervisory or therapeutic encounter. It is the supervisor's and therapist's professional responsibility to consciously and continuously work on her or his personal issues triggered in the encounter and not project them onto the supervisee or client or become paralyzed in the role of supervisor or therapist.

Supervisors must realize and accept that race is often the proverbial elephant in the room. Supervisors must take responsibility and be accountable for helping therapists to face racial perceptions, attitudes, biases, and values, not shield them. Shielding therapists by not addressing race in supervision will likely lead to client-blaming and ineffective treatment of the most vulnerable clients. Having done our own work, supervisors can deal with race without becoming defensive or reactive. Supervisors must be able to engender trust by demonstrating respect for supervisees; putting into perspective supervisees' development of internalized racial biases; engaging supervisees on an ongoing basis to acknowledge and challenge racial bias; and encouraging supervisees to confront race in the therapy room so they can better see their clients and relate to their clients' issues.

By example, supervisors must help therapists to realize the confluence of the personal and professional (Watson, 1993). Thus supervisors must make race central in the supervisory process so we can better understand, feel, and work with the self of the supervisee/therapist. Supervisors' willingness and skill in dealing with race can motivate supervisees to validate rather than ignore race as a powerful organizing principle in their own as well as their clients' lives.

I see commitment, integrity, courage, and responsibility as pillars of the supervisory process. Commitment involves motivating supervisees to sit and stay at the table. Integrity inspires supervisees to have trust and confidence in the process. Courage allows supervisees to be authentic, honest, vulnerable, and take risks. Responsibility encourages supervisees to be accountable to self and clients.

As a supervisor, I am intentional about creating candid processes that encourage all supervisees to be introspective, challenging them to face race honestly and to take responsibility for their learning and growth. Only by talking about race might we finally be able to make overt and end the prevailing narrative of white superiority and black inferiority, and decisively advance human equality and social justice in America.

Navigating cross-racial and same-racial interactions in supervision

The following is my map for establishing an authentic relationship with cross-racial and same-racial supervisees. As a structured guide, my hope is that it will prevent intractable cross-racial and same-racial conflicts. Also, it is hoped that it will lead supervisees to be connected to the self to allow more effective work with all clients but especially clients of color.

Normalize race. Beginning with sharing my philosophy of supervision and approach to therapy in the first supervisory session, I make clear that race matters. Throughout supervision, I hold supervisees responsible and accountable for their racial perceptions and for exploring race as a critical dimension of therapy. I require supervisees to do a written case presentation on each client. One of the questions asks supervisees to identify person-of-the-therapist issues, including the therapist's race, and how they intersect with the case. Another question asks supervisees to describe the influence of contextual variables, including race, on the problem and family. Hence every supervisory session includes attention to race.

As part of the introductions in the first supervisory meeting, I ask each person to provide her/his name, race, ethnicity, and a fun fact. I usually start the process to set the tone. I distinguish between race and ethnicity to encourage supervisees to begin thinking specifically about race. Also, I give supervisees a sheet of paper defining privileged and targeted identities and ask them to fill in their privileged and targeted identities. I use these to promote understanding and connection in cross-racial situations. For example, a white female therapist might use her understanding of sexism to connect with a black client's experience of racism rather than feel guarded because of her whiteness. I feel obliged to say this is about the white female therapist really connecting and using her humanity (vulnerability) to relate to the black client, not minimizing racism by talking about sexism.

Additionally, I offer supervisees a historic frame—the myth of white superiority and the myth of black inferiority—for understanding the importance of race and how potently messages of racial inequality still reverberate and resonate in our minds. My belief is that supervisors and therapists should defy the myths of white superiority and black inferiority by making them overt. Doing so might be a good starting point for cross-racial trust and, in some cases, same-racial trust; particularly since racial tension also may exist in same racial situations stemming from the myths of white superiority and black inferiority.

Maria, a self-identified white-Hispanic Argentinian supervisee, was helped to see how the myth of white superiority and black inferiority related to her signature theme (fear of vulnerability). Maria described being a white-Hispanic as having dual access in that she could identify with and be accepted by whites as well as Hispanics. She selectively used her dual access to fit the situation. Thus she did not have a coherent racial identity as a white-Hispanic, which tapped into her fear of vulnerability and unconscious correlation of vulnerability with inadequacy. Maria was encouraged to explore the myth of white superiority and black inferiority as a means to deepen her connection to the self and alleviate her struggle with being guarded, which served to protect her from feeling weak and incompetent as a person of color.

Internalized white superiority and black inferiority reside mostly in the unconscious mind. Hence, I refer to them as the white shadow and black shadow (Watson, 2013). Because internalized white superiority and internalized black inferiority are disowned or projected away, they largely have negative power, manifesting in silence, shame, guilt, and complicity with racism.

For example, Jayda, a black female supervisee, was assigned a white female client at the psychiatric hospital where she was interning. When Jayda tried to meet with the client, she said, *"I don't want to talk to another nigger today."* Jayda's on-site white male supervisor dismissed the client's comment (and Jayda) by saying only that the client had stopped taking her medication. When Jayda presented the case in off-site supervision with me, she appeared emotionless. Going beneath Jayda's "be strong" mask, I asked Jayda to tell me about her black shadow and how it intersected with the case. Jayda began to cry, expressing her feelings of not being good enough and not having a voice. Jayda was particularly ashamed of condemning her black relatives, accusing them of playing the race card when they talked about racism. The client was released without Jayda seeing her again. Jayda decided to seek therapy for work on her black shadow.

Acknowledge whiteness. According to McIntosh (1998) and Kendall (2006), whites learn not to be aware of race. Whiteness usually is neither acknowledged nor examined in the discourse on race. Thus race is about the other and the other's concern. As such, most whites don't think about race, while most blacks, and probably other people of color, think a lot about race. Therefore there seems to be little reason for whites to talk about race. Holding a mirror up to whiteness through its inclusion in conversations on race is necessary for openness and honesty in cross-racial supervision and therapy. Denying privilege, upholding individual goodness, and confusing safety with discomfort tend to be barriers for whites in cross-racial conversations. For effective cross-racial communication, whites need to be able to go there, to acknowledge white privilege as part of the white collective. Asking, *"What does it mean to be white?"* can help white supervisees to develop self-knowledge and build authentic relationships with self and other, as illustrated by my student Rema:

> Reading about all the oppression, brutality, exploitation and discrimination that white people have inflicted upon their fellow people of color, I felt an urge to dissociate myself from all that is White. I wanted to protect myself from feeling hurt and disappointed. At first I was in denial, I thought that I am not part of the American culture, thus my whiteness was never a threat to the people of color. I wanted to be alienated from the process. I was protecting myself by saying that I am not part of this culture, and I never was, hence I never was a part of all the unfairness and brutal acts against people of color. It was funny how I kept on fighting my thoughts. I was barely participating, and I was always trying my best to be a passive listener without identifying with any material discussed—until, one day, I decided to allow myself to be vulnerable and to discover how all what is being said and read relates to me as a Middle Eastern female. It was a struggle and a challenge for me to allow my whiteness to become visible. I started comparing myself to the people of color in my country, Lebanon. The concept of racism suddenly struck me, and I went into a deep thought. It was hard to accept that I might have been racist or I might have had racist practices. Freeing myself from all my defense mechanisms, I realized I possess racist attitudes. I was racist by my ignorance and silence. I realized that even if I had not had overt racist behavior toward minorities, but still, by normalizing all the exploitations, masking it with classism, and staying silent, I was practicing unspoken racism.

Validate people of color's experience of race. According to Wilkins et al. (2012), more literature is needed in the field of couple and family therapy to assist practitioners in understanding and ascertaining the impact of clients' cultural histories on their presenting problems. While this may be true, believing that racism is real and validating people of color's experience of racism can go a long way in helping therapists to talk with clients of color about race and how it impacts their lives. Clients of color, particularly blacks, often avoid talking about race or cautiously talk about race with white therapists (and some therapists of color) because they have learned not to share their racial pain due to marginalization and/or dismissal. By not validating people of color's experience of racism, we take away their voice and blame the victims, whether we intend to or not.

I engage supervisees in discussions about relevant race matters from the media as a way of encouraging them to think about people of color's experience of racism and delve more deeply into their views about racism. Also, I do this to encourage cross-racial conversations about race. For instance, I asked my group of supervisees (two white, three black, and one Asian) what they thought about the Ferguson, Missouri, racial uprising in response to the police shooting of an unarmed black youth, a story that was dominating the media. After waiting a few minutes without anyone saying anything and everyone looking a little anxious, I asked what they were feeling about being asked to comment on Ferguson. One of the black supervisees said she and her black friends talked about Ferguson but that she was not comfortable talking about it with whites. The other two black supervisees echoed her response. One of the white students said she didn't think about it because it wasn't relevant to her, and the other white student said she thought about it but felt helpless. The Asian supervisee said she didn't want to think about race. The supervisees' responses were very revealing. Upon further examination the black supervisees feared being seen as playing the race card or angry if they shared their true feelings about racism. One of the white supervisees was afraid of being seen as a racist, and the other was afraid of not being a good white person. The Asian supervisee didn't want to take sides, so she tried to stay neutral by not thinking about race.

Developing awareness of these undercurrent feelings was important for these supervisees' knowledge and management of self with clients. For example, when Emma, the white female supervisee who wanted to be a "good white person," presented a videotape of a low-income, depressed, single black mother, she talked excessively, appearing to lecture the client. Emma was anxious for the black client to see her as a good white person, and that dictated her lecturing to avoid being vulnerable and feeling helpless. I suggested that Emma take a risk and share with the client her strong desire to help and invite the client to help her to "see and feel" the client's life experience through the client's racial lens. Emma was encouraged to focus on being present to the client's story and connecting with the client, not worrying about what to do next. As well, Emma was encouraged to continue working on her racial self because it was getting in the way of her really helping the client.

The following supervisory case exemplifies my work with a black supervisee to validate a black client's experience of racism.

> Nadine, a light-skinned middle-class African American supervisee, presented a case of a 21-year-old dark-skinned black female who insisted she was a white boy. When giving her history, the client identified all her relatives as black. Yet she was adamant that she was a white boy. Nadine focused only on the client's gender identity, ignoring the client's racial identity. This was not surprising, since Nadine was anxious about working with low-income dark-skinned black female clients. Growing up, Nadine was accused of thinking she was better than dark-skinned girls. Also, Nadine's on-site dark-skinned black female supervisor at her previous practicum site accused her of not understanding low-income black clientele. Nadine's own black shadow made her feel vulnerable and incompetent, so she avoided race. The first task for Nadine was to embrace her black shadow. Nadine was asked to connect her experience of feeling marginalized and isolated as a light-skinned black female to the client's disconnection to self as a dark-skinned black female. Affirming that Nadine could understand and relate to low-income black female clients, I asked her to embark on a second task—locating her own and the client's experience in the wider structural context of racism—as a way of deepening the connection between the supervisee and client. The third task was for Nadine to use her reflections and struggles of being a light-skinned black female in a racist society to be more emotionally available to the self and client. The fourth task was for Nadine to open the door for the client to speak about her emotions and experiences of racism. Thus I asked the supervisee to engage the client in talking about her emotions and experiences of racism with the following: *"Tell me why being a white boy is better than being a dark-skinned black female in a racist society."* The client opened up about being bullied and called names in school because of being dark and overweight, including negative feelings about light-skinned black girls. (Nadine was more emotionally available to herself, having explored her own black shadow, and therefore could remain emotionally available to the client.) Also, the client talked about being raped at age 14. The fifth task for the supervisee was to introduce the concept of the myth of white superiority and black inferiority to deepen and validate the client's experience of racism.

Invest in self. The greatest power a therapist has to help is to know his- or herself, because the self is the instrument of the therapist (Aponte et al., 2009). Knowledge gives you insight and helps you to see more options. Also, it helps you to be authentic. Knowledge can help end our silence and passivity about racism, helping us to talk openly about race. Engaging in sustained self-examination about how whiteness (white privilege) or blackness (black inferiority) affects us, supervisors and therapists are better positioned to have power to our feelings and less likely to become victims of our feelings, limiting our use of self and the ability to be in relationship with supervisees and clients (Krestan, 2000). I recommend books (e.g., *Waking Up White: And Finding Myself in the Story of Race, Facing the Black Shadow, Between the World and Me*) and films (e.g., *Skin, Fruitvale Station, 12 Years a Slave*) to supervisees to aid in doing self-of-the-therapist work.

Go the extra mile. Be prepared for fractures in the cross-racial relationship because of historical racism. According to Kendall (2006), black-white relationships are superficial, which also is probably true for whites and other groups of color. Overall, people of color are likely to know much more about whites than whites know about us because of white dominance, increasing the likelihood of cross-racial misunderstandings. The challenge for whites will be staying engaged when the deference and softness usually afforded whites are missing. The challenge for people of color will be managing the tendency to rescue, comfort, or protect whites from feeling uncomfortable.

Advocacy. The privileged tend to offer spoken support for diversity but then can't be counted on to stand up for racial justice. Self-knowledge can help supervisors and therapists to move from support to action. Self-knowledge by necessity entails being clear about your motivation and expectations. Looking for thanks or appreciation or acting out of guilt as the motivation to work for racial justice is likely to result in disappointment. Recognizing that taking action is in your best interest is the best way to circumvent a harmful cross-racial misunderstanding (Kendall, 2006).

Trust. Trust starts with self and is a great liberator. Trust is empowering because it conveys shared responsibilities and common interests. Trust asks that we meet each other halfway, which is within our respective control to do. With will and the resolve to tolerate discomfort, we can hold on to trust when we fear being vulnerable. By holding ourselves accountable for our privileged social locations, we can create a trusting environment that allows us to stand in solidarity in cross-racial relationships. An assumption of those in power groups (e.g., race, class, gender) or positions (e.g., supervisors, managers, executives) is that they deserve to be trusted. Trust, however, cannot be separated from what disempowered groups (e.g., people of color, women, LGBTQ community, immigrants, workers) have known and experienced from interacting with and being impacted by policies, laws, beliefs, and practices of those in power.

Embrace truth. Face the myth of white superiority and the myth of black inferiority. Resist the lie of black inferiority that obscures people of color's humanity. Commit to making a difference in cross-racial relationships by doing your own work. In the words of James Baldwin (n.d.), "*Not everything that is faced can be changed but nothing can be changed until it is faced*" (p. 1).

References

Aponte, H. J., Powell, F. D., Brooks, S., Watson, M. F., Litzke, C., Lawless, J., & Johnson, E. (2009). Training the person of the therapist in an academic setting. *Journal of Marital and Family Therapy, 35*, 381–394.

Aponte, H. J., & Kissil, K. (2012). "If I can grapple with this I can truly be of use in the therapy room": Using the therapist's own emotional struggles to facilitate effective therapy. *Journal of Marital and Family Therapy, 40*, 152–164.

Baldwin, J. (n.d.). James Baldwin Quotes. *Goodreads.* Retrieved from http://www.goodreads.com/quotes/14374-not-everything-that-is-faced-can-be-changed-but-nothing (accessed March 24, 2016).

Kendall, F. E. (2006). *Understanding white privilege: Creating pathways to authentic relationships across race.* New York, NY: Routledge.

Krestan, J. (2000). Addiction, power, and powerlessness. In J. Krestan (Ed.), *Bridges to recovery: Addiction, family therapy, and multicultural treatment.* New York, NY: Free Press.

McIntosh, P. (1998). White privilege: Unpacking the invisible knapsack. In M. McGoldrick (Ed.), *Re-visioning family therapy: Race, culture and gender in clinical practice.* New York, NY: Guilford Press.

Watson, M. F. (1993). Supervising the person of the therapist: Issues, challenges and dilemmas. *Contemporary Family Therapy, 15*(1), 21–31.

Watson, M. F. (2008). Voluntary childlessness and the myth of choice. In M. McGoldrick & K. V. Hardy (Eds.), *Re-visioning family therapy: Race, culture, and gender in clinical practice* (2nd ed.). New York, NY: Guilford Press.

Watson, M. F. (2013). *Facing the black shadow.* http://www.drmarlenefwatson.com/ (accessed March 24, 2016).

Wilkins, E., Whiting, J., Watson, M., Russon, J., & Moncrief, A. (2012). Residual effects of slavery: What clinicians need to know. *Contemporary Family Therapy, 35*(1), 14–28.

7

LESSONS LEARNED IN QUEER-AFFIRMATIVE SUPERVISION

Deidre Ashton, MSW

> *"Being an affirmative therapist…is not simply a set of interventions or something to do; it is rather, someone to be." (Stone Fish & Harvey, 2005, p. 4)*

The stance of the therapist articulated by Stone Fish and Harvey reflects the stance that I strive to enact as a queer affirmative clinician and supervisor. First, I will self-identify, socially locate myself, explain my language choices, and review some of the literature on queer affirmative clinical supervision. Then I will identify and describe ways I learned to enact this stance through my experiences as a supervisor in an oppressive and complex setting.

I identify as a Black, African American, queer, lesbian, upper-middle-class ciswoman, who grew up working class and for many years identified as heterosexual. I was raised in the African Methodist Episcopal church, where queer identity existed but was not named or validated, received my elementary education in a Christian evangelical school where queer identity was not acknowledged as a possibility, and currently identify as nonreligious. I am a US-born, English-speaking, able-bodied person. I lived with depression/dysthymia until I came into myself as a queer woman during my adult life. My gender presentation mostly conforms to dominant culture standards and, because we live in a world that conflates gender expression, gender identity, biological sex, and sexual orientation, people often assume that I am heterosexual. Thus I am the beneficiary of cisprivilege, and if I choose to pass, heteroprivilege. Because of my skin color, I am the beneficiary of light (i.e., closer to white)-skin privilege. I also hold privilege along the dimensions of social class, nationality, language, and physical and intellectual ability. The oppressed and privileged aspects of my identity and social locations are constantly and simultaneously interacting within me, my relationships, and in my roles as clinician and supervisor providing therapy and supervision that endeavors to affirm the totality of clients and supervisees.

Sexual orientation and gender in context

Although sexual orientation and gender identity are different aspects of identity, I speak to sexuality and gender because I strive to operate from the perspective of intersectionality. I will use the term "queer" to reference LGBTQ people because it is inclusive of a range of sexual and gender identities that fall outside of the dominant culture's biologically determined, binary construction of both sexual orientation and gender. Once used to criminalize, pathologize, ostracize, and other, the label "queer" has been reappropriated to empower and celebrate. I recognize that for some, "queer" is incredibly painful language, and for many LGBT communities of color it conjures up images of white gay and trans men (Johnson, 2005). I respect the position of those who reject this language, and carry awareness of their pain and politics as I move forward using this terminology. One of the first acts of culturally sensitive practice is respecting the right of others to name themselves. I choose to name myself and use the language, "queer," in alignment with Stone Fish and Harvey's description of queer,

> Being queer is also about recognizing the ways that one represents otherness, the unexplored, or the disallowed, then, despite prejudice and injustice, insisting again and again that one belongs and that one is gifted, not in spite of these queer differences but because of them (Stonefish & Harvey, 2005, p. 4),

and in honor of Johnson's definition of "quare" (African American vernacular for queer):

> one who thinks and feels and acts committed to struggle against all forms of oppression – racial, sexual, gender, class, religious… one for whom sexual and gender identities always already intersect with racial subjectivity (Johnson, 2005, p. 125).

Essential queer affirmative approaches

The various codes of ethics that guide our practice as clinicians, researchers, advocates, educators, supervisors, and helpers require that we operate from a place of cultural competence (American Counseling Association [ACA], 2014, American Psychological Association [APA] 2010; National Association of Social Workers [NASW], 2008). The NASW standards for cultural competence highlight the need for self awareness and awareness of other cultures from a stance of humility, and they require that we address power dynamics in the healing relationship and oppression at the micro and macro levels (NASW, 2015). Therefore, we must provide affirmative services when working with queer children, adults, couples, and families. Stone Fish and Harvey (2012) regard queer affirmative therapy as one that nurtures queerness and challenges the therapist to examine self in relationship to sexuality and gender, explicitly claiming their own identities while simultaneously examining those parts of self that have been disavowed in order to claim the identity of man, woman, gay, straight, etc. along with racial, class, ethnic, spiritual, etc. identities. Queer affirmative therapy validates and values queer people as multicultural beings, and addresses the impact of oppression based on sexual orientation and gender identity (Ritter & Terendrup, 2002; Stone Carlson & McGeorge, 2012). It also requires that the therapist takes leadership in examining how heterosexism, gender oppression, heteronormativity, and cisnormativity are influencing the therapeutic process, the presenting problem, and the lived experiences of both client and therapist outside the therapy room. Since no aspect of identity or location exists separate and apart from the others, queer- affirming therapy must be affirming of all aspects of social location and challenge all forms of oppression.

Queer-affirmative clinical supervision models hold that supervision must be a safe space that validates and embraces all sexual orientations, gender identities, and forms of gender expression, and that challenges all forms of oppression. In that relational context, the supervisee is supported to acquire knowledge about the experiences and needs of queer communities and to develop the skills to effectively work with individuals, couples, and families (Garcia et al., 2009; Halpert, Reinhardt & Toohey, 2007; Hernandez & McDowell, 2010; Singh & Chun, 2010). Just as it is the clinician's role to take leadership in addressing sexual and gender oppression, it is the supervisor's responsibility to take leadership in supervision. Regardless of the supervisor's own social locations, she must demonstrate this leadership by engaging in an ongoing process of self-interrogation regarding her own attitudes, values, beliefs, biases, areas of power/privilege/oppression, how she uses power, her participation in upholding systems of oppression, the impact of multiple forms of oppression on queer communities, and the ways in which she copes with, or transcends, oppressions through acts of resilience (Halpert et al., 2007; Hernandez & McDowell, 2010; Singh & Chun, 2010). The supervisor's transparency about the professional development process can facilitate growth of relational safety so that supervisees can self-examine and share their work in the service of the ongoing development of skills and competence in working with diverse queer communities (Hernandez & McDowell, 2010).

My evolving approach to queer affirmative supervision is based on ideas from social constructionism, intersectionality, systems theory and socially just practices and was honed through my experience of supervising mostly Christian, Black, African American, heterosexual, cismen and ciswomen, clinicians and human service professionals working for a justice-oriented family therapy agency in an economically, racially, sexually, and gender oppressive, cis and heteronormative, community. It draws on the work of Hernandez and McDowell (2010) and Garcia, Koustic, McDowell, and Anderson (2009), who discuss clinical supervision from a position of intersectionality, and the work of Singh and Chun (2010), who specifically focus on supervision of queer affirmative therapy by queer people of color (QPOC) supervisors through the lens of intersectionality. The work of implementing queer affirmative supervision did not take place as an isolated supervision process but was part of an overall approach to supervision anchored in a social justice metaperspective.

Supervisory context

Many of the talented and dedicated clinicians whom I've had the benefit of supervising are fervent believers in religious traditions that condemn queer sexuality and gender. As I prepared to write this chapter, I explored the possibility for co-authorship with supervisees, but it did not work out for a variety of reasons, including personal crises and logistics. However, I did convene a group of supervisees to include their experience of supervision. Five core truths seemed to emerge: 1) the co-creation of respectful relationships in which each supervisee felt validated and valued by the supervisor and other supervisees made all difficult discussions possible, 2) a common bond around resilience in the face of racial oppression strengthened our resolve to respectfully connect in areas of difference, 3) shared commitment to supporting the children we served to survive and thrive in the most difficult circumstances held us together through the most difficult conversations, 4) the supervisor's knowledge of queer communities was reassuring and facilitated development of supervisees' knowledge and skills, and 5) the supervisor's membership in a queer community was sometimes intimidating.

Affirmative supervision practices

The mission of the organization that employed the professionals that I supervised in a school-based counseling program emphasized delivery of just and culturally competent/humble practice and trained staff to work from a contextual, systemic approach. As part of my preparation for supervision, the agency director, a White, heterosexual, ciswoman to whom I was out, shared with me her observations of the ways in which heterosexism, heteronormativity, and sexism, racism, and classism operated in the community and among the staff I would be supervising. We discussed the meaning of my identity as a Black nonreligious cislesbian social worker taking over the role of supervisor from a White, heterosexual cisman psychologist. I also examined how I would use my power, how supervisees might perceive my power, and identified areas of disempowerment and potential blind spots. I was attentive to the ways that I might misuse power to protect myself from heterosexism and cisgenderism and the ways that supervisees might experience my queer-affirming stance as invalidating.

I decided to begin the supervisory relationships with a self-identification and social location exercise modeled by me and then extended to supervisees. I felt empowered to do so by professional ethics, agency endorsement, and personal values. Socially locating and self-identifying were not acts of generating a list of adjectives but instead were performances of narrative that highlighted the contextual development of identity and location. We listened to each other respectfully and allowed ourselves to be moved by one another's stories. It became immediately apparent that faith was a core aspect of identity for most of the supervisees, as it was a key source of resilience in their stories of surviving racial oppression, and that their faith traditions did not allow queerness.

I communicated to supervisees that the profession, the agency mission, and I required practice of queer-affirmative therapy and that I was aware of the challenge this directive might hold for some staff. To my knowledge, none of the staff engaged in conversion therapy. They either assumed that everyone was heterosexual and cisgender or were mostly silent around these issues. I noticed that the queer children in this setting either did not use the counseling services, or if they did, they did so without challenging assumptions or silence, as acts of self-protection. These acts of resilience gave us time to cultivate affirmative therapy practices.

After building some trust in supervision, I would hear statements from supervisees such as "There are no gay kids here," or "It's just a phase," or "There are so many gays in the media, kids think it is OK to try it." When I walked through the schools I would hear teachers, administrators, and support staff putting each other down by calling each other "faggot" or "dyke" in a derogatory manner or referring to gender-expansive people, and it heightening my concern for the children in this setting and activating my rage. At times, I would struggle to manage these responses. As suggested by Singh and Chun's (2010) resilience-based model of supervision for queer people of color supervisors, I would process these experiences with trusted colleagues who challenged me to view these behaviors through the lens of intersecting oppressions and to use my energy to facilitate change. I found the comfort and challenge of other queer lesbians of color to be particularly healing and restorative.

To further the work of self-awareness and to nurture the supervisory alliance, I led supervisees in constructing the cultural genogram (Hardy & Laszloffy, 1995), through which they were asked to name and discuss racial, ethnic, class, education, sexual orientation, gender identity, spirituality, physical ability, and identifications of at least three generations of family and how these social locations impacted family narratives of strength, power, resilience, dominance, oppression, and subjugation. Specific attention was paid to the ways that intersecting locations shaped and informed our ways of working. As a supervision group we shared racial pride and educational success, as we were all raised with the belief that education was critical to survival and success as Black people. I began to consider how I could use our common ground as a racially marginalized people to cultivate understanding of marginalization around sexual orientation and gender identity. I also began to consider how the religious beliefs that were protective in the face of racism could also be useful in developing affirmative therapy practices even if those religions condemned queerness.

As we grappled with the dilemma of how supervisees could live their spiritual beliefs and practice affirmative therapy, I encountered the work of the Family Acceptance Project that focuses on cultivating family acceptance of queer youth. Ryan (2010) conceptualizes acceptance as a continuous construct and promotes acceptance by sharing data on the risk of negative outcomes for queer youth who do not have family acceptance, and framing family acceptance as a key protective factor for queer youth. So I conceptualized the cultivation of affirmative therapy in a similar manner.

The goal was to help supervisees view affirmative therapy as protective without directly challenging their beliefs. The work of supervision was to cultivate a *both/and* perspective regarding race, religion, sexuality, and gender identity in the service of queer-affirmative therapy.

We would utilize the genogram as specific aspects of identity became more salient in the therapeutic work. We would specifically examine family narratives and beliefs that emerged about sexuality and gender identity and how the larger social context shaped these beliefs. For example, Serena, a lead therapist, used supervision to prepare for a family session with a student and his African American lesbian parents in response to the student's behavioral issues. Serena stated that she wanted to effectively work with the family and believed that she could as long as the parents did not discuss their sex life. I validated and affirmed her honesty and sense of efficacy. I asked her if parents, assumed to be heterosexual, discussed their sex lives in a school-based therapy session about their child's behavior. When she indicated that she had not had this experience, I asked her why she thought these parents would. We engaged in a very focused dialog about her assumptions about lesbians, the values and beliefs in which these ideas were rooted, and used her genogram to examine her beliefs about sexuality and gender. We also examined the ways that her concerns mimicked the stereotypic construction of Black women as oversexualized. Serena was able to release her fear so that she could consider all the systemic factors influencing the presenting problem and form an effective working alliance with the entire family. We considered the possibility that if the parental sex life emerged as relevant to the presenting problem, Serena would respectfully refer them out because of her limited knowledge and skills and the need for ongoing work around her biases.

Tools to enhance self-awareness

Various tools to enhance self-awareness, strengthen the supervisory alliance, and counter gender and sexual oppression included common ground, power and privilege (CUSSW, 2000), and cinema therapy–like exercises. The purpose of these exercises was to cultivate a sense of shared experience, enhance capacity to view self and others as multifaceted beings, facilitate cognitive and emotional awareness of the ways that each person holds power and privilege and is simultaneously oppressor and oppressed. The supervisor's minority status along the dimension of sexual orientation sparked dialog within the supervision group about the complexity of power and fostered connections between supervisees' experiences of racial marginalization and the marginalization experienced by queer-identified people of color specifically. The lack of diversity regarding gender identity within the supervision group engendered conversations that remained more intellectualized and lacked some emotional resonance.

Film (*A Girl Like Me: The Gwen Araujo Story*, 2006; *Always My Son*, 2010; *Coming Out Stories*, 2008; *La Mission*, 2009; *Our House: Kids of Gay and Lesbian Parents*; 2000; *Pariah*, 2011; *Transgeneration*, 2005; *Unlearning Homophobia Series: De Colores*, 2004) was used to foster empathetic connection and develop knowledge about the experiences of queer communities. In my drive to cultivate affirmative attitudes toward queer communities, and perhaps operating from the subjugated parts of myself, I used a film that directly challenged religiously based heterosexism and gender oppression (*For the Bible Tells Me So*, 2007). However, because of the transparent discussions about power and the quality of the supervisory context, supervisees were able to voice how the film impacted them and challenged my thinking and use of power. I took responsibility for the impact of my actions on staff without attempting to justify, revisiting my actions with trusted peer colleagues and rededicating my efforts to practice affirmative supervision. Other more successful uses of film were those that highlighted narratives of the strengths and resilience of queer people and their family members who used their cultural narratives as resources in reconciling faith or cultural beliefs with the queer identity of their family member. These films tended to demonstrate how cultural/religious beliefs that seem to invalidate queer existence became the belief systems that brought families to acceptance.

Lessons learned

Once we collaborate with supervisees to develop critical consciousness around sexual orientation and gender identity and a strong, safe, and nurturing supervisory system, acquisition of knowledge and skills to work with queer people will follow. Although my experiences do not convey a specific model of queer-affirmative supervision, lessons can be summarized as follows:

1. Supervision that values, validates, and respects supervisees as whole persons can be used to generate queer-affirmative supervision.
2. All supervisors must engage in ongoing self-examination by developing nuanced understanding of their own development of the multiple aspects of identity, especially the dimensions of race, ethnicity, sexual orientation, gender identity, and religion, and address the following questions:
    a. Do I value all sexual orientations, gender identities, and expressions?
    b. What assumptions do I make about gender identity? How do I privilege and uphold cisgenderism? How do I devalue gender expansiveness?
    c. What assumptions do I make about sexual orientation? What assumptions do I make about sexuality based on gender assumptions? How do I privilege and uphold heterosexuality?
    d. How do other aspects of my identity shape my attitudes and beliefs about sexuality and gender?
    e. How do intersecting oppressions shape my attitudes and beliefs about gender and sexuality?
    f. What power do I hold as a supervisor, and how do I use it? How do I maintain awareness of my use of power? How will I be held accountable?
3. Supervisors must understand sexual and gender oppression in the context of other forms of oppression.
4. Supervisors must take the lead in cultivating a safe learning environment by clarifying the organizational and professional expectations for queer-affirmative practice; disclosing social location and identities; discussing issues of power and its use in supervision; and eliciting, listening, and validating supervisees' identities, social locations, and narratives regarding strength, empowerment, oppression, resilience, and survival.
5. Supervisors must take the lead in facilitating self-awareness and professional growth of supervisor and supervisees through the use of focused dialog, exercises with full supervisor participation, and ongoing examination of person of the therapist in the context of case presentations.

References

American Counseling Association. (2014). ACA code of ethics. Retrieved on September 10, 2015, from http://www.counseling.org/Resources/aca-code-of-ethics.pdf

American Psychological Association. (2010). Ethical principles of psychologists and code of conduct. Retrieved on September 10, 2015, from http://www.apa.org/ethics/code/principles.pdf

Barbosa, P. (Producer), & Barbosa, P., & Lenoir, G. (Directors). (2004). *Unlearning Homophobia Series: De colores.* USA: Woman Vision & Eye Brite Productions.

Bratt, B., Bratt, P., & Patel, A. (Producers), & Brat, P. (Director). (2009). *La mission* [DVD]. USA: Screen Media Films.

Columbia University School of Social Work (CUSSW). (2000). Self-awareness for practice in a multicultural world training manual. Unpublished manuscript.

Cooper, N. (Producer), & Rees, D. (Director). (2011). *Pariah* [DVD]. USA: Chicken and Egg Pictures.

Garcia, M., Koustic, I., McDowell, T., & Anderson, S. (2009). Raising critical consciousness in family therapy supervision. *Journal of Feminist Family Therapy, 21*(1), 18–38.

Goodman, K., & Simon, K. (Producers), & Goodman, K., & Simon, K. (Directors). (2008). *Coming out stories: Season 1* [DVD]. USA: Viacom, International.

Halpert, S., Reinhardt, B., & Toohey, M. (2007). Affirmative clinical supervision. In K. Bieschke, R. Perez, & K. DeBord (Eds.), *Handbook of counseling and psychotherapy with lesbian, gay, bisexual, and transgender clients*, (2nd ed.) (pp. 341–358). Washington, DC: American Psychological Association.

Hardy, K., & Laszloffy, T. (1995). The cultural genogram: Key to training culturally competent family therapists. *Journal of Marital and Family Therapy, 21*(3), 227–237.

Hernandez, P., & McDowell, T. (2010). Intersectionality, power, and relational safety in context: Key concepts in clinical supervision. *Training and Education in Professional Psychology, 4*(1), 29–35.

Johnson, E. P. (2005). "Quare" studies, or (almost) everything I know abut queer studies I learned from my grandmother. In E. P. Johnson & M. G. Henderson (Eds.), *Black queer studies*, pp. 124–160. Durham, NC: Duke University Press.

Karslake, D. (Producer), & Karslake, D. (Director). (2007). *For the bible tells me so* [DVD]. USA: First Run Features.

Long, J., & Groute, J. (2012). Queer supervision. In J. Bigner & J. Wetchler (Eds.), *Handbook of LGBT-affirmative couple and family therapy* (pp. 409–418). New York, NY: Routledge.

National Association of Social Workers. (2008). Code of Ethics. Retrieved on August 27, 2015, from http://www.socialworkers.org/pubs/code/code.asp

National Association of Social Workers. (2015). NASW standards and indicators for cultural competence in social work practice. Draft for public comment, May 6, 2015. Retrieved on August, 27, 2015, from http://www.socialworkers.org/practice/NASWStandards/culturalCompetence/Contents%20for%20Draft%20CC%20Standards%20and%20Indicators%2015-3.pdf

Ritter, K., & Terndrup, A. (2002). *Handbook of affirmative psychotherapy with lesbians and gay men*. New York, NY: Guilford Press.

Rosati, F. (Producer), & Holland, A. (Director). (2006). *A girl like me: The Gwen Araujo story*. USA: Braun Entertainment Group.

Ryan, C., & Kleinman, V. (Producers), & Kleinman, V. (Director). (2010). *Always my son* [documentary film short]. USA: Libra Films.

Ryan, C., Russell, S., Huenber, D., Diaz, R., & Sanchez, J. (2010). Family acceptance and adolescence and the health of LGBT young adults. *Journal of Child and Adolescent Psychiatric Nursing, 23*(4), 205–213.

Singh, A., & Chun, K. (2010). From the margins to the center: Moving towards a resilience-based model of supervision for queer people of color supervisors. *Training and Education in Professional Psychology, 4*(1), 36–46.

Smothers, T. (Producer), & Simmons, J. (Director). (2005). *Transgeneration* [DVD]. USA: World of Wonder Productions.

Spadola, M. (Producer), & Spadola, M. (Director). (2000). *Our house: Kids of gay and lesbian parents* [DVD]. USA: Icarus Films.

Stone Carlson, T., & McGeorge, C. (2012). LGB-affirmative training strategies for couple and family therapist faculty: Preparing heterosexual students to work with LGB clients. In J. Bigner & J. Wetchler (Eds.), *Handbook of LGBT-affirmative couple and family therapy* (pp. 395–408). New York, NY: Routledge.

Stone Fish L., & Harvey, R. (2005). *Nurturing queer youth*. New York, NY: Norton.

Stone Fish, L., & Harvey, R. (2012). Raising lesbian, gay or bisexual youth: An affirmative family therapy approach. In J. Bigner & J. Wetchler (Eds.), *Handbook of LGBT-affirmative couple and family therapy* (pp. 183–187). New York, NY: Routledge.

8

INTEGRATING AND ADDRESSING RELIGION AND SPIRITUALITY IN SUPERVISION AND TRAINING

Argie Allen-Wilson, PhD

Integrating and addressing religion and spirituality in supervision and training is a process that is often fraught with complexity and many inherent challenges. Walking the tightrope of attending to, acknowledging, and respecting religiously and spiritually based values in supervision and training without imposition is not an easy feat. In this chapter, I discuss lessons learned from faith-based and clinical training to guide how to integrate religion and spirituality into supervision and training. This approach engenders respect for differences while also encouraging difficult conversations regarding the intersection of religion, spirituality, and clinical training.

Conceptualizing two constructs: Religiousness and spirituality

Keep in mind that religiousness and spirituality have been a part of the human experience throughout the length and breadth of human history (Zinnbauer & Pargament, 2000). The terms "religion" and "spirituality" have been used interchangeably over the years (Spilka & McIntosh, 1996). According to Goldberg (1990), fundamental descriptions that were once applied to religion are now becoming the province of spirituality. Spirituality has come to represent an overarching construct regarding a dimension of the human experience involving individuals' efforts at reaching a variety of sacred or existential goals in life, such as finding meaning, wholeness, inner potential, interconnections with others, and a search for universal truth (Goldberg, 1990). This construct can be within or outside of formal religion, through family of origin, cultural heritage, or a connection with nature and humanity. In contrast, religiousness is substantively associated with formal belief, group practice, and institutions often portrayed as peripheral to these existential functions (Pargament, 1999). For most, this encompasses a belief in God or a Higher Power. Often those who describe themselves as religious also identify themselves as spiritual. Thus the distinction between the two constructs may not be that useful with regard to meaning (Hill & Pargament, 2003; Miller & Thoresen, 2003). Additionally, those who describe themselves as spiritual may not identify themselves as religious. While the terms "religion" and "spirituality" are not entirely interchangeable, they often have overlapping meanings (Hage et al., 2006), thus will be referred to from an inclusive perspective throughout this chapter.

Training programs: Commitment to the integration

The extent to which supervisors attend to these issues related to religion and spirituality also appears to be strongly connected to the training programs from which they gained their supervisory experiences. It is postulated that for programs charged with designing educational experiences aimed at cultural competency, spiritual and religious diversity need to be considered along with other areas of diversity, such as culture, ethnicity, and gender, as key components of sensitive multicultural training (Hage et al., 2006). Further, Hage et al. (2006) suggest that while many clinical training programs have reported being open to further inclusion of spirituality and religiosity within their core curricula including supervision, it appears that they facilitate limited integration of spiritual and religious content into the educational process.

Acknowledging the importance of conversations on religion and spirituality in supervision

Hage et al. (2006) suggest that the awareness of clients' religious background has become even more important as the diversity of religious traditions continues to increase due to immigration and other factors that have increased the plurality of religious life here in the United States. For some marginalized groups (e.g., African Americans), spirituality and religion have also been identified as major sources of strength and survival (Boyd-Franklin & Lockwood, 1999; Mattis, 2002). These groups have utilized their religious connections to heal from the residual effects of slavery. Even though navigating the arduous terrain of addressing religious and spiritual beliefs and values in supervision may prove daunting, it has become imperative that supervisors find unique and innovative ways to integrate these constructs within the realm of supervision. Otherwise the opportunity may be missed to include the potential for growth with not just the supervisees but their clients as well. Whether supervisors are compelled to integrate religion and spirituality into the training process largely depends on their awareness of locating their own religious and spiritual selves (Aponte & Winter, 2000; Hage et al., 2006; Watson, 1993). This can be a difficult task while also attempting to maintain a healthy respect for our universal differences and simultaneously embracing our universal similarities.

Social location of self

I locate myself as an educated, middle-aged, middle class, heterosexual, cisgender, non-disabled, and married female who also identifies as a Christian Baptist African American woman. Additionally, I identify as a black woman who has enjoyed the privilege of being raised by educated parents who had professional careers, were married for 58 years, separated only by death, and as a daughter, sister, niece, auntie, friend, wife, mentor, and mental health professional. I grew up in the black Baptist church community with lots of hardworking extended family members who also identify as black Baptist Christians priding themselves on being both very religious and spiritual.

I'm excited about this chapter because it challenges me as well as the readers to think about the inherent mistakes in supervision we are bound to make related to religion and spirituality. We all have the potential to slip up as supervisors when we are in the trenches with our supervisees as well as their clients. Additionally, this chapter will help the reader to celebrate the major opportunities we have as supervisors to create space for what I like to call courageous conversations. While highlighting questions regarding religious and spiritual beliefs can create some discomfort for the supervisor/supervisee relationship, locating powerful resources that may be available to those we seek to help through the diverse connections to their religious and spiritual values can enhance the therapeutic process (Hage et al., 2006). With this in mind, supervisors must be careful to not impose their spiritual or religious beliefs onto supervisees, hence fostering an isomorphic paradigm (Lee & Everett, 2004), which in turn has the potential to negatively impact the therapeutic process for their clients.

It can be expected that mental health professionals will encounter diverse client populations with a broad range of spiritual and religious backgrounds during the span of their career (Richards &

Bergin, 2000). How the supervisor assists the supervisee in finding avenues of exploration to tap into the vast resources of religious and spiritual values remains a fundamental question as the climate of diversity continues to expand.

The integration of religion and spirituality in supervision: When it works

Early in my career, when I was in my mid-20s, I recall a potential new supervisor who was the director of a women and children's drug and alcohol program, giving me one of my first tools to carry with me on a long journey as a clinician of color in the mental health field. I was young and somewhat naïve to all the complexities required of a clinician, yet full of passion, empathy, and a sincere desire to make my contribution by helping underprivileged families who were struggling due to the social injustices of humanity. This program was located in the heart of urban northeast Philadelphia. Little did I know that this supervisor, who located herself as an educated middle-aged, middle class, heterosexual, African American Christian woman, would become my boss, my mentor, and ultimately my friend. The tool she imparted to me was in the form of a question followed by a powerful answer. With that said, the powerful answer did not come from me. Even as a new and eager supervisee, my answer seemed lackluster at best, as I reflect on the interaction many years later—so lackluster that it is my belief that my new supervisor decided to answer the question herself. The answer she provided to her question turned out to be one of the most powerful revelations I have ever experienced and ultimately shaped my clinical style of practice and provided much of the foundation for my relationships both personally and professionally. What I did not take into consideration then, but am acutely aware of now, is how that very same question/answer scenario could have had a very different result if the supervisor was not a Christian woman of color similar to the identified characteristics that I possess.

What was the question followed by my supervisor's answer? Well, I'm glad you asked. The question was, "What makes you think you can do this clinical work with this population of primarily poor, disenfranchised, black, drug- and alcohol-addicted older women and their children who are trying to recover from years of trauma if you've never had any of their personal experiences, especially with drugs and alcohol, and you have no children of your own?" This question left me a little dazed and slightly paralyzed, without a good rationale for how I was equipped to accomplish the task presented to me. I mustered up enough courage to at least say that I wasn't sure, but that I was determined to learn. And so the learning began with my first lesson related to self of the therapist (Aponte, 2002; Baldwin, 2000). My supervisor took a pregnant pause and then proceeded to answer her own question by saying to me, "If you are going to be successful at doing this very difficult clinical work with those who are relegated to living in the margins of humanity, you must always remember: There but for the grace of God go I."

While I had heard this saying before, given that I had grown up in the church and considered one of my selves to be "a good church girl," I had not ever heard this phrase used in the context of a work-related conversation such as supervision. In that moment I recall internally and intently acknowledging a spiritual connection between myself and my supervisor and a realization that the work we were about to embark on was much bigger than she or I individually. There was a collective spirit that united us, even though I had much to learn from my supervisor as well as my assigned clients and their families. This connection appeared not to be about specific religion or denomination, but more about the ways in which we were spiritually connected to the mission of making a contribution to humanity in our small corner of the universe. I continued to work as a therapist receiving supervision for several years at this program and believe that I gave and received many rewarding experiences both from my clients and from my former supervisor. This gift from my supervisor that I now entitle as my mantra, "There but for the grace of God go I," has become the foundation through which I've governed myself while completing thousands of clinical hours over the past 20 years. It has helped me to better understand my clients and their families through the lens of humility while making valid attempts to treat them without judgment and support them through the prism of our spiritual connection to the universe.

Additionally, this awareness continues to allow me many years later to still utilize this mantra as a tool that helps to ground and regulate me as a female clinician of color. I have learned to utilize my spirituality to connect to a greater source, which helps me to access internal resources to support those I supervise and treat. In doing this I'm careful to make inquiries, not assumptions that might border on imposing my religious or spiritual value system. I'm acutely aware that if I impose my religious or spiritual values onto my supervisees or my clients, I run the risk of very easily abusing my power, causing harm to the very people I am trying to help.

The integration of religion and spirituality in supervision: When assumptions thwart growth

While the aforementioned supervisory experience worked out very well for me, given that I still utilize this mantra today in my clinical work and in my personal life, if the supervisor and supervisee had come from very different religious, spiritual, and racial backgrounds, this may have fostered a very different outcome. Hence, this process offers the potential to devalue the supervisee who may have had a vastly different religious or spiritual perspective. The assumption by the supervisor that the supervisee even believed in God may have been an inaccurate assumption, not giving room for engaging in a discussion that fosters mutual respect for both perspectives. Given the fluid way in which we experience social constructs, it's important to note that a supervisor can border on the edge of a slippery slope by assuming that those we supervise possess the same cultural belief system about religion and spirituality.

The intersection of religion, spirituality, and racial identity in supervision: Integrating alternate approaches

It is extremely important for supervisors to pose questions regarding the ways in which supervisees views religion and spirituality in their own lives. This approach offers the advantage of helping supervisees gain a better understanding of themselves as well as offering techniques regarding how they might gather information about the religious and spiritual value systems in their clients' lives. Further, engaging in this kind of respectful dialogue regarding similarities and differences might also foster the supervisees' ability to integrate this kind of inquiry into the therapeutic process with clients regarding religious and spiritual values.

In creating a multicultural supervisory training environment, one should also keep in mind that it's very possible to be quite presumptive in assuming that because there is a shared racial identity, the supervisor/supervisee relationship also encompasses the same shared religious and spiritual identity. In the example with my previous supervisor from many years ago, I did share the same racial and spiritual/religious identity. However, one cannot assume that this will automatically be the case. Additionally, if the supervisor is white and the supervisee is black or of mixed race, it is essential to understand the power and privilege differential in order to thwart stereotypical presumptions about the religious and spiritual background of the supervisee. While it is important to attend to the integration of religious and spiritual inquiries within the supervisory process, it is equally important to pay close attention to the intersection of the aforementioned social constructs with racial identity in the context of clinical training. Failure to attend to the intersection of these critical constructs has the potential to create barriers, impeding the growth process for all parties involved.

The integration of religion and spirituality in supervision: When therapists' values are different from their clients'

During my early 30s I considered myself to be a young, fairly naïve supervisor-in-training who was just beginning my journey in the complex world of supervision. I had experienced what I considered to be both excellent and horrible supervision as an MFT student. From those experiences, many lessons were learned, mostly encompassing what not to do as a supervisor. Admittedly, during this time I was still a bit confused regarding what I should be doing as a supervisor.

The program I was working for at the time had a Clergy track, and I found myself drawn to working with a group of budding clinicians who had been formally trained in theology. These supervisees' formal training as theologians appeared antithetical to the clinical work I had been accustomed to in my secular training. I recalled having the internal desire when I began my academic journey to take what I learned in the secular institution and integrate those concepts with religious and spiritual principles. Thus, working with clergy from all different religious backgrounds clearly engendered a connection to my spiritual core. Additionally, I was acutely aware that the lens through which many of them assessed the presenting problems of their clients seemed riddled with judgment and blame as opposed to compassion and empathy. I too connected with those constructs in that I had grown up in the church and certainly could recall those "well-meaning" religious folks appearing extremely critical and destructively entitled at times, especially when they had little tolerance or acceptance of difference. I included myself in that category, so I considered this a process by which we would all be learning together. I became very focused on my attempt to assist these pastors/ministers/clinicians with strategies in supervision that would dually honor their commitment to religion and spirituality while helping them to raise uncomfortable questions that they may never have asked in their clergy role. During this process many of them adapted my old mantra that I had learned over a decade prior, "There but for the grace of God go I." This seemed to resonate with many of them, yet it was very apparent that helping them to engage in the therapeutic dialogue regarding spirituality and religion was more arduous when the religious ideology of their clients was different than their own belief system. That said, we continued to struggle together, and what evolved seemed to be a level of trust related to our shared experiences that permitted room for growth. In many cases, we have to create room for differences in order to embrace similarities. Many of my supervisor/supervisee relationships emulated an isomorphic paradigm shift that often benefited their clients and families. They became more open to the possibility of exploring all religious and spiritual beliefs, versus just their own, while recognizing that their role as a clinician was quite different from their clergy role. Both roles could be cloaked under the umbrella of ministry but with very different methods of care.

In reflection, had I shut down, becoming paralyzed as a supervisor by what appeared to be an extreme level of criticism and judgment, I would not have been able to utilize our shared spiritual connection to foster bridges between these clergy and their clients. Engaging in difficult conversations in supervision for the purpose of integrating religion and spirituality has become a very necessary part of the growth process. Those who shy away from it may be hindering a very important role in the expansion of the multicultural learning process.

The intersection of religion, spirituality, and racial identity in supervision: Walking the tightrope

For the purpose of this case example, I will call my supervisee Jeff. Well over a decade ago, I was assigned to supervise a 30-year-old heterosexual, cisgender, African American male father of a 5-year-old son. Jeff was aspiring to become a family therapist, had completed about half of his course work, and was struggling to accumulate the clinical hours necessary for completion of his Post-Master's Certificate in Marriage and Family Therapy.

While he was not a part of the Clergy track, he did disclose to me during the initial stages of our work together that he was born and raised as a Christian and that his mother and father had been married for many years. He expressed a desire to marry one day, but was very focused on completing his education and launching his professional career.

Jeff presented a case during supervision where he was working with a 42-year-old Caucasian, nonreligious, single mother of two. Her presenting problem was trying to get out of a toxic relationship after recently finding out that she was pregnant. She also needed support to help make a decision with regard to whether or not she should terminate the pregnancy.

After reviewing the video of the session, I asked Jeff why it appeared that he was sitting so far away from his client in the therapy room. Initially, Jeff resisted the notion that he had positioned himself at the furthest distance from his client while in session. Upon closer inspection of the videotape, it was determined that Jeff was sitting closest to the door and his client was sitting on the other side of the room, with an empty chair between them. I asked Jeff to think about what he was thinking when he positioned himself near the door. At first, Jeff's reply was that he was just going through the checklist of what he wanted to cover in the therapy session. After further exploration and a quick field trip down the hall to the vacant office where he had conducted the session, Jeff began to share what he was really thinking while facilitating the session with his client. He shared that he was afraid to be in a closed room with a white woman, because his mother, who was a schoolteacher who grew up in the South, always told him that he should never get caught with a white woman behind closed doors. He further shared that it was against his religion to support his client getting an abortion, so he wanted to avoid the conversation as much as possible.

Once I had a better understanding of what Jeff was going through, I was able to assure him that his job was not to tell the client what to do. Moreover, his responsibility was to walk the tightrope of holding on to his core beliefs but not imposing them upon his client. I encouraged him to ask his client questions related to her own spiritual and religious background. During that inquiry it was determined that they shared more similarities than differences. Even though she was not religious, she did articulate that she shared a universal spiritual belief about life and that she was unwilling and unable to go through with the termination of her pregnancy. Jeff and I also explored the residual impact of historical trauma, which helped him better understand his fear of being in a closed room with a white woman. He was able to make the connection that even though his mother's concerns were valid through her lens, his protective factors in the work setting were able to ease his fears about being falsely accused of impropriety. I believe that the connection that was formed out of our shared religious, spiritual, racial, and familial experiences allowed room for the growth process.

The intersection of these constructs may sometimes present itself in multiple ways that contribute to disconnection versus connection. If Jeff's supervisor was racially or spiritually located differently, the stretch to address the intersection of these coexisting constructs may have proved more challenging but not unobtainable. Having the courage to walk the tightrope by engaging in these necessary conversations not only honors our commitment to our supervisees, but it demonstrates a commitment to those diverse clients we serve as well. These families are counting on our field of helpers to be culturally aware and sensitive to the unique ways in which religion and spirituality impact humanity.

The integration of religion and spirituality in supervision: Reflective questions for further exploration

It is important to note that many of us as supervisors arrive at this place of cultural awareness and sensitivity with regard to religion and spirituality through trial, error, and a sincere willingness to expose our own vulnerabilities. Often, becoming more culturally aware is what happens when we've survived the many pitfalls and mistakes encountered in supervision. Additionally, as we become more comfortable challenging our own religious and spiritual biases, prejudices, and stereotypes, we have the potential to become much more equipped to assist our supervisees to walk the tightrope of engaging themselves as well as their clients in these delicate yet powerful conversations.

While embarking on this multicultural supervisory process, it's important to embrace reflective questions that stimulate both awareness of and sensitivity to religious and spiritual barriers as well as bridges. The following reflective questions can be used as tools when considering how to integrate religion and spirituality within the context of supervision.

1. What is your rationale for the inclusion or exclusion of religious or spiritual questions within the clinical process?
2. What are the essential ways to search for connections versus disconnections when there are clear differences within the intersection of religion, spirituality, and racial identity in the clinical process?
3. What are the elements in your personal history that contribute to your avoidance and/or inclusion of religious and spiritual exploration in the clinical process?
4. What are the ways in which you might utilize your religious and spiritual historical connections to engage with those who might use their religious and spiritual beliefs as resources for growth?
5. How do you utilize previous negative experiences with religion and spirituality as a point of reference and/or a potential resource in the clinical process?
6. How has the inclusion of religious and spiritual inquiry impacted the clinical process when utilized as a resource?
7. How has the exclusion of religious and spiritual inquiry impacted the clinical process when not utilized as a resource?
8. What would you do differently when the integration of religious and spirituality in the clinical process has gone wrong?
9. What are the strategies that you employ to adhere to your personal religious and spiritual values while respecting the rights of others?
10. How do you self-monitor your biases, judgmental beliefs, and lack of acceptance of spiritual and religious differences?

In conclusion, it is important to remember as mental health professionals, whether we are the supervisor or the supervisee, our first commitment is to do no harm. Maintaining a level of honesty and integrity in supervision means that we must continue our due diligence and commitment to cultural diversity. As agents of social change, the exploration of our religious and spiritual blind spots is imperative, as is being unafraid to identify and address areas where we have the potential to fall short. By avoiding this responsibility, we miss valuable opportunities for personal growth as well as miss out on assisting our clients with the utilization of their religious and spiritual resources; hence, potentially causing more harm than good.

References

Aponte, H. (2002, January/February). God and therapy. *Family Therapy Magazine, 1*, 16–21.

Aponte, H. J., & Winter, J. E. (2002). The person and practice of the therapist: Treatment and training. In M. Baldwin (Ed.), *The use of self in therapy* (2nd ed.) (pp. 127–165). New York, NY: Hawthorne.

Baldwin, M. (Ed.). (2000). *The use of self in therapy* (2nd ed.). New York, NY: Hawthorne.

Boyd-Franklin, N., & Walker Lockwood, T. (1999). Spirituality and religion: Implications for psychotherapy with African-American clients and families. In F. Walsh (Ed.), *Spirituality resources in family therapy* (pp. 90–103). New York, NY: Guilford Press.

Goldberg, R. S. (1990). The transpersonal element in spirituality and psychiatry. *Psychiatry Residents Newsletter, 10*, 9.

Hage, S. M., Seigel, M., Payton, G., & DeFanti, E. (2006). Multicultural training in spirituality: An interdisciplinary review. *Journal of Counseling & Development, 82*, 504–507.

Hill, P. C., & Pargament, K. I. (2003). Advances in the conceptualization and measurement of religion and spirituality: Implications for physical and mental health research. *American Psychologist, 58*, 64–74.

Lee, R. E., & Everett, C. A. (2004). *The integrated family therapy supervisor.* New York, NY: Routledge.

Mattis, J. S. (2002). Religion and spirituality in the meaning-making and coping experiences of African American women: A qualitative analysis. *Psychology of Woman Quarterly, 26*, 309–321.

Miller, W. R., & Thoresen, C. E. (2003). Spirituality, religion, and health: An emerging research field. *American Psychologist, 58*, 24–35.

Pargament, K. I. (1999). The psychology of religion and spirituality? Yes and no. *The International Journal for the Psychology of Religion, 9*, 3–16.

Richards, P. S., & Bergin, A. E. (Eds.). (2000). *Handbook of psychotherapy and religious diversity.* Washington, DC: American Psychological Association.

Spilka, B., & McIntosh, D. N. (1996, August). *Religion and spirituality: The known and the unknown.* Paper presented to the annual conference of the American Psychological Association, Toronto, Canada.

Walsh, F. (Ed.) (1999). *Spiritual resources in family therapy.* New York, NY: Guilford Press.

Watson, M. F. (1993). Supervising the person of the therapist: Issues, challenges and dilemmas. *Contemporary Family Therapy, 15*, 21–31.

Zinnbauer, B. J., & Pargament, K. I. (2002). Working with the sacred: Four approaches to working with religious and spiritual issues in counseling. *Journal of Counseling and Development, 78*, 162–171.

9

IMAGE AND EXPERIENCE IN MULTICULTURAL SUPERVISION AND TRAINING

J. Leonardo de la O, MA

We were told that up ahead we would find the American Indian petroglyphs. Supposedly it was a place that few knew about. It was off the beaten path and was difficult to find. In fact, my brother-in-law, a park ranger at Joshua Tree, said that the site was not spoken about to "outsiders," because of the fear of desecration by vandals. I was told that people and the environment itself had damaged many other sites. I recall leaving our van on the service road and beginning the ascent up the somewhat difficult slope. The soil beneath me was made of broken rock and would easily give away as we attempted to gain ground. It was late in the afternoon and there was talk of perhaps returning to our campsite before it got too late, which would make the return trip more difficult in the dark. However, we decided to push on a bit more, thinking it could not be much farther. It was shortly after this discussion that I recall stepping across what can only be described as an imperceptible line in the topography of the land and yet, once on the other side of the landscape, the surroundings itself felt quite different. Here, there was a complete melancholy stillness.

Up ahead, perhaps 15 yards further, were the petroglyphs. As I looked at the lines and figures drawn into the rock, I was overtaken by a grief unlike anything I had felt before. As I looked across the desert landscape, I felt that I was in a place of vast immutability. This profound sense of loss was not located in me but rather in this desolate vacuum of desert space. I felt that the land was holding on to the trauma of a vanished people and a wounded land. Perhaps it was the disconnection between desert itself and those who once lived in this area. However, what became conscious to me was that the conquest of the Americas, which began in 1492, was still held in the land and very much alive in me and in the descendants of the conquest. The experience of that day confirmed a felt sense that people of the Americas, and the land itself, continue to hold the trauma of what Mexicans often vividly refer to as *"La Chingada,"* the conquest of the Americas. *La Chingada* is an image that preoccupies much of the Mexican psyche. Jung writes: "Concepts are coined and negotiable values: images are life" (*Collected Works* [CW] 14, 1953d, p. 180) He also states that "the image is a condensed expression of the psychic situation as a whole, and not merely, or even predominately of unconscious contents pure and simple" (CW 6, 1953b, p. 242). In other words, Jung argues that image is psyche. *La Chingada* is such a profound expression of the Chicano psyche that supervisors cannot hope to deepen their understanding of the Chicano and other Latin Americans without thoroughly understanding this image and the psychological split which resulted from the separation of Gods, nature, and an indigenous way of life. Supervisors must also understand their own relationship to *La Chingada*, which began in 1492 and continues to shadow the Americas.

As therapists, we are required to hold difficult emotional material, which simply and not so simply occurs in everyone's life, and yet, ethically, we are now called to do more. We must also hold the client's conscious and unconscious cultural experiences, which not only includes the trauma of the conquest, *La Chingada*, but also includes ongoing social and political oppression. It has been my experience, both in Joshua Tree and as a supervisor and professor, that many Chicano and Mexican clients bring experiences of what has been referred to as "transrational reality" (Bernstein, 2014). Vestiges of the Conquest of the Americas or experiences of nonrational reality may appear in the psyche of Latino clients. The Conquest and the resulting separation from the indigenous soul are clinical concerns that should be acknowledged and addressed in clinical supervision and in educational programs. As we shall see, this separation impacts all people living in the Americas. Not only is *La Chingada* in the land, it is also present in the consultation room.

Culture in psychotherapy

Before moving forward it is necessary to briefly define what is meant by "culture." Edward T. Hall, the late cultural anthropologist, writes that culture is "a way of life of a group of people—the sum of their learned patterns, attitudes, and symbols that they accept, generally without thinking about them. Different cultural groups think, feel, and act differently" (1959). Clinical psychologist Pamala Hays (2008) concurs with Hall and informs us that "most anthropologists would agree that the term 'cultural' includes traditions of thought and behavior such as language and history that can be socially acquired, shared and passed on to new generations." Hall argues that it is important to acknowledge "the broad extent to which culture controls our lives." In other words, the lens through which we, as supervisors, view the world is bound by one's cultural perspective.

In fact, Hall (1959) says that the examination of culture leads one to a greater self-knowledge.[1] The clinical supervisor and psychotherapy instructor is not exempt from this dynamic. Not only do student clinicians bring their personal history and their cultural lens with them into supervision but, more importantly, so do clinical supervisors and instructors. This includes racial biases and cultural experiences as well as a culturally defined value of mental health (Sue, 2012). The supervisor's cultural lens will affect his or her impact on student learning and case management. It is therefore necessary that the supervisor begin any supervisorial role with a deeper look into his or her own cultural background and worldview.

The use of self

As a Chicano professor and clinician working with students in multicultural classes, or as an instructor in the clinical practicum courses, I find it necessary to disclose a bit about myself. If I am asking students to begin with their cultural experiences, then it is necessary that I model my own personal work in this area.

Sharing my own experiences as a Person of Color allows for a significant change in perspective. Where diversity was once a discussion about "them," my voice, the voice of the "other," is now part of the discourse. The importance of this shift cannot be overstated. On the one hand, we are no longer talking around the issues of racism and oppression but meeting them head-on in a dialogue that allows for everyone's voice. In addition, the voice of Whites is no longer just about that of the oppressor. An open dialogue allows for Whites to express that part of themselves which is often not admitted into the discussion, the ways in which racism has impacted their lives as well. What is required in multicultural training is a sense of openness that allows for honest discussion of those moments in our life when we experienced racial bias and prejudice as well as experiences of pride.

The supervisor must begin with himself or herself. Only then can we call upon students to openly discuss their own cultural background. The instructor, in the role of educational leader and role model, must deal with her or her own fears, bias, wounds, and anger. This is necessary if we are to create a safe container that will allow students to feel supported as they begin their own cultural inventory. We must begin with the professor and the supervisor if we are going to train "culturally responsive therapists" (Hays, 2008).

My evolving cultural identity

I was born and raised in Echo Park, downtown Los Angeles, where Spanish was my first language. My parents, who lived in Texas in the 1920s, experienced a form of racism that can best be described as the results of the Mexican War that raged in Texas and much of the Southwest, but can also be understood as a result of internal colonialism. The Mexican people "had been defeated in the U.S./ Mexican War, leaving Mexico's northern lands and barrios as the New Southwest, a colony within the continuous territory of the Anglo-American empire" (Chavez, 2011).

My parents' resulting internalized racism meant that they wanted me to flourish by identifying with and embracing the culture of White America. Images of America in the '50s, such as *See the U.S.A. in your Chevrolet* and *Walt Disney's Wonderful Word of Color,* stood as portraits of success and happiness for my parents. However, I experienced the shadow side of the American Dream of the '50s through childhood experiences of racism, such as segregation and tracking in schools and negative racial encounters in my neighborhood. I recall going to the home of my best friend, who was White, and being served a bowl of beans by his father many times. He would say with laughter in his voice, "Lenardo, you like beans, don't you?" I would sit there eating the beans, as my friend would be served his lunch (which did not include beans). As I recall that story now, I want to kick myself not because I sat there like a fool eating those beans. What I find troubling is that those beans weren't even *mi jefita's*[2] pinto beans. They were damn pork and beans and from a can!

Segregation and tracking in school meant that I interacted only with other Latino children, and I found this to be the beginning of pride in my Raza.[3] But it wasn't until I entered college as an Education Opportunity Program (EOP) student, the beginning of the Chicano Movement, and my work with the United Farm Workers that I found a deep well of a cultural heritage and dignity. It was during my late teens and early twenties when I traveled extensively throughout Mexico that I experienced a cultural shock that allowed me to view reality through a different set of cultural lenses and alter my view from my childhood mentality. I share this story because it is my belief that in the classroom there is no other way but self-disclosure, and this must begin with the supervisor or instructor.

Role-play vignettes and the subject of race

As a result, and with a desire to get my students to take seriously the culture of others, I have found it advantageous to bring in guest speakers to role-play multicultural vignettes. I have invited Black, Asian, and Latino therapists from the community for these role-plays, which the students have found challenging and anxiety-provoking but, nevertheless, invaluable. The guest speakers take on the role of client. I ask the speakers to submit a vignette prior to class. I review and make suggestions so that the role-plays are focused on cultural diversity, as well as clinical material. The submitted vignette also allows for the guest speakers to "own" and "know" their character and bring a depth of realism to the role-play. The vignettes should not focus on negative stereotypes of a particular ethnic group or a representation of the society's negative projections. I refrain from using obvious red-flag issues, as the students will focus, quite appropriately, on these issues and not on the cultural diversity material.

The vignette should have a feel to it that culture in itself is not the problem but rather a strength and potential resource in the community and within the client. Cultural diversity is not pathological, and it is imperative that instructors and supervisors communicate the "beauty and strength that can be found in diversity" (comments to the author from California Lutheran Latino students citing Maya Angelou, 2014). After the roles, which are an hour in length, the students have the opportunity to receive important feedback from the guests. The students also have the opportunity to ask questions and to informally process the role-play. On one occasion the evening class concluded with the guest therapist reading his poetry about being a Chinese American in the United States. This was an insightful experience for both student and instructor, which allowed for a genuine connection with his experience as an Chinese American. The reader is referred to Chapter 18, where the Multicultural Role-Play Exercise and Asian American Role-Play vignette are presented.

The subject of culture in counseling

The subject of race and culture is difficult and continues to be a threatening and an emotionally laden topic in our society today. I once had a student who asked me why it is necessary to even consider culture and race in counseling psychology. In fact, there is at least one student each year who believes it is wrong to bring race into psychotherapy training because, in their view, we are all the same, and true healing occurs on a deeper level. In response, I have found it prudent to begin a multicultural class or a supervisory group with an open discussion as to why we even bother with a consideration of cultural diversity in psychotherapy.

After this discussion I begin with the following exercise. I will ask my students and trainees to do a "Think, Pair, Share" (Kagan & Kagen, 2009). I ask students to bring to consciousness a cultural image or an experience in their own lives. Another useful activity is to ask students or interns to reflect on the following: What is your connection to your ancestors, your lineage, and your cultural background? Students in the past have shared both positive and negative experiences with these prompts. For the person of color, born in the United States, many feelings of *La Chingada* have surfaced that included, anger, fear, and their own sense of loss and alienation from an inability to fit in their cultural world or that of the White dominant culture.

One Latino student spoke of his traditional upbringing and how his mother would still make *tortas* for him as a way to save money while he attended graduate school. He spoke of this with awkwardness but also with a firm sense of connection to his family's way of life. The students were deeply moved by his sharing, and we all felt compassion for this student's vulnerability. I responded by saying that I was imagining his mother making *tortas* for the entire class. He responded by saying, "You know my mother would do that for us."

A supervisor's blind spot

My past work with White students allowed me to realize a huge oversight. In fact, I was not seeing the White students. I was more concerned with my cultural wounding. I would move into issues of power differentials, White privilege, and stories of societal oppression without acknowledging that my "other" students also had painful and emotional experiences in American culture. These experiences need to be witnessed and talked about. I often have White students who feel totally alienated from their ancestry. It has been said to me, "I don't have a culture," or "I'm not connected to my family's history." There is a profound reservoir of alienation as a result of our Western way of life that must be addressed by instructors and clinical supervisors. I have found that White students need to express what it is like to be White in America. Perhaps what is being communicated is a desire to heal from the disconnection and isolation of a culture and society that is no longer involved in the mystery of nature and its sanctity. This is perhaps the modern-day *Chingada*.

It should also be noted, and must be emphasized by the supervisor or professor, that the Western alienation that the White students feel is intensely different from what Latinos and other People of Color have experienced. As mental health professionals, we must not discount or dismiss injustice caused by racial oppression or White economic and academic privilege. Conversely, it must be noted that the shadow side of the American racial dynamic makes it possible, and perhaps far too easy and desirable, to only see things from one's own side of the tracks. As supervisors, we are called upon to hold this opposing tension and to be empathetic to the wounding of all our interns and students.

It is of paramount importance that the clinical supervisor validates everyone's cultural experience in order to more fully look at cultural diversity and its influence on alienation, race, privilege, and oppression.

> We still attribute to the other fellow all the evil and inferior qualities that we do not like to recognize in ourselves, and therefore have to criticize and attack him, when all that has happened is that an inferior "soul" has emigrated from one person to another. The world is still full of bêtes noires and scapegoats, just as it formerly teemed with witches and werewolves.
> —C. G. Jung (1970)

Renewed conscious awareness of racial tension has become more common as American demographics change. It is important to acknowledge the "bêtes noires and the scapegoat" that lie in the shadow of racial bigotry. We must acknowledge that racial and ethnic hatred is a two-way street. I recall living in Spain and being in a store where I was verbally attacked for being an American. I totally agreed with the accusations, and I found it strange to be called an "American"; I have never truly felt to be an American without a hyphen or some reference to being a "minority." However, the shop owner who had witnessed this confrontation apologized for the rude behavior of the customer. I said that America has a dark past and I agreed basically with what that guy had said about the United States.

The shop owner was quick to point out that no country is without a dark side. His argument was, "Look at Spain." His point was well taken.

In our role as supervisors, we must remember that hubris and inflation are always a danger. Constant vigilance is required in order to remain unencumbered by the power dynamic in supervision and our own biases and agendas. The danger is that the supervisor falls victim to his or her own narrow and one-sided view of race and culture. Can I truly see my students? Can I see their souls? Racism is an issue that impacts everyone negatively, and the effectiveness of any course on cultural diversity rests on understanding that the damage it does can be healed only by an understanding and appreciation of everyone's diverse backgrounds and our shared experiences as human beings.

I had one White student who sought me out because one of the Latino students had said to her that she had never suffered because she was rich, born into White privilege, and that she could never understand racial prejudice because she was White. She was being judged and not seen as a person in her own right. I have found it important to tell my students that we are in this together and that I do not view anyone in class as a racist, but rather that we are working to hold this racial tension and become healers who tend to wounded individual psyches and to souls in and of this fragmented world.

As supervisor, I realized that I had been examining cultural experience from only one side of the street. This needed to be corrected. In supervision and in the classroom, the supervisor must acknowledge how racism wounds everyone in this country. Students have also expressed feelings of White guilt for the racism of the past, for White Privilege, and for being a part of a system that has and continues to oppress cultural minorities and other diverse groups. My response to students has varied, but White students need to deeply process and understand this guilt and that it must not become the racial complex that, in the countertransference, rules the session. This will prevent the prospective clinician from truly seeing diverse clients both on a personal and cultural level.

Derald Sue suggests that we must "first experience and learn from as many sources as possible." Sue suggests frequenting minority-owned businesses and attending street fairs as well as a variety of churches, temples, and synagogues. He also suggests living in culturally diverse communities (Sue, 2012). I believe that in clinical supervision and the classroom we can learn from each other as well.

Working in both worlds

The supervisor and instructor must be able to move between his or her cultural worldview and the cultural perspective of the "other." The clinical supervisor must also model what it means to be a responsive and competent multicultural therapist by doing her or his work. This requires a willingness to be genuine, continue self-assessing for cultural biases and projections, and have empathy for students and supervisees.

After I told my pork and beans story to my students one year, a student approached me to say she was sorry. I told her that she shouldn't be, that she needed to take her feelings of sorrow and guilt and find a way to give back and to be of service as a therapist and citizen. I said that, in fact, as therapists we are of two worlds for we are privileged to move between the transrational world of psyche and soul, and the other of wounding and healing. This student then added, "But I had no idea." I then told her that I once received a passionate course evaluation from a White student that said I did not see her or make room for her experience as a White woman in class. When I read those words, I had wanted to respond in exactly the same way as this student, but never had the chance—I had no idea. After all, on some level, we are all *hijos de la Chingada*, and this is where we begin.

Notes

1 I include Edward T. Hall in here because of his important insight, which directly impacts the supervisor's obligation to see beyond his or her own cultural lens. Perhaps Hall says it best when he states, "One of the most effective ways to learn about oneself is by taking seriously the cultures of others. It forces you to pay attention to those details of life, which differentiate them from you" (1959, p. 31). Plainly speaking, the supervisor must be able to see beyond his or her limited cultural frame of reference in order to meet the challenges of our multicultural society.
2 Mexican/Chicano slang for *Mother*, an endearment.
3 A reference to the *mestizo*, or race; a mix of American Indian and Spanish heritage.

References

Angelou, M. (2014). *Rainbow in the cloud: The wisdom and spirit of Maya Angelou*, p. 6. New York, NY: Random House.
Bernstein. J. S. (2014). Nonshamanic Native American healing. *Psychological Perspectives: A Quarterly Journal of Jungian Thought, 57*(2), 129–146.
Chavez, J. R. (2011). Aliens in their native lands: The persistence of internal colonial theory. *Journal of World History, 22*(4), 785–809.
Hall, E. T. (1959). *The silent language*. Garden City, NY: Doubleday.
Hays, P. A. (2008). *Addressing cultural complexities in practice: Assessment, diagnosis, and therapy*. Washington, DC: American Psychological Association.
Jung, C. G. (1953a). *Symbols of transformation*. Princeton, NJ: Princeton University Press.
Jung, C. G. (1953b). *Psychological types*. Princeton, NJ: Princeton University Press.
Jung, C. G. (1970). *Civilization in transition*. Princeton, NJ: Princeton University Press.
Kagan, S., & Kagan, M. (2009). *Kagan cooperative learning*. Moorabbin, VIC, Australia: Hawker Brownlow Education.
Sue, D. W., & Sue, D. (2012). *Counseling the culturally diverse: Theory and practice*. New York, NY: Wiley.

PART III

Strategies for Promoting Cultural Sensitivity in Supervision and Training

10

FROM INVISIBILITY TO EMBRACE

Promoting culturally sensitive practices in supervision

Jessica L. ChenFeng, PhD

I am a second-generation Taiwanese American, Christian, non-disabled, heterosexual, educated female therapist, professor, and supervisor of marital and family therapy. These identifiers, though helpful, barely begin to tell of how I know myself and how I hope to be known as a whole person. I believe the same holds true for our clients, students, and supervisees. I hope my experiences thus far serve to build a collective hope and persistence in the difficult work of moving toward cultural sensitivity and humility in a world where difference oftentimes feels overwhelming and exhausting.

My cultural history and context

Taiwanese American upbringing in the suburbs

In the suburbs of Los Angeles and Orange County where I grew up, the vast majority of my friends were second-generation Asian Americans—the children of Chinese, Taiwanese, or Korean American immigrant parents. This community, along with my Taiwanese American conservative Christian church and my own immigrant Taiwanese parents were the context that shaped the core pieces of my identity.

When I was in middle school, I had the customary Chinese American experience of "ching chong" yelled to my face while I was at the mall with my mother, younger sister, and the women of another Taiwanese American family. This was one of the more vivid memories of racial discrimination growing up. For the most part, however, the messages I internalized about being minority and insignificant came through more covert systemic avenues, such as rarely seeing people in the media whose images reflected what I saw in the mirror. Day-to-day life up through my college years was relatively devoid of intentional, consciously fear-inducing, overt racial discrimination. I know this is a privilege that many children of Asian immigrants have not had. But because of this, it was deceptively easy to be disconnected from the racism I had internalized. Because all my friends and their families seemed to share similar Asian American family values, work ethic, respect, and communication style, I also had very little awareness of my own cultural identity. Life at home was fairly congruent with life outside of home—the expectation of academic success, commitment to faith, honoring of your family and others. All of it seemed "normal."

Difference and invisibility

Though my parents taught that I would have to work harder, write better, and learn more vocabulary as the daughter of immigrants, experiential consciousness about my racial and cultural identity did not surface until I began graduate school in marital and family therapy. Almost all my professors and supervisors, and the majority of my classmates, were white. Suddenly, I had the perpetual feeling of being different and invisible. I never knew that I had grown up in a world where I had grown accustomed to and unknowingly desensitized to microaggressions. However, I had no terminology, vocabulary, or conscious awareness that my internal workings were any different from that of a white or other-minority colleague.

In group conversations, I could not speak up as quickly or as loudly as others, because I did not know how to. In my Asian community, I was taught to be respectful and wait until I was called upon, or to wait until there was a clear pause to speak. This led me to believe I was less competent. I needed to improve my communication skills, my self-esteem, and just be more assertive. I had to adapt to the way things worked around me. It was as though everyone knew and felt the differences, and yet no one knew how to speak of them. My culture went ignored, unknown, silenced.

Being a Taiwanese female, I implicitly learned that being quiet, compliant, and subservient made me more likeable and helped to keep peace. So for many years, I functioned in this way: I tried to be the hardworking intern who listened to her supervisors and performed well. All the while, the beautiful pieces of my cultural identity were becoming more lost and my voice more hidden.

Transformative encounters

Disconnect

When I became a doctoral student, I faced some of the most hurtful experiences with oppression and subjugation. These encounters were certainly not the only ones, but they give a good picture of what I experienced once I began to live life outside of my upbringing in an Asian American–majority context.

At a national conference in our field, I was at an interest group whose interest was a subject very dear to my heart. I arrived at the meeting place and found myself amongst ten other members, all of whom were my elders. All were white but three non-Asian minority individuals. After going around the circle for initial introductions, I cannot pinpoint what happened, but all I knew was that my anxiety increased over time: my feelings of being excluded, different, and invisible were becoming actualized. Though we were facing each other at a circular table, no one made any eye contact with me throughout the next hour of discussion, and when addressing issues that would seem relevant to someone like me, an Asian and immigrant, no one looked at me or asked me anything. I felt that there were so many reasons why I could not speak up—my age, my age with my gender, my age with gender and Asian ethnicity, and some vague sense that there was a class difference. I left the meeting feeling invisible and irrelevant.

Another encounter was related to what was spoken by someone on the main stage of a conference. The speaker was critiquing the female author of a book on Asian American parenting in such a way that put her and all Asian American mothers in a negative light. I thought I might be overreacting as I sat there growing flustered, when my white friend next to me nudged me and said, "I can't believe he's saying that!"—at which point I realized what I was hearing was true. To a room of hundreds of mostly white therapists, this person was making statements that put Asian American mothers in a negative light. In that moment, I felt not only was I unknown, but also my people were unknown and were becoming wrongly known. After the session I waited to share my sentiments with the speaker. He asked if I had been raised in the same way that the female author described as

Asian American parenting, and when I replied "Yes," he said, "I'm sorry you were raised like that." I left feeling saddened that my parents' parenting, which I felt to be courageous and resilient, he assumed to be negative without first asking me about my experiences. That feeling of disconnect and relational loss between myself and someone different from me was a terrible feeling, and it became my hope to make every effort in my life to create something different.

Though feeling invisible, dismissed, and unknown has become something with which I am now familiar, I share these experiences to give a glimpse of what it has been like to be an Asian/Taiwanese American female therapist in our community. Some of the most poignant culturally insensitive encounters have taken place among family therapists. I know I am not alone in having these experiences. This is heartbreaking and sobering for us as educators and supervisors in an increasingly diverse field.

Redemption

I am grateful that my experiences do not end here. Some of the most redeeming encounters of embrace and acceptance have also taken place in my relationships with dear friends and colleagues in our field. For four years in doctoral studies, a few significant professors and supervisors modeled a way of being that allowed me to know that I mattered and my culture mattered to them and to our field. They were well versed in dynamics of power, privilege, and marginalization and thus knew to elicit my voice and be genuinely curious about the things they did not know or understand. Though I might have perceived them as having power over me (white older women and men), they allowed my life and my stories to influence them and to shape their worldviews. This allowed for a community of safety in which I could further explore my own identity without the threat of ever feeling one-down or unvalued. This was true empowerment toward my own knowing and acceptance of self and others.

My beliefs about teaching, diversity, and social justice

I share so much with you about my personal history because I have no other way to tell you how I have come to think and be as an educator and supervisor. I resonate with Parker Palmer (1998), who shares that "good teaching comes from the identity and integrity of the teacher." Out of my own process of moving toward personal wholeness comes the desire I have to teach and see this experienced by students such that they might encounter a fullness in themselves that calls them out to impact a world in need. Teaching is a pursuit of wholeness discovered by the self of the teacher and by the students, so that together we can live more fully with one another for the purpose of transforming our societies toward communal wholeness.

Diversity is a beautiful but often nebulous idea. What does it mean to value diversity? I believe we must go beyond learning about our differences and develop reflexivity (Mangione, Mears, Vincent & Hawes, 2011) and contextual consciousness (Esmiol, Knudson-Martin & Delgado, 2012). It is one thing to learn about the culture of a people through a lecture or book, but it is an entirely different thing to be in relationship with another human being such as with our students and supervisees. Esmiol et al. (2012) define contextual consciousness in three dimensions in terms of a therapist's work with clients. I believe these dimensions can also apply to a supervisor/educator's work with the supervisee/student, which I have adapted here. As supervisors and educators, our contextual consciousness should have (a) consciousness about existing power differentials in the supervisee's social context; (b) sensitivity to the supervisee's unique experiences in different contexts and with different clients; and (c) attention to how the larger social context intersects with the supervisee's clinical work and with supervisory relationships.

The process is isomorphic: If we hope for our students to have the capacity to embrace the tensions and complexities of their clients' lived realities, then this process must be reflected in the supervisor/supervisee relationship. Teaching and supervising in our field is indeed social justice work. The individuals and families we serve come seeking help because they are disenfranchised, downcast, oppressed, and stuck. Only as we experience feeling liberated and empowered can we facilitate this process in another.

Liberate and empower

Liberation and empowerment of self

So what might it look like to facilitate reflexivity and contextual consciousness in our students and supervisees? I believe the first step is to allow for reflexivity in our own lives so we can walk toward liberation from internalized privileges and oppression. This process continues to be cultivated by the safe and meaningful relationships and communities in my life.

Some ideas that can support us in facilitating reflexivity and contextual consciousness:

- having a safe colleague of a different social context with whom we can ask questions and share openly
- recognizing our own assumptions and internalized privileges
- processing through our own experiences of marginalization and oppression
- pursuing accountability with someone who is in a position to be able to do so, and remaining connected to a community of colleagues/friends who value such work

Liberation and empowerment with students

Only once we are open to seeing ourselves more clearly can we begin to consider supporting students toward liberation from their own internalized privileges and oppression. This begins to happen as the supervisor creates a setting that allows a sense of safety and support for the supervisee (Mangione, Mears, Vincent & Hawes, 2011). As this is established, the supervisee can feel more at ease with addressing complex and uncomfortable contextual issues. As concerns involving power differentials surface, the supervisor or supervisee can initiate discussion about the supervisory relationship or process. There will be circumstances where feelings of discomfort surface, and these situations require both supervisors and supervisees to sit in discomfort and remain open and engaged in the process (Christiansen et al., 2011).

In a society where we largely attempt to avoid authentic, honoring conversations of difference, we have few models of this done well. The supervisory relationship has the potential to be the opportunity in which supervisees experience for the first time how identity can be explored in a way that leads to connection and embrace. When supervisors are willing to be emotionally available, share their work and internal process, and speak about professional activities in an open personal way, there can be positive learning and role-modeling (Mangione et al., 2011).

As Esmiol et al. (2012) suggest, we must learn to be conscious of the supervisee's social context and be aware of the inherent power differential in the supervisory relationship. We can impact, knowingly or not, the "degree to which the supervisory system supports the free expression of racial identity attitudes. Given the supervisor's power, his or her racial identity attitudes may shape the racial attitudes and behaviors of the supervisee and, indirectly, the client" (Garcia, Kosutic, McDowell & Anderson, 2009).

The majority of my supervisory work has been with other minority female supervisees. Here are some foundational yet critical process examples of what I use to create a safe supervisory space:

- In my humanness, I have assumptions and prejudgments, so I seek to *maintain an open and curious posture*, reminding myself to *always suspend judgment*, even if I think I understand something.

- *Take initiative* in bringing discussions about culture and difference into the supervisory relationship.
- *Be accountable* for when I make mistakes, apologizing if my supervisee has felt wrongly understood.
- *Share personal examples* that I have processed, of how I came to recognize my own experience of privilege or marginalization.

Questions we can ask/statements we can use with supervisees that can support this process include the following:

- "How do you see your own culture and social context as contributing strengths to your development as a clinician?" When I have asked this question, it has challenged supervisees to reframe experiences they internalized as negative aspects of their cultural heritage. For example, an Asian American supervisee was told by other supervisors that she had to be more direct and "go deeper" with clients. She felt incompetent and that what she had learned to value in her Asian heritage—to be socially gracious and honor others by not being so intrusive/direct—were irrelevant to her development. Asking this question allowed her to see ways in which her Asian heritage and values could contribute to her growth as a clinician.
- "Is there anything that I do/model that feels like it could be different from the way you think or might want to approach clinical work? Help me to understand the way this is important to you."
- Checking in about the supervisory power dynamics. For example, with a younger Vietnamese American supervisee I might say, "I know sometimes in Asian culture, we're taught to be respectful and not disagree with those older than us. How is it for you to have me, an older Taiwanese American woman, be your supervisor? I want to invite you to communicate openly with me, even if it's about something you're not typically comfortable saying to an older person."
- "I know it's not always easy or natural to think and talk about our cultural identity, but I want you to know that I value you in your being [contextual identity] and that you will grow more competent and effective as a clinician as you integrate all of who you are into your work."
- "In my Taiwanese immigrant upbringing, I internalized ideas that I was less than the white Americans I was trying to become, so it wasn't easy for me working with older white clients. How about for you? What might be some clinical challenges related to ideas you have internalized from your context?" When I have posed questions like this, supervisees seemed to be more at ease in sharing with me the very real struggles they have that are connected to their contextual identities. I have had supervisees express anxiety about how their accent might make them come across as less competent to "American" clients, or that they're not as good a therapist as their white American colleagues who are comfortable talking so directly about feelings.

The journey toward social justice requires patience and persistence. Change does not come easily, because we are reaching beyond individuals to the histories, systems, and contexts that have constructed us. In our field, we have the privilege of creating sustained hope through building relationships anchored in mutuality and authentic encountering of one another. As we demonstrate with our supervisees that human diversity and difference is not about arriving at clean and clear conclusions but rather about sitting in tension with one another, we will experience true connection and embrace. This is the liberation and empowerment we hope for.

References

Christiansen, A. T., Thomas, V., Kafescioglu, N., Karakurt, G., Lowe, W., Smith, W., & Wittenborn, A. (2011). Multicultural supervision: Lessons learned about an ongoing struggle. *Journal of Marital and Family Therapy, 37*(1), 109–119. doi: 10.1111/j.1752-0606.2009.00138.x

Esmiol, E. E., Knudson-Martin, C., & Delgado, S. (2012). Developing a contextual consciousness: Learning to address gender, societal power, and culture in clinical practice. *Journal of Marital and Family Therapy, 38*(4), 573–588. doi: 10.1111/j.1752-0606.2011.00232.x

Garcia, M., Kosutic, I., McDowell, T., & Anderson, S. A. (2009). Raising critical consciousness in family therapy supervision. *Journal of Feminist Family Therapy, 21*(1), 18–38. doi: 10.1080/08952830802683673

Mangione, L., Mears, G., Vincent, W., & Hawes, S. (2011). The supervisory relationship when women supervise women: An exploratory study of power, reflexivity, collaboration, and authenticity. *The Clinical Supervisor, 30*(2), 141–171. doi: 10.1080/07325223.2011.604272

Palmer, P. J. (1998). *The courage to teach: Exploring the inner landscape of a teacher's life.* San Francisco, CA: Wiley.

11

BALANCING CULTURE, CONTEXT, AND EVIDENCE-BASED PRACTICES IN SUPERVISION

Benjamin E. Caldwell, PsyD

Early in the supervision relationship, I will tell a new supervisee, "As you may have noticed, I'm a white guy." I'll even take it much farther: As an educated, financially stable, heterosexual, cisgender, taller-than-average, non-obese, Caucasian, non-disabled male who speaks English as a first language, I am a veritable walking, talking *pile* of privilege. I have a wide variety of social advantages that easily can be—and for much of my life, were—taken for granted.

It is therefore understandable that students, supervisees, and colleagues raise eyebrows at the notion of my leading useful discussions on cultural diversity and the various elements of power and privilege that come with it. Where issues of cultural oppression arise, my demographics put me almost always in the category of the historical oppressors. And it often doesn't go well to have an oppressor in the position of setting the terms for a discussion of how the oppressed are impacted.

So I understand and even welcome the skepticism that arises as I attempt to address issues of culture in the supervision room. It isn't unusual for supervisees of color to have heard supervisors (particularly white supervisors, and especially white men) say the right things about diversity at first, only to bristle when confronted on an area of cultural awareness that they lack. **Opening a conversation about culture and difference isn't the same thing as *being open* to it**.

A good supervisor should do both. As I regularly remind supervisees, the very foundational concepts of family therapy—a profession I love and with which I strongly identify—are about understanding how each generation of a family is impacted by the actions of prior generations. That extends quite naturally to the community and cultural levels. In short, I do not believe it is possible to be a competent family therapist without understanding, on a fairly deep level, how issues of culture and context create advantages for some and disadvantages for others. The supervision process in therapy provides an excellent opportunity for everyone involved to further that understanding, and to act based on what they learn.

Who I am

I was born and raised in Lawrence, Kansas, a middle-class, middle-sized university town near the middle of the United States. While Lawrence was in many ways an ideal place to grow up, you may not be surprised to hear it was not tremendously diverse, making many of those avenues of privilege even easier to ignore. When I moved to California to go to graduate school, I went through a fair amount of culture shock.

Like many of my peers, it was only in and after graduate school—and often through failures in my work with clients—that I started the process of becoming aware of my various levels of privilege. I use the term *started* because I am keenly aware that it isn't finished; I learn more on a regular basis about the advantages these various elements have brought me, often unfairly. Where this developing awareness has brought me is into agreement with Hardy (2001) that privileged groups have not just the opportunity but the obligation to recognize that privilege and actively use it to benefit those without it.

Today, much of my professional work focuses on advocacy. I supervise MFT interns for Caldwell-Clark, a nonprofit counseling agency with offices in San Diego and Los Angeles. The interns I supervise work with clients who present a wide variety of cultures and presenting problems, as Caldwell-Clark was built with the specific intent of serving these diverse communities. (As an aside, I use the term "client" broadly to refer to the unit of treatment; a client may be an individual, couple, family, or other constellation.) I also teach for Alliant International University in Los Angeles, where multiculturalism and internationalism are key parts of our mission. The university has offered me the opportunity to travel to Mexico City and Hong Kong to teach classes, though I can say with humble gratitude that I learned far more than I taught there. For several years now, I have been involved with the Legislative and Advocacy Committee for the California Division of AAMFT, donating a great deal of time to push for changes in public policy to improve the lives of MFTs and those we serve.

Core beliefs

There are three core beliefs that drive much of my supervision work. Indeed, almost every intervention I use in supervision finds roots here.

1. **All practitioners have a responsibility, set forth in our professional codes of ethics, to strike an effective balance between (1) recognition and respect for the influence of the social context, and (2) recognition and respect for the knowledge that has emerged from research in our field over several decades**. Neither of these offers adequate excuse to simply ignore the other. Balancing them is hard work, and therapists who don't want to do the work of responsible treatment planning sometimes use issues of culture and context as an excuse to avoid doing that work. (The same can be said, by the way, for supervisors and supervision planning.) They believe they can use what they know about a client's context (or, worse, their own hunches) to dismiss recommendations from, well, anywhere: scientific literature, colleagues and supervisors, sometimes even the clients themselves. It is hard to blame busy practitioners for wanting to simply default whenever possible to their treatment model of choice. But treatment decisions must be based on what is likely to be best for the clients, and not simply what will be easiest for us.

2. **Regardless of whether privilege is earned or unearned, privileged groups have not just the opportunity but the obligation to recognize that privilege and actively use it to benefit those without it.** This is, to me, a moral imperative, so much so that I would be unlikely to work with a supervisee who did not share this perspective; I believe it is at the very foundation of the field of family therapy. The desire to advocate for a more level playing field, for power to be distributed fairly, and for those who have been disadvantaged to be helped drives much of my professional life. My supervision work is a purposeful act of advocacy for my supervisees and the clients they work with.

3. **Awareness means nothing without action**. This applies everywhere: therapy, supervision, education, politics, and interpersonal relationships. There isn't much point in developing awareness of cultural differences if you are not willing to act based on what you have learned.

Sometimes that action is simply an apology for having misunderstood another's intent or action, one that with the right contextual information makes much more sense. Sometimes that action is a specific change in your therapy (or my supervision) work going forward. Whatever the resulting action is, I don't want a new awareness to be met simply with a "huh, interesting" and then for us all to go back to carrying on as before.

With that summary of my background and beliefs, I hope that the specifics of how I supervise will not only make sense but will feel like the only logical way that I *could* supervise. Of course, the particular way that I address culture and context in supervision is not the only useful way of doing so. As is the case in so much of therapy and supervision, there is not a singular "right way" we should be pursuing; our responsibility is to find the most effective way we can of accomplishing what we set out to accomplish. My way works for me—indeed, it's the only logical way for me, given my context—but, as the saying goes, your mileage may vary.

Basic framework: Culturally competent, evidence-based treatment planning

Similarly to how I teach students about law and ethics, and certainly consistent with my view of supervision as an act of advocacy, when I am supervising I want my interns to not be satisfied with a *good enough* course of action. It is not especially difficult to reach a minimally acceptable standard of care. Instead, I push them to actively consider what is *best* for their clients. What represents the intern's *best* effort in terms of case conceptualization, their *best* recognition of the elements of context and culture at work in a particular case, and their *best* application of a theoretical model in a complex and multicultural environment? These should not be easy questions. I worry much more about supervisees who present quick certainty in the face of these questions than I worry about those who are willing to take the time to sort through their doubt.

Patterson, Miller, Carnes, and Wilson (2004) outlined a specific conceptualization for evidence-based practice for marriage and family therapists, and it is one I have taken to heart. It embeds issues of culture and context in the treatment planning process. Evidence-based practice should not simply mean providing therapy from a list of approved treatments; not only does this fail to take in the full context in which clients live, it also devalues the clinical judgment therapists spend years developing. Instead, **evidence-based practice should be about making thoughtful and defensible treatment decisions that have the greatest chance of success *with the specific case in front of you.*** As Patterson et al. (2004) describe it, this means active consideration of four sets of factors:

- **Client factors**, including their motivation and readiness for change, their strengths, their resources, and their struggles.
- **Therapist factors**, including the therapist's level of knowledge and skill with various treatment models and interventions. This also refers to the therapist's ability to conduct model-neutral clinical tasks, like building a good relationship with multiple family members.
- **Contextual factors**, including the setting of the therapy and the larger cultural and social environment.
- **Research literature**, including studies of the specific problem, the specific population, and the specific model the therapist is considering using. Ideally, studies would be available that match the current case on all three of these, but such specific studies are often not available; studies with one or two of these may still be helpful. Even in the presence of large-scale quantitative data, qualitative studies and single-case studies also can provide valuable information.

Exercise: Tasks of culturally competent, evidence-based treatment planning

With this framework, I ask my students and supervisees to conduct the task of *culturally competent,* evidence-based treatment planning. It generally follows these steps:

1. **In order to develop a defensible treatment plan with the best chance of success, gather information relevant to this case from *all four* of the domains of evidence-based practice**. Cultural issues should be part of *every one of them.*

    Client factors would obviously include the cultural and family background of the client, information that hopefully every therapist gathers at initial assessment. Admittedly, it can be confusing to know what elements of culture best belong in client factors and what belong in contextual factors, but I think about it like this: If an individual client identifies as gay, then his sexual orientation, his stage in the coming-out process, and his feelings about his sexuality are client factors. His family's and community's levels of acceptance or hostility toward people who identify as gay is an important contextual factor. Ultimately, it matters less where one draws the line between these two categories, and more that no important matters of culture or context fall through the cracks.

    Therapist factors include the cultural background of the therapist, and any key areas of difference between therapist and client. This area can become particularly challenging when addressing biases they have toward the client, especially differences that may bring up moral judgment, such as clients in sexually open relationships (Zimmerman, 2012). If I have done my job well in building a trusting relationship with a supervisee, a tilted head and a raised eyebrow should be all it takes to move them from "I don't have any biases toward anyone in this family" at least to "Well, there is this one thing." But I am fine with it taking more than that, as it can for newer supervisees or especially difficult issues. Part of this is modeling; during case discussions in supervision, I try to make my biases, as well as their origins and intensities, clear before offering feedback or suggestions on any particular case. I also do my best to account for those biases when making suggestions, and I allow supervisees to see my process in doing so. For example, I may say in supervision, "When I see video of your session with this family, I find myself ignoring or dismissing the oldest daughter's complaints. Now, I can tell that oldest daughter uses that sort of country slang, which I get bothered by for reasons that have nothing to do with her. She also is the only child here who was born to her mom's ex-husband. Is ignoring her something that happens in the family? Or is it just that if *I* were in that family, *I* would ignore her?" Through these kinds of questions, supervisees can see how my clinical judgment is impacted by biases (to the degree that I'm aware of them), and take my suggestions with the appropriate grain of salt. I also work to create an environment where supervisees are comfortable calling each other out, and calling me out, on biases of which we may not immediately be aware. Doing so obviously requires the development of a strong level of trust.

    Contextual factors are where considerations of culture most obviously fit. Even so, in the United States there is a tendency to train therapists to think about culture largely in terms of race (and, more recently, sexual orientation). Much of the rest of the world thinks about culture primarily in terms of social class, the impacts of which are often hidden or stretched to mythology in the United States (Laszloffy, 2008). It is interesting to consider whether a poor Latino family would have more in common with a rich Latino family or a poor White family. Social context also does not always fit neatly into those classes protected from discrimination (age, gender, race, marital or relationship status, and so on). One of the most rewarding experiences I've had as a supervisor came from watching a pair of supervisees, who were both working with the same family, come to understand how the family's behavior in therapy—their unwillingness to show up for more than a bare minimum number of sessions, and once there, their reluctance to say much—had been impacted by their years-long involvement with the justice system. In that context, the smartest thing for the family to do was the bare minimum to stay out of trouble, without saying anything that could be in any way used against them. The supervisees used this new understanding to revisit conversations with the family about the therapists' roles, though in my eyes the positive changes that occurred after this point had more to do with the therapists shifting from a stance of blaming the clients for their perceived resistance into a stance of crediting the clients for what had been an intelligent adaptation to an intrusive system. This is an excellent illustration of social context that extends beyond attention to protected classes.

Supervisees sometimes struggle with integrating culture into their exploration of the **research literature**. We have come some distance, though there is far to go, in identifying treatment models that are effective for specific cultural groups. There is not, however, great literature suggesting when a client from a particular background—let's say African American here (or, to make things more complex, a family that *partially* has that background, such as a multiracial family) —is better served with a culturally specific and less-researched treatment, or a more generally accepted but less culture-specific treatment. Here is where the supervisee's clinical judgment must come in, balancing the client's cultural embeddedness with all the other factors, including the therapist's ability to deliver the culture-specific treatment.

2. **After thoroughly investigating all four of the domains above, come up with at least three viable treatment options**. We then can go through the four domains and resulting options together, and see where our clinical judgment leads us. I often will ask the supervisee to include an initial recommendation for his or her preferred option, understanding that this will be discussed and debated in supervision.

3. **Working together with the supervisor (and, if applicable, the supervision group), determine the course of action *most* likely to be successful with this particular case**. Group supervision is wonderful for this, as the debate about which treatment is likely to work best and why teaches everyone present that they need to be making thoughtful and defensible treatment decisions—and that our field remains a balance of science and informed judgment, one where culture and context cannot be separated from anything we do.

I have used the "Exercise: Tasks of Culturally Competent, Evidence-Based Treatment Planning" as a written exercise for my classes, and as a verbal/presentation exercise in supervision, and in my experience it works fairly well in either setting. As a written exercise, it can get students into the habit of consulting the literature when making treatment decisions; as a presentation exercise in group supervision, it helps supervisees understand both the need for, and the method of, defending their treatment decisions as being both scientifically sound and culturally and contextually aware.

I should caution that this exercise is best suited to relatively newer therapists and those with broad practices. For those who are more specialized, it still can be helpful, though at that stage it may be more to address the question of whether to treat a particular case or refer.

Addressing power and privilege in the moment

The exercise above is intended for a thoughtful and structured effort at treatment planning. Of course, in the supervision process, not every discussion is (or should be, in my opinion) so structured—creativity often goes hand in hand with spontaneity. One consequence of spontaneity is that it can allow issues of power and privilege to arise in ways they otherwise might not: an offhand comment, a choice of gendered language, a moment of inappropriate deference.

I have very fond recollections of a supervisee, who I knew to be quite confident, remarking as an aside that she gave a great amount of deference to the men she was working with in therapy, especially if she perceived them as older, intelligent, or powerful. She started to go on discussing the case she had been describing, and I interrupted. "Really?" I asked with a smile. "You don't do that with me." I wasn't sure whether to be proud that our supervision relationship had transcended this habit of hers, or troubled that she perhaps didn't see me as being quite as smart as I hoped my supervisees would. (Looking back on it, I wonder whether my interrupting was an effort to assert power—I could have waited until the end of her next paragraph.) She stopped for a moment and thought this over. "No," she said, "I do." And that simply, we began a very rich conversation about gender, power, and perception, one that we often returned to in supervision after that.

While these conversations are important, I also don't want to make the mistake of investing them with so much gravity that they take up the entire room. (There are occasional exceptions where that's actually fully appropriate, but this is a general guideline.) That can scare supervisees away from entering into them. So some of the other ways I might take us down that path would be questions and comments like these:

- (When discussing a couple or family case) "Would you have heard that differently if it had come from him instead of her [or vice versa]? What would have been the difference?"
- "I can tell that you really like [or dislike] this particular client. What is it about them that you're connecting with so well [or struggling to connect with]?"
- "It seems like there's something missing here. What do you know about their background or history that might make [an unexplained, seemingly senseless, or angry behavior] more sense?"

Challenges

One of the most difficult relational issues to manage in supervision is that of the therapist's role. I ask my supervisees to give me deference where legal and ethical issues are concerned, but that we should operate largely as colleagues when it comes to clinical decision-making. Ideally, this is mutually understood as the limited way in which I choose to exercise position power (Fine & Turner, 2014), but to some it can seem to be a mixed message. Regular assurance that "I trust your clinical decision-making; I wouldn't have taken you on as a supervisee otherwise" can be helpful. I have also found it useful to offer multiple perspectives on a particular case rather than simply one preferred perspective, which the supervisees might feel unduly obligated to take on themselves. Walking through how therapists of different theoretical orientations might treat a particular case, or even figuring out multiple possible interventions within the therapist's existing theoretical frame, reinforces my role as a clinical consultant rather than a higher-ranking therapist.

Takeaways / Reflections

It's funny, I suppose, that I've been seeing clients for 15 years now and yet I still think of myself as young, career-wise. Becoming a supervisor is different from my other areas of privilege, in that it wasn't a by-product of the genetic lottery. (Not directly, at least.) In any event, whether a position of power and privilege is earned or culturally bestowed, I believe it comes with responsibility. I've done my best to turn my responsibility into defined action.

As supervisors, we can use our positions of power to ensure the highest quality care possible. Considering knowledge and context together in the supervision process **is an act of advocacy for client and supervisee alike**, one that should have lasting effects for them both.

References

Fine, M., & Turner, J. (2014). Minding the power in collaborative systemic supervision. In T. C. Todd & C. L. Storm (Eds.), *The complete systemic supervisor: Context, philosophy, and pragmatics* (2nd ed.) (pp. 297–313). Malden, MA: Wiley.

Hardy, K. V. (2001). African American experience and the healing of relationships. In D. Denborough (Ed.), *Family Therapy: Exploring the field's past, present, and possible futures* (pp. 47–56). Adelaide, Australia: Dulwich Centre Publications.

Laszloffy, T. (2008). Social class: Implications for family therapy. In M. McGoldrick & K. V. Hardy (Eds.), *Re-visioning family therapy: Race, culture, and gender in clinical practice* (2nd ed.) (pp. 48–60). New York, NY: Guilford Press.

Liddle, H. A. (1988). Systemic supervision: Conceptual overlays and pragmatic guidelines. In H. A. Liddle, D. C. Breunlin, & R. C. Schwartz (Eds.), *Handbook of family therapy training and supervision* (pp. 153–171). New York, NY: Guilford Press.

Patterson, J. E., Miller, R. B., Carnes, S., & Wilson, S. (2004). Evidence-based practice for marriage and family therapists. *Journal of Marital and Family Therapy, 30*(2), 183–195.

Reiner, P. A. (2014). Systemic psychodynamic supervision. In T. C. Todd & T. L. Storm (Eds.), *The complete systemic supervisor: Context, philosophy, and pragmatics* (pp. 166–185). Malden, MA: Wiley.

Zimmerman, K. J. (2012). Clients in sexually open relationships: Considerations for therapists. *Journal of Feminist Family Therapy, 24*(3), 272–289.

12

REFLEXIVITY, COMPASSION, AND DIVERSITY

Teaching cultural sensitivity in supervision

Diane R. Gehart, PhD

Invitation

Having trained new therapists in California for nearly 20 years, one of my greatest challenges has been teaching supervisees how to meaningfully conceptualize and effectively work with human diversity. My approach has evolved over the years using social constructionist and Buddhist psychology concepts as well as my personal experience of cultural identity. The ideas in this paper are oriented toward helping therapists to be more effective in session with clients one-on-one. These concepts do not directly confront social inequalities on a broader scale; other models do this more directly (Monk & Gehart, 2003). Instead, the approach described here is intended to enable new therapists to quickly learn how to compassionately address diversity in ways that help their clients live more fulfilling lives.

Using social constructionist reflexive processes and Buddhist-informed models of compassion, my approach promotes a supervision culture that embodies the concepts it tries to teach. This process is grounded in collaborative and dialogic methods designed to expand a person's sense of compassion, humility, and humanity (Anderson, 1997). This chapter provides an outline of the key concepts of this approach, which may feel a bit like a whirlwind tour as we explore logical philosophical concepts, personal details I rarely share, and a typical day in my supervision group. However, for me, these multiple, contradictory realities reflect the process of engaging diversity itself: multifaceted, jarring, disordered, and imperfect. Before I introduce the theory behind my supervision practices related to diversity, I would like to contextualize these by sharing about my own personal journey.

My journey

My personal experience of diversity has followed an unusual pattern, one that is closest to the experiences of invisible minorities. Although my life does not include the type of marginalization, injustice, and abuse that many others endure, I spent many painful years feeling profoundly "other." Because my differentness is invisible to most in this country (but not abroad), I did not become fully aware of my otherness until a young teenager. At that time, I had no sense that my differentness had to do with my family's cultural and immigration status. My experience was simply that I did not fit in: I was a "freak" (my term of choice at the time). Looking back, it is clear that I had inherited a "map of life" (i.e., a set of culturally defined "goods") that would have helped me skillfully navigate life in communally organized, pre-industrial agricultural societies, such as a Medieval village in Southern or Eastern Europe.

But, it really was not practical for surviving in middle-class Los Angeles suburbia during the Valley Girl era. Every aspect of my early teen life—friendship, fashion, dating, family, music, sports, etc.—seemed impossible to make sense of in the way my peers could. The only exception was schoolwork: because it involved hard work, the one thing in which my rural cultural legacy excelled. Everyone in my life seemed to believe I shared fully in a common culture, a shared set of suburban American values. Inside, however, I knew I did not. The world around was foreign, and I struggled daily to navigate it. I came to the only seemingly logical conclusion that I was an utter failure who had no useful place in this world, which led to four years of profound depression. Ultimately, it was numerous experiences living as an "other" abroad and in various corners of the United States that helped me slowly realize that the despair I experienced was due to my cultural differentness.

My father shares his stories of how he emigrated from Austria as a young adult, having grown up in a small self-sufficient village on the Austrian-Czech border. All the necessities of life—food, clothing, and housing—were met within the village. The only commodity his family needed to purchase was salt. The villagers were keenly aware of how they needed each other to survive. Stealing was impossible, as everyone knew whose hammer or plow was whose, and harvest time involved everyone helping everyone else. Each New Year's Eve, the blacksmith would come by, and my grandfather would pay him for services during the year—all done on one's word of honor without written records. The village was held together by honesty, integrity, and generosity.

In Greek, my mother's mother shared tales of how she grew up as a semi-migrant goat herder in the region between Sparta and Argos. They lived in simple stone houses with dirt floors, surviving off a deep sense of spirituality and a limited number of crops and animals that could survive in the stark land. Cooperation, collaboration, and spirit were essential for survival. She immigrated between the World Wars, marrying my grandfather who, like many poor, illiterate immigrants in the early 1900s, did hard labor in mines and building railroads, which led to his early passing. After she left, most of the males in her village were executed by a Nazi-affiliated group.

These humble and often traumatic family histories provided little guidance for navigating the individualist and competitive culture in which I was born. Yet, learning more about my own differentness fostered a greater awareness of how we are all profoundly shaped by the multiple and often contradictory cultural discourses that inform our lives, whether or not we are consciously aware of them. Few of us fit comfortably into the check-boxes often used to measure diversity. No matter how a person appears, it is fair to assume there is a unique and more complex and multilayered cultural story than anyone could possibly imagine.

Social constructionist and collaborative foundations

Trained as a collaborative therapist (Anderson, 1997; Anderson & Gehart, 2007), I engage the processes of therapy, teaching, supervision, and research, using primarily a social constructionist lens (Gergen, 1999). Social constructionists maintain that an action can be interpreted only within the context of its particular form of life (Gergen, 1999; Schwandt, 2000). As a simple example, the comments of a teenager should be interpreted within the teen's social context to determine its meaning. However, ultimately, I, as a therapist, can never fully understand the meanings of another, since I can engage them from only my constructs and worldview (Gadamer, 1975). Thus, although therapists can inquire to learn more about the origin and meaning of certain comments, they can never fully grasp their full significance as the teen does—one's own teen and adult experiences color one's understanding.

Yet, in my sincere attempts to understand the worlds of my clients, students, supervisees, and research participants, we enter into dialogues in which we negotiate new meanings, understand the familiar in new ways, and—at times—literally transform how we experience our worlds

(Anderson, 1997). Alternatively stated, I never actually arrive at the same meanings as those others, but in my attempts to better understand and in their willingness to engage in the process, we transform both our worlds. Thus, as I explore my teen client's worldview, both our understandings of contemporary culture shift, deepen, and typically become more complexly nuanced. This process is the heart of collaborative approaches (Anderson & Gehart, 2007) and provides the foundation for my supervisory work.

Social constructionist understanding of culture: Negotiating the good

A social constructionist definition of culture can be particularly useful for therapists when engaging diversity (Gergen, 2001, 2009; Shotter, 1993). Although many definitions are proposed even within social constructionist literature, the following definition is perhaps the most conducive to developing not only a humane approach to diversity but a practical one that promotes positive outcomes in therapy specifically:

> *Culture:* A set of "goods"—in the form of values and meanings—that a community uses to coordinate joint action.

This definition is largely based in John Shotter's (1993) work that describes the social construction of meaning arising from a fundamental human need to coordinate joint action (i.e., doing something together). In order to coordinate action and live together in relative harmony, humans must distinguish "good" or "appropriate" behavior and "unacceptable" behavior. For example, knowing whether a particular hand gesture is a symbol of friendship or attack has been essential for survival in primitive and modern civilizations. The fabric of our daily lives is woven together with countless threads of socially negotiated gestures and actions that have evolved over time to coordinate life within a given community: a handshake, cup of coffee, traffic light, kiss, party, all have specific meanings that coordinate community interactions. Such actions enable the members of the community to navigate both personal and communal life. Without such shared meanings, it would be nearly impossible to coordinate action in order to form families, feed ourselves, and develop the complex processes that characterize civilization. The "goods" to which a particular culture aspires also serve to define the "good life" to which its members aspire.

Within culture oppression

However, this socially agreed-upon set of goods has limits even within the particular cultural group (Shotter, 1993). Identifying a specific behavior or value as "good" inherently implies something is "bad." To function, every culture must oppress—to some degree—certain behaviors and beliefs: It is impossible to successfully coordinate human behavior without identifying some behavior as acceptable (these are the things we agree to do) and those behaviors are unacceptable (we agree to not do these other things). This allows for humans to coordinate action and jointly make meaning. The critical question then becomes what role do the minority voices play within the culture. If the minority voices are allowed expression in a context that allows for true dialogue—an exchange of ideas—this promotes *self-reflexivity*, the questioning of one's own position (Gergen, 1999).

Reflexivity allows for the culture to evolve and grow and has a profound *humanizing* effect on a society. Without reflexive processes within the society, even the "best" society becomes inhumane. If the minority voices are not allowed any form of expression, this has a dehumanizing effect on all involved. For instance, if a particular culture has organized itself with formal religion as a "good," the extent to which it allows for alternative forms of non-formal expressions of spirituality or atheism determines the degree to which its members experience the culture as oppressive. If the minority voices are allowed to be part of social discourse, the culture is likely to slowly evolve new definitions of the "good" and acceptable religious behaviors. If the minority voices are silenced, they experience a problematic sense of marginalization that may eventually threaten the foundation of the community itself. For example, American culture has allowed for the voices of alternative sexualities to partake in social dialogue, and a slow shift in the definition of the "goods" and "acceptable" sexuality is measurable in the society (Dillon, 2014; Jang & Lee, 2014). This shift does not mean all oppression has ceased, but the ongoing dialogue reduces its severity and enables members to engage in a communal meaning-making process that is more humane and humanizing for all involved.

Cross-cultural differences and tension

A different set of tensions arise when we consider interactions between persons from different social cultures, because each uses different definitions of "good" and "appropriate." Such conflict is inevitable in our global age (Gergen, 2001). Whenever we interact with others from a different cultural group (race, ethnic, gender, social class, age, profession, sexual orientation, religion, region, etc.), to one degree or another we have different visions of polite conversation, appropriate touch, emotional expression, personal space, etc. From this perspective, *virtually all conversations are cross-cultural in one way or another*. Even with those from a similar ethnic and general cultural background, there is variance in the definition of good and appropriate behavior based on age, generation, social class, etc. Using the framework of "culture as a set of goods," promotes a more humane and curious approach to our inherent differences in values, behaviors, and expectations. This framework engages the challenges of differentness with the assumption that *each person's behavior is organized around some from of good, even if I don't agree with or understand it*. When tension or confusion arises, this means the other's good is at odds with one's own. From within the social constructionist approach, such moments demand *relational responsibility* in which one seeks to understand—not necessarily agree with—the good behind the other's actions (McNamee & Gergen, 1999). This willingness to understand promotes the humanity of both; anything else detracts from it.

A Buddhist-informed compassionate stance

Buddhist psychology, with its emphasis on compassion, has also informed my approach to diversity in supervision (Gehart, 2012). In a Buddhist context, *compassion* refers to a spiritual embracing of "what is" and the fullness of what it means to be human: the good, the bad, the desired, and undesired (Gehart & McCollum, 2007). Unlike empathy in other therapeutic traditions, which focus on the subjective lived experience of one person (i.e., a phenomenological worldview), the Buddhist concept of compassion emphasizes a universal embrace of the struggles that come with being human. When combined with the social constructionist understanding of culture as described above, this informs a compassionate understanding of the struggles implicit in all forms of cross-cultural engagement. Coordinating meaning with a person who aspires to a different set of "goods" is difficult—it can be one of life's most painful challenges. It is also at the heart of all social interaction. Approaching this ongoing challenge from an unwavering position of compassion requires a strong commitment to continually seek to understand and respect the good to which others aspire, even when radically different than one's own. This is no small task, whether in our most intimate relationships or across nations. But often the ability to do so requires a person delve deep into their own personal experiences of sameness and differentness to cultivate the humility and insight necessary to practice such compassion, a premise that is particularly helpful back in my urban Southern California classroom.

Creating a culture of reflexivity and compassion in training contexts

Because I train students in a highly diverse area, Los Angeles, the ability to effectively work with clients who are different than myself is essential. Learning about a handful of particular cultural groups is a beneficial beginning, but in no way suffices for the profound task ahead. Rather than specific content or readings, I have found the most effective way to prepare students for working with diversity is to create a training culture of reflexivity and compassion. Similar to others (Christiansen et al., 2011), I prefer group supervision for teaching cultural sensitivity: Academic classes tend to be too large, and individual supervision does not provide sufficient relational complexity. Within the group context, the supervisor creates a culture of reflexivity and compassion through the supervisor's way of being in relation to supervisees, theoretical ideas, local community, and life more broadly. Readings can be supportive, but the heart of the process is using the supervision experience to consistently demonstrate a compassionate and profound ability to embrace the difficulties, hypocrisies, and challenges of being human and of being different. Trainees learn to struggle with their judgments of self, peers, and clients within a profoundly accepting yet unapologetically honest context. Three of the strategies that I find most useful in creating such a context are as follows:

- Taking an appreciative stance: Finding the good
- Promoting tolerance of tensions: Reflective processes
- Teaching mindfulness, acceptance, and self-regulation

Taking an appreciative stance: Finding the good

Within the existing therapeutic literature, one of the most useful concepts for developing a training culture that embraces diversity is the concept of taking an appreciate stance using the practices of *appreciative inquiry* (Cooperrider, Sorenson, Whitney & Yaeger, 2000). Appreciative inquiry refers to a social constructionist consultation model that transforms through a curious and supportive exploration of strengths and challenges. These methods have been piloted in clinical supervision contexts (Fialkov & Haddad, 2012; González, 1997). As a supervisor, I explicitly teach and role-model an unwavering appreciative stance related to all persons and discourses that arise in the supervision process, including clients, classmates, clinical theories, other professionals, personal struggles, societal processes, county agencies, etc. This process is fostered by asking appreciative questions such as the following:

- What good is this person [process, agency, etc.] trying to achieve with his/her/their position?
- Why might this make sense in that context?
- What other struggles might there be that we (or they) are unaware of?
- What other goods and strengths do you notice?

By relentlessly pursuing the good intentions and strengths of others whose actions we do not understand, we typically soften our position of judgment and become more compassionate. For example, in a recent supervision session, a trainee shared a story of how a low-income African American father lost custody of his stepchildren due to what seemed to my student to be the surprisingly racist position of the African American social worker, who wanted the children to have better life opportunities. We used appreciative inquiry to explore the possible "goods" behind the social worker's position, imagined other struggles that we may not be privy to that might make his position make more sense, and openly discussed difficult social realities. This process helped the trainee re-engage this challenging political situation from a more compassionate and yet more confident position.

Promoting tolerance of tensions: Reflective processes

To teach students to meaningfully engage diversity, supervisors must not only teach appreciative practices but also direct engagement of the conflicts and tensions that define diversity. This is not a comfortable process, but I believe it necessary to teach students to skillfully manage the tensions that are inherent in all human relationships. Thus, I see tolerating tensions as the natural corollary to appreciative practices, which could easily become Pollyanna if difficult conflicts are ignored. I typically introduce students to these skills with an overt discussion about the differences between members in the group, a somewhat less threatening set of differences to explore. Setting a context of relentlessly appreciating all sides of these tensions provides a foundation for helping students to address the dynamics of the more difficult conflicts related to other forms of diversity. For example, in the early formation of the supervision group or class, I might start a discussion such as the following:

> I also want to share with you my observations of how we all evolve as therapists, which inherently includes working with many opposite tensions and sensibilities. Most of us begin lopsided and can naively be arrogant in our lopsidedness. By this, I mean we have strengths in certain areas that almost necessarily imply a weakness in another, but initially we don't see the need for the virtues in the opposite position or ability. For example, in supervision groups such as this one, I often observe a dichotomy related to empathy versus confrontation. Most have a natural propensity for one or the other, with the majority in this program favoring the former. If a group is lucky, there is at least one person who excels in confrontation rather than empathy. As the odd one out, however, this person is often labeled, pathologized, and sometimes ostracized by the group. So, as we watch each other do therapy, I want you to keep this in mind when you are tempted to judge another. And you will be tempted. I believe there are almost an infinite number of ways to be helpful to the various clients we encounter; each of us should try to master as many ways as possible, and this often means learning from those whose ways are different.

Over the course of supervision, I often raise difficult issues that students may be tempted to gloss over. For example, recently in supervision we discussed the situation of a political asylum immigrant from the Middle East who aspired to many American values, complained about her traditional marriage, but never spoke of divorce. However, my supervisees were quick to move in this direction because they saw the relationship as controlling by American standards. I encouraged them to consider the multiple layers of her situation, which included a trauma, marginalization, religious beliefs, language barriers, employment struggles, conflicting gender identities, Los Angeles culture, etc. We discussed the multitude of values she embraced and the various possibilities of what it could mean to be "culturally sensitive." The conversation invited them to slow their judgments, become curious, and wrestle with having no simple, easy answers.

Also, as part of this process of learning to engage tensions, I use Anderson's (1997) "as if" reflecting process. In this supervision exercise, each person in the group is instructed to listen to the therapist present a case "as if" he/she was a member in the client system. For example, if the client was a family with a social worker and teacher involved in the discussion of the problem, members of the supervision group would listen as if they were the mother, father, child client, sibling(s), teacher, social worker, therapist, etc. The supervision group then has a reflecting team process within the supervision context [no clients are listening] in which they speak "as if" they are the person, from a first-person stance. This exercise can be helpful in demonstrating the multiple, valid realities of each person involved as well as in developing an ability to tolerate the tension of contradictory realities. Once identified, these tensions are then used to help identify ways for the trainee to be helpful to the client.

Teaching mindfulness, acceptance, and self-regulation

Engaging diversity is difficult and requires a significant level of maturity and self-knowledge. I have found introducing mindfulness and acceptance an exceptionally gentle and effective means to teach this. I use a curriculum described in detail elsewhere (Gehart, 2012; McCollum & Gehart, 2010) that involves teaching students to practice mindfulness-based meditations to increase their ability to accept themselves and others and to manage distress. One of the most notable outcomes of having students practice mindfulness is that they increase their ability to self-regulate emotions and actions, which means they are able to more effectively engage the difficult interactions and conversations that arise related to diversity (McCollum & Gehart, 2010). Also, students report that this process enables them to be more accepting of the complexity and contradictions of human condition, thus having greater compassion for their clients' struggles. Any judgment becomes harder to justify. Thus, when social justice issues arise, the conversation begins to shift from one of finger-pointing and blaming to one of compassion for those who suffer, recognition of the systems that create it, and a curiosity for how to transform the injustice. For example, one student reported that mindfulness increased her understanding of the many conflicting thoughts she has each day; this enabled her to have more compassion for an immigrant Latino woman struggling with an abusive relationship while caught between two cultures—two sets of shoulds. The student didn't expect the woman to have one consistent opinion, which was liberating for her, the client, and the therapeutic process and allowed her to help the client explore these two sets of values with fresh eyes. Having experienced transformation through reflexivity and compassion themselves, they are far more capable and confident in their ability to make a difference in the lives of their clients and society at large.

Concluding reflections

The journey of understanding human diversity is lifelong, an ever-unfolding series of trials and insights that touch us at the core of our being. Therapists can use the basic process of striving for humanizing dialogue and interaction with others—including appreciative, reflexive, and mindfulness practices—to help navigate this difficult territory. The struggle is often to maintain a sense of humanity when we bear witness to and feel outrage about the painful and deeply human consequences of social injustice, ignorance, and the darker side of human nature. To be transformative, this outrage must be balanced by compassion for and an honest acceptance of the complexities and contradictions of being human. This is not an easy task or a struggle with simple answers, but I find it is exactly that struggle that renews our sense of humanity and inspires us to imagine new forms of communal good.

References

Anderson, H. (1997). *Conversation, language, and possibilities: A postmodern approach to therapy.* New York, NY: Basic Books.

Anderson, H., & Gehart, D. (2007). *Collaborative therapy: Relationships and conversations that make a difference.* New York, NY: Routledge.

Christiansen, A., Thomas, V., Kafescioglu, N., Karakurt, G., Lowe, W., Smith, W., & Wittenborn, A. (2011). Multicultural supervision: Lessons learned about an ongoing struggle. *Journal of Marital and Family Therapy, 37*(1), 109–119. doi:10.1111/j.1752-0606.2009.00138.x

Cooperrider, D., Sorenson, P. F., Whitney, D., & Yaeger, T. F. (Eds.). (2000). *Appreciative inquiry: Rethinking human organization toward a positive theory of change.* New York, NY: Stipes.

Dillon, M. (2014). Asynchrony in attitudes toward abortion and gay rights: The challenge to values alignment. *Journal for the Scientific Study of Religion, 53*(1), 1–16. doi:10.1111/jssr.12096

Fialkov, C., & Haddad, D. (2012). Appreciative clinical training. *Training and Education in Professional Psychology, 6*(4), 204–210. doi:10.1037/a0030832

Gadamer, H. (1975). *Truth and method.* New York, NY: Seabury.

Gehart, D. R. (2012). *Mindfulness and acceptance in couple and family therapy.* New York: Springer Books. doi:10.1007/978-1-4614-3033-9

Gehart, D., & McCollum, E. (2007). Engaging suffering: Towards a mindful re-visioning of marriage and family therapy practice. *Journal of Marital and Family Therapy, 33,* 214–226.

Gergen, K. (1999). *An invitation to social constructionism.* Thousand Oaks, CA: SAGE Publications.

Gergen, K. (2001). *Social construction in context.* Thousand Oaks, CA: SAGE Publications.

Gergen, K. (2009). *Relational being: Beyond self and community.* New York, NY: Oxford University Press.

González, R. (1997). Postmodern supervision: A multicultural perspective. In D. B. Pope-Davis & H. K. Coleman (Eds.), *Multicultural counseling competencies: Assessment, education and training, and supervision* (pp. 350–386). Thousand Oaks, CA: SAGE Publications.

Jang, S., & Lee, H. (2014). When pop music meets a political issue: Examining how "Born This Way" influences attitudes toward gays and gay rights policies. *Journal of Broadcasting & Electronic Media, 58*(1), 114–130. doi:10.1080/08838151.2013.875023

McCollum, E., & Gehart, D. (2010). Using mindfulness to teach therapeutic presence: A qualitative outcome study of a mindfulness-based curriculum for teaching therapeutic presence to master's level marriage and family therapy trainees. *Journal of Marital and Family Therapy, 36,* 347–360. doi: 10.1111/j.1752-0606.2010.00214.x

McNamee, S., & Gergen, K. (1999). *Relational responsibility: Resources for sustainable dialogue.* Thousand Oaks, CA: SAGE Publications.

Monk, G., & Gehart, D. R. (2003). Conversational partner or socio-political activist: Distinguishing the position of the therapist in collaborative and narrative therapies. *Family Process, 42,* 19–30.

Schwandt, T. A. (2000). Three epistemological stances for qualitative inquiry: Interpretativism, hermeneutics, and social constructionism. In N. K. Denzin & Y. S. Lincoln (Eds.), *Handbook of qualitative research* (2nd ed.). Thousand Oaks, CA: SAGE Publications.

Shotter, J. (1993). *Conversational realities: Constructing life through language.* Thousand Oaks, CA: SAGE Publications.

13

EXPANDING THE HUMAN SPIRIT

Pathway to promoting cultural sensitivity

Kiran Shahreen Kaur Arora, PhD

Expanding the human spirit

As a professor who is also a South Asian, Brown-skinned, Sikh, and Punjabi woman, I believe that educating for critical consciousness is an ethical imperative. Paulo Freire described critical consciousness as a social and educational concept, which encourages an in-depth analysis of our lives while deepening the understanding of the social and political contradictions that permeate our worlds (Freire, 1970). Whether teaching a formal course in diversity or a traditional course in marriage and family therapy, the role of the educator in the twenty-first century must prepare the next generation of therapists to practice with cultural sensitivity, humility, and competence. I do this by transforming the classroom into a microcosm for "Expanding the Human Spirit." This involves traversing fear, understanding what unites us, and creating meaningful communities. Engaging in dialogue is a modest way to begin to cross boundaries and form relationships with people and ideas that seem foreign to us. In the classroom, communities can be created to understand the need for social change and develop practices that promote compassion, kindness, and freedom. My pedagogy is informed by ten principles, which I will discuss throughout this chapter: (1) examining the self; (2) making a commitment to learning and mentoring; (3) using storytelling; (4) exploring cultural selves; (5) addressing the sociopolitical nature of psychological and relational injuries; (6) having difficult dialogues; (7) cultivating curiosity, respect, and compassion for those who are different; (8) encouraging risk-taking; (9) moving beyond known parameters and comfort; and (10) committing to relationships.

Examining the self

Having an in-depth understanding of one's social location is critical in understanding others (Hardy & Laszloffy, 2002). Ultimately, we are products of our environments, and our social contexts are significant factors in our understanding of human relationships. Our families of origin and respective sociopolitical histories shape our worldviews, how we relate to one another, and address suffering and healing. An acute awareness of self requires an ongoing examination of historical and current experiences in our lives. I am aware that my life as it has unfolded serves as a foundation for my pedagogy and my clinical work and therefore requires transparency.

The ongoing experiences of racial and religious bigotry have crystallized my commitment to social justice both inside and outside the classroom. I grew up in Vancouver, Canada, during a time when there was much unrest in the Sikh community. I have been affected by the more recent events concerning Sikhs as the rise for an independent Sikh homeland grew in Punjab, India, and spread through the diaspora community. My family members have been personally impacted by the state-sponsored attacks in Punjab, India, during the 1980s and 1990s, including but not limited to Operation Blue Star, Operation Woodrose, and the Anti-Sikh Pogroms. These crackdowns included attacks on Sikh spiritual spaces, disappearances, murder, torture, rapes, and psychological warfare against Sikhs, in the thousands. I grew up looking at faces of identifiable turbaned Sikhs on the front pages of Canadian newspapers daily, who were unfairly under suspicion. Any protest against the human rights violations was viewed as supporting militant activity in Punjab. These tensions fractured my morale as a young person by creating fear and voicelessness.

When these events began to simmer I found myself in the midst of another transnational crisis, 9/11. On the one-year anniversary of 9/11, I was arrested and detained by the federal police in Canada. I maintained my stance of mistaken identity and was released several hours later when authorities realized the gross error they had made. Being "Brown" during this time of heightened terrorist rhetoric is not lost on me. Between several interrogations, I had moments of intense clarity where I understood my arrest to be an exercise in deepening my understanding of the dynamics of oppression and trauma as it relates to minority communities. My compassion for those who are racially targeted by police intensified. I am aware that racial and religious bigotry, as I have experienced it, acts as a compass in much of my work today. Working to understand the underpinnings of racism and other dynamics of oppression is a political act. It is my way of both embracing the traumas I have experienced and resisting the painful effects of them. While my life experiences are a wealth of resources that inform my work as an educator and clinician, they also sometimes limit and bias my perspective. I regularly draw attention to my biases in the classroom, in an effort to demonstrate the influence of experience as it relates to interpretation.

Making a commitment to learning and mentoring

In 2005 I joined Syracuse University's marriage and family therapy doctoral program, where I engaged in self-of-the-therapist and diversity training. This rigorous learning was only possible due to the strong mentoring relationships I had with the faculty who laid the framework for my learning. I was encouraged to introspect deeply and examine my self in relation to various dimensions of diversity. Initially I felt apprehensive about this philosophy. I was defensive during clinical supervision. As a woman of color I had had so many experiences of feeling exposed and humiliated by dominant groups of people such as men and white people that any posed inquiry to my personhood felt like an exercise in indignity. I felt trapped in my body, often overflowing with emotion yet silencing verbal expression. Further, I had so much pent-up rage that I had hardened over others who seemed to be a threat. Over time I began to understand the connection between my *self* and how I relate to the world, as I became more comfortable with stating my opinions, defining my experiences, and articulating past hurts. With the faculty's interest in my growth as a human being and as a marriage and family therapist, I began to concretize my thinking around the person and educator I wanted to be. My clinical supervisor, Kenneth V. Hardy, helped me in coming to terms with my own fluctuating identity as a Brown woman. My training involved sorting through various therapeutic models, strategies, research orientations, and developing my own theory of therapy. However, in clinical supervision much attention was devoted to my practice of family therapy in a field that is mostly ignorant and apathetic to the dynamics of injustice. While early contextual experiences had shaped my desire to become a therapist, in graduate school I learned how these same experiences shaped my ability to relate and love another. Through ongoing trusting and caring relationships with my inner circle of colleagues, I continue to learn to transform my heart. My commitment to mentoring students is a direct correlation to the quality of mentorship I received in my training program at Syracuse University. I make ongoing efforts to engage with students in hopes of creating lasting communities that inspire and heal.

Using storytelling

Like many people of color, I am the descendant of a people who use testimony and the transmittance of cultural knowledge through storytelling. In this regard, as a professor I have fully embraced storytelling as a method of discussing difficult and intricate topics. Telling my own stories has allowed students to have a window to my life and witness my mistakes and learning edges as a marriage and family therapist. It also invites them to take their own risks. I encourage students to share their family and community stories as they relate to the topics at hand.

In an effort to use my own learning as an example, I tell students of a time when this was most highlighted for me. Given my personal political experiences in Vancouver, I had formed a compassionate and forgiving perspective on what the media termed "Sikh militants." This group of Sikhs was often described as those who were on the front lines of the struggle in creating an independent homeland. However, the term "militants" was often blurred to include all turbaned Sikh men who looked like "terrorists." The Canadian and Indian media had created a powerful discourse on branding traditional-looking Sikhs (mostly men) as turban-wearing terrorists and militants. My protectiveness toward my father and brother, both turban-wearing Sikhs, and my own sensitivities toward the plight of my community, including those who were advocating for an independent homeland, confused my thinking. While I held segregated thinking and resisted the discourse on the militant/terrorist, I also let go of a possibility for any Sikh to commit harm to another community member in this struggle. This perspective was challenged when I interviewed a Canadian Sikh woman for my dissertation. The goal of the interview was to gain an understanding of her experiences of the political violence in Punjab, India, as a diaspora Sikh. She shared that during a trip to Punjab in the 1990s she witnessed the men in her family being tortured by other Sikhs who claimed to be militants (Arora, 2009). Further, they forced the family to feed them and hand over foreign currency as they hid from the Indian state police. Unable to hold a both/and perspective toward the Sikhs who were committing crimes during the struggle, I was shaken to my core when confronted with this story. I could not deny the participant's experience. Yet I couldn't comprehend these Sikhs being both victims and perpetrators. Examining lived experiences in dichotomous and segregated categories limits our perspective. Embracing a both/and perspective opens us to the possibilities that all experiences are connected, and that we can inhabit a number of contradictory positions in life (Hardy & Laszloffy, 2002). While beginning to comprehend that Sikhs too had been perpetrators in asserting their political and human rights, I held compassion for this woman who had been so brutally violated. Over reflection and many of my own supervision sessions I made connections between my seemingly quickly accessed feelings of compassion toward this *Sikh* woman who had been violated and my resistance toward others, mainly Hindus, who had experienced similar violations during this time of upheaval. I had experienced Hindus as the dominant group, as aggressors, and as those who misused their power and privilege; however, this segregated thinking left no room for those Hindus who were loving, fair, accountable, just, and aligning themselves with minority communities in South Asia. It left little room for Hindus to be anything other than what I had believed them to be.

Exploring cultural selves

Early on in a course I spend time having conversations with students about culture. This lays the groundwork for thinking through future ideas presented. I believe a complex analysis of how we view ourselves and mark our territory in this world is essential in acquiring and deconstructing any knowledge. My thinking is primarily informed by Hardy and Laszloffy's Multicultural Perspective or MCP, as referred to at that time, a philosophical position that posits the self as having many cultural selves (2002). The idea that no one dimension of culture is exhaustive and absolute provides infinite possibilities in how one person defines herself and understands another. While this thinking seems customary to me, I am always amazed at the receptiveness from students. The idea that culture is not only relegated to race and ethnicity but also includes gender, social class, sexual preferences, immigration status, religion, regional belonging, etc. offers students a complex and nuanced way of viewing self in relation to the other. White students are often taken aback when they begin to think of themselves as having membership in many cultures, including race and ethnicity. One white student stated, "I know that I have English heritage and culture, but I never embodied it the way I would view a Black person whose parents are from Kenya." The meanings we attach to our cultures adds substance to how we relate. Students come to understand that the meanings associated with their cultures, both intended and unconscious, shape how they interpret and respond to others. Expanding the human spirit involves both an appreciation and critique of the many cultural positions that intersect in relationships.

Addressing the sociopolitical nature of psychological and relational injuries

Healing requires addressing oppressive sociopolitical structures in which a person lives (Martín-Baró, 1994). Addressing the sociopolitical nature of psychological and relational injuries and taking positions against injustice and disparities are essential in creating transformative experiences in training and clinical work. The interconnectedness between a personal experience and the power structures that influence and subjugate is an assumption that translates into several activities and assignments in my courses. Raising socio-political consciousness and understanding the insidious impact of oppression is key in working with families. Equitable access and distribution of opportunities and the basic right to human dignity and respect are at the heart of many conversations in my classroom.

Racism is often the most distressing topic of discussion over the course of the semester. Drawing connections between the self and social conditions that uphold racist attitudes and practice can be jarring. At first some students are upset at the realization that they are the beneficiaries of someone else's pain. Many white or lighter-skinned students resist the idea that light skin privilege means subjugation for darker-skinned people. The historical realities of oppression and its deteriorating affects on mental health and relationships are critical conversations I have in the classroom.

Having difficult dialogues

Difficult dialogues are necessary in an effort to increase understanding and care between people, and to move beyond difference (Hardy & Laszloffy, 2002).

Developing greater intimacy involves having conversations that change the dynamics in people and the relationship between them. These dialogues are often marked with nervousness and feelings of trepidation, as people are encouraged to face their positions while remaining in the conversation (Hardy & Laszloffy, 2002; Stone Fish & Harvey, 2005). As a professor, I have facilitated difficult dialogues between students, encouraging them to move toward their contention and remain with their primary emotions. One light-skinned, mixed-race, second-generation Brazil female shared being made to feel invisible by a white male professor in another class. She shared stories of feeling dismissed and felt that her professor viewed her as "uncouth" and "dense." She was visibly upset over this and the realization that even in places where learning should be free of discrimination, it is not. While most of the class seemed empathic towards her, a darker-skinned Malay student from Singapore was irritated by this sharing and eventually told the Brazilian student that she was being "hypocritical." The Malay student expressed anger over feeling similarly discriminated against by the Brazilian student. In their personal interactions, the Malay student had felt like a "second-class citizen in America," and as someone who did not "belong" because of her international status and Singaporean accent. Initially the Brazilian student began to shut down when being confronted by her classmate. In an effort to keep the conversation moving towards understanding, I encouraged them to stay in the conversation, to talk *with* one another by facing each other, instead of *about* one another. While encouraging the expression of frustration and sadness, I guided the conversation so that their stories were heard. My goal was to soften the image of one to the other so they could handle their differences and find some common ground. By the end of class, the conversation had shifted to the broader dynamics of racism, and each student understood that what felt like seemingly personal injuries were in fact directly related to racial and cultural disparities that divide us. The Brazilian woman understood how she could be privileged and subjugated at the same time. The Malay student acknowledged that her classmate's experiences of discrimination were justified. While this interaction was challenging, it allowed for an increased intimacy and connectedness that was previously missing.

Cultivating curiosity, respect, and compassion for those who are different

Often students share situations from their internships or workplaces indicating some frustration or aversion toward clients. For some, clients remind them of family members they are in conflict with or early childhood reminiscences that remain unresolved. For others, clients simply are *different* and reflect dominant perspectives of distrust and suspicion toward a particular cultural group of people. Classroom discussions regularly become exercises in giving statements on personal experiences. One white Anglo Christian student shared that her work with a Brown Pakistani Muslim couple, Muneera and Ahmed, was problematic. She stated that Ahmed was "controlling towards his wife" and that he "didn't want his wife to be Americanized." The student decided that she could no longer work with Ahmed due to his "traditional" character. She gave several examples of Ahmed disapproving of Muneera's exploration of career choices. In my experience, the word "traditional" is often code for racist undertones toward a person of color. So far to me, it sounded like only a common struggle couples of all colors and faiths have in regard to balancing work and home life. I do not believe that this student would have had the same visceral reaction toward a white couple. After some further probing, she stated that she was uncomfortable with Muneera wearing a *hijab* and held Ahmed responsible for the head covering. As an instructor, I have learned to slow down and refrain from making abstract textbook type connections that does very little in educating the student. My initial reaction was to make overt connections about the internalized racist messages perpetuated by the "othering" of Muslims in America and her experience of the couple. Instead, I decided to ask her to be curious about social context and the many cultures she takes membership in. I asked her what role her context played in understanding this couple. In particular, I asked her how being white, Anglo, and Christian informed her understanding of this Brown Pakistani, Muslim couple and their lives. She eventually shared that she really did not know much about the couple other than the problem they presented her with in therapy. Further, she shared how she had associated the couples' faith with extremism and gender discrimination. While validating her effort in being transparent and introspective, I shared that I experienced her as being open to self-examination as it relates to cultural differences. The validation honored her process of learning and created space for her to be curious about an alternative story to the couple relationship. She also began to separate some of the biases she held toward Muslims and women's choices in regards to wearing the hijab. In the following class I revisited this discussion with her. She stated that she had softened toward Ahmed and realized how she had unfairly judged him. Her awareness of her own biases and the direction this took in her relationship with the couple helped her understand some of the daily prejudices the couple experiences. Keeping curiosity, respect, and compassion at the center of our practice is critical in expanding the heart toward others.

Encouraging risk-taking

Talking of oneself culturally and sharing family-of-origin stories can feel intimidating. Therefore, giving students permission to take risks in the classroom is essential in Expanding the Human Spirit. I do this first by taking risks myself early on in the semester. Sometimes it involves admitting my biases and apologizing to students for misunderstanding them; other times it involves making myself vulnerable by sharing a story that exposes my fragility as a human being.

In addition, I tell students that there will be times over the semester where they will be uncomfortable. I share the benefits of pushing oneself and being open to making mistakes. I tell them that some readings may trigger them and that I hope they will hang in there when this happens. I also offer to meet with them privately should they need compassionate ears or further clarity in regard to their learning. Early in the semester I assign a reflection paper, which asks students to reflect on themselves culturally in relation to the topic at hand. This gives me the opportunity to start to know them intimately while providing personal feedback. At this point, my goal is to encourage students to think of themselves as complex, cultural, and relational beings as they connect with course materials. Initially there are typically several incongruencies in the students' thinking. I validate their openness to being curious about themselves, as well as gently highlight the gaps as understood from my perspective. I then offer direction toward addressing some of these gaps, should they wish to do so. I usually give extensive remarks with a number of curiosities formed through questioning. Whether it be in discussion groups or individual assignments, expressing biases without punishment as they sort through these complicated topics is useful in moving the students toward thinking critically about their lives and work.

Moving beyond known parameters and comfort

As an educator I have a responsibility to hold myself accountable and move beyond known parameters and comfort. I pay acute attention to my effectiveness as an instructor. Most often when students are struggling with a particular concept, it is a cue that I have become too "academic" and am not speaking from the human place that connects us. It is when I have stepped into traditional modes of teaching, using methods of control and authority over students, that I become most restricted and prone to ineffective teaching. Classrooms, which promote attention to emotion and feeling, collaboration, and reinvention, lead to hopefulness and reinvention (hooks, 1994). Although I am becoming increasingly astute to teaching practices that promote the human spirit, every so often I find myself unconsciously guided by dominating teaching practices that are prevalent in academia. For myself, moving beyond known parameters and comfort means to honor my inclination toward engaging in the whole student—the intellectual, emotional, and spiritual—as a means to expanding the human spirit. It means paying attention to cultural differences that may have limited my curiosity about another. In a similar fashion, I encourage students to move beyond their known parameters and comfort. I encourage them to stretch and dabble in places that feel foreign to them.

Committing to relationships

I believe in transforming the lives of people around me, and I believe in encouraging this in my students. Over time and through my own learning as an educator, I have become committed to developing personal relationships with each student. It is in these relationships that intimate learning occurs. In these relationships I have been able to promote an environment of kindness, curiosity, and critical consciousness. These relationships require time and effort. They require that I pay attention to each student's life story, their places of struggle and optimism. I work toward being present, self-aware, and mindful of my power and authority. My hope is that the potential benefits of these relationships will encourage students in committing themselves to relationships they have with clients and others as they create healing.

Conclusion

Expanding the Human Spirit involves moving toward a desire to accept, embrace, and assist human beings across all cultures. It involves coming together, all voices involved in creating justice and equality for all people. Engaging in critical dialogue with students about power and the destructive nature of oppression is key in developing clinical skills that promote relational well-being. I continue to work on expanding my human spirit by transforming my classrooms into communities that challenge authority, believe that they can create change, and place a high premium on the welfare of people from all cultures.

References

Arora, K. S. K. (2009). Breaking the silence: The impact of political violence in the Sikh diaspora. (Doctoral dissertation). Retrieved from PsycINFO. (AAI3381558).

Buchignani, N. (October 28, 2014). Sikhism. Retrieved from http://www.thecanadianencyclopedia.ca/en/ article/sikhism (accessed March 24, 2016).

Freire, P. (1970). *Pedagogy of the oppressed*. New York, NY: Continuum.

Hardy, K.V. (1995). Embracing both/and. *The Psychotherapy Networker, 19*(6), 42–57.

Hardy, K.V., & Laszloffy, T. A. (2002). Couple therapy using a multicultural perspective. In A. S. Gurman & N. S. Jacobson (Eds.), *Clinical handbook of couple therapy* (3rd ed.) (569–596). New York, NY: Guilford Press.

hooks, B. (1994). *Teaching to transgress: Education as the practice to freedom*. New York, NY: Routledge.

Stone Fish, L., & Harvey, R. (2005). *Nurturing queer youth: Family therapy transformed*. New York, NY: Norton.

White, M., & Epston, D. (1990). *Narrative means to therapeutic ends*. London, UK: Norton.

14

ENHANCING CULTURAL SENSITIVITY BY SPEAKING TRUTH TO POWER

Mary M. Read, PhD

This chapter aims to engage readers with my story, as a way of learning about their own. A crucial step in becoming multiculturally sensitive is developing an understanding of one's cultural selves through self-reflection (Comas-Diaz, 2012). Interpretation of cultural stories is couched in the sociopolitical context of cultural privilege, discrimination, and oppression (Vargas & Wilson, 2011). Sharing the resilience and uniqueness of our kaleidoscopic identities offers the opportunity for supervisors, supervisees, and their clients to bond in culturally sensitive practices. The increasing globalization of counseling and psychotherapy necessitates this sensitivity as an ethical responsibility for socially just supervision (Gallardo, Johnson, Parham & Carter, 2009). The practical exercises I use with supervisees offer opportunities to discover, express, and contextualize their cultural experiences, so that they are more able to process this sensitivity with their clients.

Who I am

At this point in my life, after six decades of growth and gradual consciousness-raising, I have come to multiple facets of awareness about my own cultural identity. My cultural inheritance as a mid-life, Irish/German, lesbian, feminist, therapist, supervisor, and counselor educator who is musical and dedicated to non-judgment is always part of the equation of my interactions. Celebrating my kaleidoscope of cultures and enjoying others' as well enriches my clinical work, and informs my supervisory practices. Theoretically, this is consistent with the Person-of-the-Therapist model (Aponte & Carlsen, 2009) and Relational-Cultural Theory (RCT) (Abernethy & Cook, 2011), both of which influence and inform my supervisory efforts.

Growing up in rural Wisconsin, I became fascinated with Celtic lore, earth religions, and all things green, especially trees. I can see that my love of music, stories, and jokes is the inheritance of many Irish generations. My tendency to be industrious, thrifty, and somewhat rule-bound flows from my German side. At times my class/socioeconomic status (SES) awareness has even more effect on me than my racial/ethnic heritage, in terms of my career choices and social "comfort zone." My dad sold Fuller Brush products door-to-door while my mom was a part-time high school librarian, influencing my tendency to be entrepreneurial and self-employed, as well as my love of reading.

Spirituality is kaleidoscopic for me, an overlay of pan-spiritual and multiethnic teachings, rooted in the Existential concepts of freedom, choice, and responsibility. My abiding sense of the compassion of the Universe and the inevitable balance of all things has marked my worldview, best represented by the maxim "Lift the judgment and allow compassion to flow." Intimately connected to my spirituality, my sexual identity has become an important cultural lens for me over time.

Although still a stigmatized identity, I cherish the deeper dialogue my "coming out" makes possible (McGeorge & Carlson, 2011). Speaking about healthy relationships and sexuality in general provides common ground with my students and supervisees (Burkhard et al., 2009), privileging the notion that all sexual orientations and gender identities are equally valid and open for discussion. Love = truth = freedom is a trustworthy guide for my spiritual practice, along with the Wiccan rede: "Do as you will, harming none."

What I do

Currently, I am the Director of Clinical Training for the Department of Counseling at California State University, Fullerton, where I have taught graduate students on their way to becoming Licensed Marriage and Family Therapists (LMFTs) and more recently Licensed Professional Clinical Counselors (LPCCs) for 25 years. I oversee the students' practicum fieldwork year and teach a couple of classes every semester. I'm a clinical supervisor at three community agencies serving a variety of cultures, and provide trainings as a consultant on a number of topics. Because I love doing psychotherapy, I also maintain a small private practice a couple of days a week, specializing in the areas of identity issues, recovery from grief and loss, and transcending addictive patterns. My other (volunteer, non-clinical) life is as a founding member of Vox Femina Los Angeles, a diverse women's chorus dedicated to giving women voice and raising awareness about issues that affect the family of women. "Through our music, we aim to create a world that affirms the worth and dignity of <u>every</u> person" (www.voxfeminala.org).

My core beliefs

I believe that knowledge is co-constructed and ever-evolving, contextual, and situated by the learners involved (Gray & Smith, 2009). Supervisors learn as they mentor, sharing the power of meaning-making. Life-as-lived, experienced both uniquely and universally at the same time, provides the tapestry framework weaving together the world, like Grandmother Spider. This epistemology embraces both diversity and equality, twin pillars of social justice.

I also believe that discussions of power and diversity must be engaged at both process and content levels in any learning environment. *Speaking truth to power* begins in the supervisory relationship so that it can translate into clinical work. Research confirms that supervisees feel more competent when the supervision process includes discussions of power and diversity (Green & Dekkers, 2010) and the supervisor is open, accepting, and flexible toward supervisees and their clients (Ancis & Marshall, 2010). Using tools like Aponte and Carlsen's (2009) *Person of the Therapist model* for case presentations helps highlight the cultural (and social, political, economic, spiritual, etc.) backgrounds of both supervisee and client, opening the ground for transparent discussions. For example, in speaking of spiritual matters I intentionally use the terms "Universe" or "Cosmic Consciousness" so as to not unduly preference one spiritual lens over another. Quoting sacred writings from multiple spiritual traditions and using folktales from many peoples helps to privilege a diverse range of cultural worldviews that informs a broad spectrum of human behavior (Sommer et al., 2009). I ask supervisees to bring in metaphors from other cultural lenses to describe their clinical work, encouraging the celebration—not just tolerance—of diversity (Suthakaran, 2011).

The origins of my commitment to social justice

My impetus toward social justice in counseling springs from my feminism—they are inseparable to me. I can clearly recall my first introduction to feminism, in the guise of a class handout in Sociology 101 about "protecting" boys in sports. The facts of girls' innate strengths were noted (built for childbirth, etc.) along with the clear fragility of boys, by virtue of their external (and therefore vulnerable) genitalia. In those few paragraphs, I felt the world shift on its axis as statements about girls in sports that I'd accepted all my life were gender-reversed. I began to actively question the paradigm privileging "male" as equal to "powerful." If that belief structure was flawed, what freedoms might come from purposefully shifting societal perspectives about gender and power? How might relationships be improved and personal potential be activated if gender equality rather than patriarchy became normative? These questions inevitably led to more, challenging heterosexism, classism, ageism, ableism, and other power paradigms, seeking more socially just, balanced perspectives. I look forward to the day I no longer need to identify as feminist, only humanist, once the worth and dignity of all persons of all ages, genders, orientations, and backgrounds are equally affirmed in global society. It's my goal to help supervisees process such perspective changes about power differentials from their own standpoints and those of their clients. It is important for me to remember that, as the one with more power in the room, it is my responsibility to raise these power conversations in an environment of safety, ensuring mutual respect for differences while building common ground through what is shared.

Helping supervisees and students move into a "recovery-oriented" worldview (Read et al., 2012) also engenders a critique of the power differentials built into the "medical model" view of clinical work, thereby fostering social justice. Supervisees are encouraged to question whether clients who are late to session may have transportation or childcare issues, for instance. Rather than frame the client who wants to run overtime in session as pushing boundaries (or "being borderline"), curiosity about other forms of social support beyond relationship with the clinician is fostered. Viewing the angry teenager from an oppressed culture as responding to decades of micro-aggressions (Sue et al., 2007) for which socially just redress needs to be sought, rather than as behaving in an oppositional or defiant way for no cause, helps supervisees address power differentials and cultural inheritance in their holistic assessment of their clients.

At times, I find it helpful to encourage supervisees to simply put themselves into the world of the client and view the therapeutic milieu from that standpoint, as in the following exercise.

"Put yourself in her shoes" exercise

Description and purpose

This exercise aims to give group members experiential practice in identifying with a cultural worldview different than their own, enhancing cultural sensitivity. After imagining the given scenario, volunteers are asked to respond to the questions below. Responses will likely include those who can and cannot understand the client's potential choices and a critique of the current social system in place to respond to the client's needs.

Applications of exercise

This exercise is helpful for developing empathy for cultural differences and choices. It can be used effectively with individuals or groups of any size.

"Put yourself in her shoes" exercise process

Group members are asked to imagine this scenario:

> You are a young woman from a traditional, hierarchical (patriarchal) society. All your life you are taught that men run the world and women are subservient to them. Your role is to please and care for your husband, no matter what. You have done your best to fulfill that worldview, even when circumstances have not been ideal. Now, imagine that an incident of domestic

violence has occurred with your husband, and a Child Protective Services worker is inter-viewing you, asking you to make a choice — leave him and enter a domestic violence shelter, or potentially lose custody of your children.

After a few minutes, ask group members the following questions:

How do you feel?

What are you thinking?

How might a counselor join you in your worldview and help you explore what is happening?

What approaches might help you feel the compassion (vs. judgment) of "the system" that aims to help you protect your children?

What other choices might you have?

What will you do now?

This exercise flows out of my experience, as a very new clinician, doing an intake session with a young Latina mother of three. Despite ongoing abuse from her husband, both her family and church demanded that she stay with him, as she indeed wished to do. After spending 35 minutes together, she stated that what she really wanted from our sessions was to feel better about herself *after* her husband beat her. I told her this was not a therapeutic goal toward which we could work, shared domestic violence (DV) recovery resources, and developed a safety plan. Not surprisingly, I never saw her again. My awareness of my failure to adequately meet this client in her cultural world informs this exercise.

How I respond to unintentional bias

Unfortunately, subtle, institutionalized biases, including heterosexism, classism, self-referenced spiritual assumptions, and racism still influence the worldviews of well-intentioned helping professionals (Sue et al., 2007). In the spirit of lifting the judgment and allowing compassion to flow, when an incident occurs in supervision (or class) that reveals the unintentional bias or prejudice of the speaker, I use the following exercise.

Unintentional bias exercise

Description and purpose

The goals of this exercise are to set the groundwork for a corrective experience when a group member has unintentionally used language reflecting bias or prejudice. Such experiential tasks help develop cultural sensitivity in an atmosphere of safety and mutual respect (Laszloffy & Habekost, 2010).

Steps for unintentional bias exercise

First, I am responsible to notice and interrupt the speaker when language reflecting bias or prejudice is used in the learning environment.

Second, after I interrupt, I state that I believe the speaker's intentions to be well-meaning.

Third, I ask for suggestions from other group members of alternate ways things might be stated. Each contributor can then say how they might have heard the words used from their own particular frame of reference and what might have been more helpful to hear.

Last, the speaker is asked to rephrase their original comment incorporating the feedback given, and to process further (and possibly privately) if needed.

Adapted from the National Council for Community and Justice (www.nccj.org).

Preventing unintentional bias by expanding supervisees' frames of cultural reference is a worthy supervision goal. Exercises for discussing different domains of cultural identity assist in this growth process. This may be as simple as asking yourself how demonstrating respect for a client/supervisee/ student requires you to honor their spiritual tradition, even as you may disagree with it, along with some steps you can take to demonstrate this honoring. This promotes a context for accessing and honoring spiritual diversity, so essential for creating a more peaceful global society.

Navigating difficult conversations

Some of the most difficult conversations I have had with students and supervisees have occurred around the deeply personal realm of spirituality, and how that impacts the clinical (and therefore supervisory) relationship. It is challenging when worldviews do not align—to demonstrate respect and openness while holding a boundary that allows for different perspectives to both enter and leave the conversation. When supervisees are looking at scarcity, coming from fear, or locked into negative judgment about clients, I try to go toward their view until I truly understand it, then offer a linkage to my own perspective without requiring them to shift to it. For example, I recall when an intern ("Vicky") had to make a Child Protective Services (CPS) call about her client, a young mother of three, who had slapped her 5-year-old son in a fit of frustration. My intern was so angry with this mom she could not access the compassion with which she usually held her clients. Despite Vicky's familiarity with the client's generational patterns of abuse, extreme poverty, and three high-needs toddlers, this one act of violence colored the mom as "all bad," in her view. When CPS did not "take" her report Vicky was outraged, and vented this in supervision.

The challenge of helping her to see the mom as a whole, real person who'd made a very unfortunate choice involved accessing Vicky's spiritual framework to look for potential flexibility. Vicky's spiritual tradition emphasized the importance of continual right action to maintain good standing. With further questioning, however, a pathway for reconciliation after making mistakes was revealed that was consonant with Vicky's worldview. Using this capacity for reconnection after wrongdoing, the group was able to help Vicky brainstorm ways this stressed-out mother could repair her relationship with her son. Even though the mom had made a mistake that it was important to stress she not repeat, reinforcing the mom for her many strengths and good choices was more clinically appropriate for Vicky, after facilitating the relationship repair. Encouraging this mom to forgive herself, as her son already had done, was only possible once Vicky could find it in her heart to see how any mom could make that choice, harmful though it may be. Without Vicky's unspoken forgiveness of the client, the therapeutic relationship would have been damaged, since compassion could not flow. And without our group process in supervision, Vicky's lack of forgiveness toward herself for judging her client would have negatively impacted her own clinical and personal development.

Conclusion

Cultural sensitivity in supervision is a crucial element in the development of socially just, recovery-oriented, empowered and empowering supervisees. By using all of one's cultural lenses to flesh out a kaleidoscopic whole, the sharing of power and meaning-making in supervision develops that sensitivity to new and transformative levels.

References

Abernethy, C., & Cook, K. (2011). Resistance or disconnection? A relational-cultural approach to supervisee anxiety and nondisclosure. *Journal of Creativity in Mental Health, 6,* 2–14. doi: 10.1080/15401383.2011.560067

Aducci, C. J., & Baptist, J. A. (2011). A collaborative-affirmative approach to supervisory practice. *Journal of Feminist Family Therapy, 23,* 88–102.

Ancis, J. R., & Marshall, D. S. (2010). Using a multicultural framework to assess supervisees' perceptions of culturally competent supervision. *Journal of Counseling & Development, 88,* 277–284.

Aponte, H. J., & Carlsen, J. C. (2009). An instrument for person-of-the-therapist supervision. *Journal of Marital and Family Therapy, 35*(4), 395–405. doi: 10.1111/j.1752-0606.2009.00127.x

Burkard, A. W., Knox, S., Hess, S. A., & Schultz, J. (2009). Lesbian, gay, and bisexual supervisees' experiences of LGB-affirmative and non-affirmative supervision. *Journal of Counseling Psychology, 56,* 176–188.

Comas-Diaz, L. (2012). Cultural self-assessment: Knowing others, knowing yourself. In L. Comas-Diaz (Ed.), *Multicultural care: A clinician's guide to cultural competence* (pp. 13–32). Washington, DC: American Psychological Association.

Falender, C. A., Shafranske, E. P., & Falicov, C. (Eds.). (2014). *Multiculturalism and diversity in clinical supervision: A competency-based approach.* Washington, DC: American Psychological Association.

Gallardo, M. E., Johnson, J., Parham, T. A., & Carter, J. A. (2009). Ethics and multiculturalism: Advancing cultural and clinical responsiveness. *Professional Psychology: Research and Practice, 40*(5), 425–435.

Gray, S. W., & Smith, M. S. (2009). The influence of diversity in clinical supervision: A framework for reflective conversations and questioning. *The Clinical Supervisor, 28,* 155–179. doi: 10.1080/07325220903324371

Green, M. S., & Dekkers, T. D. (2010). Attending to power and diversity in supervision: An exploration of supervisee learning outcomes and satisfaction with supervision. *Journal of Feminist Family Therapy, 22,* 293–312.

Laszloffy, T., & Habekost, J. (2010). Using experiential tasks to enhance cultural sensitivity among MFT trainees. *Journal of Marital and Family Therapy, 36*(3), 333–346.

McGeorge, C., & Carlson, T. S. (2011). Deconstructing heterosexism: Becoming an LGB affirmative heterosexual couple and family therapist. *Journal of Marital and Family Therapy, 37,* 14–26.

National Conference for Community and Justice. (2013). Bulletin on Racism/Anti-Racism. Retrieved on October 15, 2014, from http://www.nccj.org

Read, M. M., Avineri, M., Davis, S., Loewy, O., & Wexler, K. (2012). *The transforming system: A practical handbook for understanding the changes in California community mental health.* Santa Barbara, CA: AAMFT-CA.

Sommer, C. A., Derrick, E. C, Bourgeois, M. B., Ingene, D. H., Yang, J. W., & Justice, C. A. (2009). Multicultural connections: Using stories to transcend cultural boundaries in supervision. *Journal of Multicultural Counseling and Development, 37,* 206–218.

Sue, D. W., Capodilupo, C. M., Torino, G. C., Bucceri, J. M., Holder, A. M. B., Nadal, K. L., & Esquilin, M. (2007). Racial micro-aggressions in everyday life: Implications for clinical practice. *American Psychologist, 62*(4), 271–286.

Suthakaran, V. (2011). Using analogies to enhance self-awareness and cultural empathy: Implications for supervision. *Journal of Multicultural Counseling and Development, 39,* 207–217.

Vargas, H. L., & Wilson, C. M. (2011). Managing worldview influences: Self-awareness and self-supervision in a cross-cultural therapeutic relationship. *Journal of Family Psychotherapy, 22,* 97–113. doi: 10.1080/08975353.2011.577684

Vox Femina Los Angeles. (2014). Mission Statement. Retrieved on October 15, 2014, from http://www.voxfeminala.org

15

EXPERIENTIAL EXERCISES

Innovative pathways to promoting cultural sensitivity

Kenneth V. Hardy, PhD, and Toby Bobes, PhD

The exercises in this chapter are designed to enhance cultural sensitivity through experiential learning. The purpose of these exercises is to move participants beyond one of the common pitfalls of addressing cultural sensitivity in supervision and training. This common pitfall occurs when the focus tends to be "awareness-oriented," that is, upon understanding the other to the exclusion of self-reflective processes. This chapter will provide a series of innovative exercises which will equip supervisors and trainers to take a proactive role in creating educational experiences that promote cultural sensitivity.

Hot-button issues or trigger points will inevitably arise during emotionally charged conversations and therefore may require additional time for processing. It is essential that facilitators have the ability to encourage and tolerate discomfort and intensity. Staying with the intensity is essential and is a critical attribute for supervisors and trainers to demonstrate (McGoldrick & Hardy, 2008).

The following exercises are ones that we have found useful in our respective supervision and teaching practices. They are designed to assist practitioners in generating ideas for facilitating experiential exercises in supervision and training. The exercises may be used in training as well as supervision.

The following exercises are included in this chapter:

• Cultural storytelling	• The cultural interview
• My cultural self	• The multicultural role-play
• The difference exercise	• An ethical struggle about religious differences

Reference

McGoldrick, M., & Hardy, K.V. (2008) (Eds.). *Revisioning family therapy: Race, culture, and gender in clinical practice.* New York, NY: Guilford Press.

Cultural storytelling

Kenneth V. Hardy, PhD

Description and purpose

Cultural Storytelling is an exercise designed to encourage trainees to think critically about their respective cultural positioning and how virtually all aspects of their lives are shaped by it. The exercise is based on three salient assumptions: 1) Culture is a broad and multifaceted concept that encompasses a vast array of sociocultural dimensions including, but not limited to, gender, race, ethnicity, religion, etc.; 2) as human beings we live lives that are embedded in culture; 3) "stories" are integral to our lived experiences and constitute a platform through which we experience the world and ascribe meaning to it; 4) stories are subjective and help to shape how we make meaning in our lives; and 4) knowledge and understanding of (the) *Self* is crucial to fostering understanding of (the) *other*.

The design of the exercise is semi-structured to afford trainees the opportunity to be creative and flexible in the actual approach that might be taken to "telling one's story." In so doing, trainees are encouraged to share a significant story from their respective cultural experience that highlights the relevancy of culture in their lives. They are urged to consider the various dimensions of culture that define them as cultural beings and to recall a story that would emphasize the significance of one or several dimension(s). The goals of the exercise are to 1) stress the significance of stories and storytelling in promoting cultural awareness and sensitivity, 2) assist trainees in becoming more fluent in "cultural talk," and 3) help train and acclimate the "ears" of trainees to effectively listen for and hear salient cultural themes that underpin the experiences of those with whom they interact.

Often having a supervisor or trainer share a cultural story or simply inviting a trainee to tell one is commonly an effective strategy in getting the process started. However, in some rare instances the use of a starter question might be needed to stimulate the cultural storytelling process. The following is a list of sample starter questions that might be a useful catalyst in spearheading the process.

Sample starter questions

1. Who was the "family cultural historian" in the family you grew up in? What cultural stories do you remember? Which story was your favorite or the one you heard most often? Can you tell us your favorite story as told by the "family cultural historian" in your family?
2. What role did storytelling play in the culture that you and/or your family identified with when you were growing up? What stories about your culture did your hear? What was the nature of how the stories were told? Were they humorous, tragic, happy, triumphant, etc.?
3. What family or cultural rituals often accompanied cultural storytelling in the family you grew up in? Were stories often told at mealtime, with or without alcohol, with or without food, in large or small groups, etc.? If you were to select a favorite cultural story that was told and embellished by a ritual, what would it be?
4. Can you tell a story, real or imagined, about your culture that instilled a sense of cultural pride in you?
5. Can you tell a story, real or imagined, about your culture that generated a sense of cultural shame in you?
6. As you think of yourself culturally, what stories have you heard or told that helped you learn more about yourself culturally?

7. Can you tell a story that both summarizes and highlights who you are culturally?
8. Can you tell a story about a special event you attended (social, political, or religious) that affirmed who you are and how you see yourself culturally?
9. Can you tell a cultural "story of resilience" that you have heard and/or told that is emblematic of what it means to be a member of your cultural group?
10. Can you tell a cultural story of hardship and/or struggle that your culture and family had to overcome that has helped to shape who you are?

General guidelines for facilitators

The role of the trainer is paramount to the effective execution of the exercise. The following are some general guidelines that are helpful for trainers to remain cognizant of throughout the Cultural Storytelling process:

1. Understand that stories are subjective and can be "real" or imagined. Thus the major emphasis is on the actual telling of *the story* rather than on issues of truth, accuracy, or objectivity.
2. Emotional space must be allotted for all participants to tell their stories in their own words uninterruptedly.
3. All stories must be connected to at least one dimension of culture.
4. Be mindful that some participants will have membership in shame-based cultures, and thus cultural storytelling can be slightly more challenging (and shame-evoking).
5. The facilitator should be poised to attend to vulnerable moments with empathy and to validate the experience of participants as they tell their stories.

My cultural self

Kenneth V. Hardy, PhD and Toby Bobes, PhD

Description and purpose

This exercise will assist participants in identifying and understanding their cultural selves. A series of questions is posed to facilitate cultural sharing and storytelling. As participants share their stories and experiences, they enhance sensitivity to differences among themselves and increase empathy for the perspectives of others. Addressing the questions in this exercise expands the knowing of oneself. It is the informed knowing of self that prepares participants to become more culturally sensitive in working with people of various cultural backgrounds.

Applications of exercise

This exercise may be introduced in supervision and/or training contexts as an important first step toward becoming culturally competent. The questions are useful in working with individuals and in group settings.

Facilitation of exercise

Facilitators who lead discussions that involve an exploration about one's cultural selves must first identify the multiple and complex aspects of their cultural beings. The use of oneself through cultural sharing promotes a climate of safety, risk-taking, and transparency in dialogues. This begins the process of becoming culturally competent (McGoldrick & Hardy, 2008). As participants share their stories and experiences, they enhance sensitivity to differences among themselves and increase their empathy for the perspectives of others.

EXERCISE: MY CULTURAL SELF

1. Who am I (race, gender, culture, sexual orientation, class, etc.)?
2. Which dimensions of my self are easy to own and embrace?
3. Which dimensions of my self are not easy to own and embrace?
4. Which dimensions of my self are the sources of my greatest personal discomfort?
5. Which dimensions of my self are the sources of my personal pride?

From: *The couple is telling you what you need to know: Couple-directed therapy in a multicultural context* (p. 34). Bobes, T. & Bobes, N. (2005). New York: Norton. Reprinted with permission.

References

Bobes, T., & Bobes, N. (2005). *The couple is telling you what you need to know: Couple-directed therapy in a multicultural context* (p. 34). New York, NY: Norton.

Hardy, K. (2000, November). *Bridging differences: Working with strained relationships.* Workshop at the Southern California Counseling Center, Los Angeles, California.

McGoldrick, M., & Hardy, K.V. (2008). Re-visioning training. In M. McGoldrick & K. Hardy (Eds.), *Re-visioning family therapy: Race, culture, and gender in clinical practice* (2nd ed.) (pp. 442–460). New York, NY: Guilford.

The difference exercise
An ethical stance: Exploring attitudes about difference in supervision and training
Toby Bobes, PhD

Description and purpose

The major objective of this exercise is to assist participants in accessing their personal experiences of difference. We believe this process of self-examination is essential to enhancing cultural sensitivity. Exploring one's attitudes about difference evokes a wide range of emotional responses and visceral reactions to the experience of difference. The ethical guidelines of our profession require that we are aware of and sensitive to how one's own cultural identities, values, and beliefs affect therapeutic and supervision processes. Therefore, we need to increase awareness of our attitudes toward difference. Specifically, we need to increase sensitivity to contextual variables such as gender, race, class, sexual orientation, ethnicity, and so on. This exercise is intended to deepen our empathy and promote understanding in working with individuals of different cultural backgrounds.

Applications of exercise

This exercise is valuable in a number of group settings, including supervisions, trainings, classrooms, and workshops. The exercise is useful in small and large group settings.

Facilitation of exercise

The facilitator begins the exercise by inviting participants to share their stories: "I invite you to think about a time in your life when you felt 'different from' or devalued. It may be a difference related to gender, race, physical ability/disability, sexual orientation, scholastic achievement, or any other aspect of difference. It can be in current time or in a past time in your life."

The facilitator shares a personal story first, briefly. Then participants are invited to tell their stories with the following questions:

- Would anyone be willing to share a story?
- Would you tell us about your experience?
- What was the experience like for you? What happened?
- What emotions did you experience?

After everyone who wishes to respond to the exercise has spoken, the group processes the experience. The group processing that follows the exercise offers an opportunity for participants to continue the conversation to talk about what it was like to bear witness to each other's stories of oppression and devaluation. An important part of this process is that each person's experience is validated. People often tell stories that reflect courage, resilience, and strength. It is important to allow ample time for processing so that the range of emotional experiences may be heard and validated.

Questions for discussion and reflection

- What did you learn about yourself as you reflected upon this experience?
- What kinds of difference are you most comfortable with? (Rambo & Shilts, 2002, p. 91)

- What kinds of difference are you most uncomfortable with? (ibid.)
- How might your personal experience of difference(s) inform your clinical work?

Reference

Rambo, A. H., & Stilts, L. (2002). Four supervisory practices that foster respect for difference. In T. C. Todd & C. L. Storm (Eds.), *The complete systemic supervisor: Context, philosophy, and pragmatics* (pp. 83–92). Lincoln, NE: Authors Choice Press.

The cultural interview

Toby Bobes, PhD

Description and purpose

The goals of this exercise are to create a cross-cultural experience for group members, enhance sensitivity to differences between self and other, and increase empathy for the perspectives of others. During the interview and the processing that follows learners often discover "their culturally based emotional triggers" (Hardy and Laszloffy, 1995, p. 228).

A group member volunteers to participate, the interviewer asks questions that are culturally based, and, at the conclusion of the interview, group members are invited to express their personal reactions. These reactions reveal the group members' own cultural selves as they respond and comment on the interviewee's stories. Thus the dialogue expands to include all the voices among and between group members.

Applications of exercise

This exercise has broad application for a variety of learning contexts. It may be used in small and large group settings.

CULTURAL INTERVIEW QUESTIONS

- What were the stories around the migration of your family, and how did these stories organize, affect, or influence you? (Steiny, 1998)
- We all have different ways of defining what "family" means. How do you define family?
- Who are some of the people—non-family members—who influenced you? In what ways did they influence you?
- How did your family interact with others in the community?
- How did your family view or design their celebrations, reunions, rituals, and so on? (Steiny, 1998)
- How does your ethnicity contribute to the ways you respond to others?
- What were the messages you grew up with around what men do? Around what women do?
- If I had visited you in your early family setting, what would I have particularly noticed? (Steiny, 1998)
- What were your family's reactions around issues of crisis?
- How did your family respond to troubling or tense times? (Steiny, 1998)
- How did family members react to the usual life changes of marriage, divorce, death, loss of job, and career changes?
- In what ways did religion or spirituality play a role in your family?
- What were some of the legacies and loyalties you embraced when you were growing up? Which of them are most/least valued by you today?
- How would your family members define social class?
- In what ways did you view your family as different from your friends' families?
- How did your family view racial differences?

(continued)

- How did your family view religious differences?
- How were differences expressed and negotiated in your family?
- Are there any particular questions you wish I had asked you?

From: *The couple is telling you what you need to know: Couple-directed therapy in a multicultural context* (p. 104). Bobes, T. & Bobes, N. (2005). New York: Norton. Reprinted with permission.

References

Bobes, T., & Bobes, N. (2005). *The couple is telling you what you need to know: Couple-directed therapy in a multicultural context* (p. 104). New York, NY: Norton.

Falicov, C. J. (1995). Training to think culturally: A multidimensional comparative framework. *Family Process, 34*, 373–388.

Hardy, K. V., & Laszloffy, T. A. (1995). The cultural genogram: Key to training culturally competent family therapists. *Journal of Marital and Family Therapy, 21*(3), 227–237.

Steiny, N. (1998). *The cultural interview*. Presented at Southern California Counseling Center, Los Angeles, CA.

The multicultural role-play

J. Leonardo de la O, MA

Description and purpose

The goals of the Multicultural Role-Play are to 1) give student therapists in training experience working with multicultural case material in a classroom setting; 2) open dialog and provide feedback from the culturally diverse role-players, the instructor, and peers; 3) enhance cultural sensitivity and increase empathy; and 4) become aware of unconscious biases and assumptions about ethnic and racial groups.

Classroom setting

1. If possible, divide class so that there is a maximum of no more than 12 students per group.
2. The small groups will meet in separate classrooms. In each classroom there should be a large circle for the students and three chairs in the middle, one for the role-playing "client," and one for the student-therapist. A third chair (the jump-in chair) is placed to the side, which will allow other students a turn at role-playing the therapist.
3. Total length of Multicultural Role-Play class session is 3 hours:
   a. Thirty minutes for instruction and small group setup.
   b. Two hours for the role-plays.
   c. Thirty minutes for debriefing and processing of the role-plays.

Application of exercise

Before the role-play begins students are given the following guidelines. These directions are given to the whole group:

1. There are four role-play therapy sessions, with each therapy session lasting 10 minutes followed by a 5-minute group discussion to process the dyad role-play and case management.
2. The class is usually divided into two groups so that the small groups do not exceed 12 students, if possible.
3. Select a student to act as timekeeper for each role-play therapy session and instruct that student to give a 2-minute warning. Time management is particularly necessary in classes with a large group of students, as the role-playing guests will repeat their vignette for the other group.
4. Explain *Jump-In Chair*—the small group proceeds to read the vignette, Asian American Role-Play, and to choose someone to begin the role as therapist. Explain to the students that the idea of a Jump-In Chair is to allow other students a turn at being "therapist." The students in the outside circle may enter the circle by taking a seat in the empty third chair. At an appropriate pause, the student changes places with the acting therapist, returning to the large circle. In addition, if the student-therapist is feeling stuck, or would like to opt out, they simply need to raise their hand, thus signaling for a classmate to take their place.
5. At the beginning of the role-play, the student-therapist meets and invites the "client" into the session and begins with the assumption that they have knowledge of what brought the client to therapy. In other words, in order speed up things up it is assumed the student therapist and the students in the large circle know the material contained in the case vignette. Again, it is important to state that there are no red-flag issues.
6. Once again, depending on the class size, the vignette is repeated by having your vignette's guest switch groups in the second hour.
7. At the conclusion of the role-plays, students return to the whole group to process, ask questions, and receive feedback from the guests in the final thirty minutes.

Asian American role-play: A sample vignette

Keith Mar, MA

Jeremy Lau is a 30-year old, third-generation Chinese American male who entered psychotherapy after medical exams and tests revealed no organic etiology for the headaches he suffered. His physician then referred him for psychotherapy. He initially felt shame at having to see a therapist because his Asian culture tends to attach stigma to help-seeking behavior.

He dropped out of a previous brief attempt at therapy because his therapist, in his words, "didn't understand his culture." Jeremy felt conflict because his parents were opposed to his interracial relationship. His therapist concluded he was "overly dependent" on his parent's approval and tried to convince him to just do "what felt right to him." Furthermore, he felt the therapist dismissed his growing awareness and concern with experiences of racial discrimination. After describing one incident at work, the therapist minimized it by stating, "I'm sure he didn't mean it."

In truth, his headaches reflected an array of internal conflicts in addition to his relationship issue. He feelings of failure about not advancing in his career led to depression. As an acknowledged expert in his field, he was repeatedly asked to train new hires, who eventually were promoted over him.

Adding to the conflict are feelings of anger and helplessness. Typically, he has used suppression to handle strong emotions. The result is a lack of concentration, which has affected his work. When he addressed his lack of promotion with his employer, he eventually forced his boss to admit that he did not believe that Jeremy was ever going to be "leadership material."

This incident served as a catalyst to address his racial identity. Growing up, he has attempted to deny his racial identity because he felt shame about being Chinese. He was the target of racial bullying at his primarily white grade school.

His lifelong exposure to demeaning media depictions of Asian males as emasculated geeks who were the butt of jokes or sidekicks who never got the girl reinforced his negative self-image. As a result of such experiences, he developed a strong racial self-hatred.

For a time, his adaptation to his environment has been to engage in the fantasy that if he acted white enough, he would be accepted as white. However, the episode at work is forcing him to come to grips with his authentic racial identity and racial relationships in the United States, and because of the continued physical complaints, he is now willing to give therapy another try. There are no red-flag issues.

An ethical struggle about religious differences

Toby Bobes, PhD

Description and purpose

This exercise is based upon the article by Benjamin Caldwell, "The Dilemma: Can a Religious Therapist Refuse to Treat Gay and Lesbian Clients?" (Caldwell, 2011, pp. 50–52). Participants must read the article which highlights the *Julea Ward Case* and address the questions posed. Through group interaction, participants have the opportunity to address their values, beliefs, biases, and stereotypes. Although centered upon religious differences, this exercise has relevance for discussion about any aspect of difference.

Applications of exercise

This exercise has broad applications in a variety of learning contexts. It may be used in small as well as large group settings.

Julea Ward case

In 2009, Julea Ward, a counseling student at Eastern Michigan University, was in her school-assigned practicum when she was assigned a same-sex couple for treatment. She went to her supervisor and said she could not provide treatment to the couple, citing a conflict with her religious beliefs. The couple ultimately was assigned to a different counselor at the same agency, who did not have the same conflict. Julea thought she had handled the issue appropriately, as the client received the treatment they had sought and she was not put in a position of needing to hide or compromise her beliefs. She understood the issue to have been successfully resolved.

Her graduate program, however, did not. The university began a disciplinary action against Ward, citing the non-discrimination clause of the ACA Code of Ethics. The ACA Code, like the AAMFT Code, contains two clauses that appeared to conflict in Ward's case:

- Mental health professionals do not discriminate based on sexual orientation or religion, among other factors.
- Mental health professionals do not treat clients outside of the professional's scope of competence (2011, p. 50).

The following questions may be useful for group discussion:

- As a supervisor, how would you handle Julea's request not to treat a same-sex couple? How might your own values, attitudes, and beliefs affect the conversation?
- How did you respond to William Northey's view in Caldwell's article: "I am personally not comfortable with MFTs refusing to provide services on religious grounds or any other value system." How is your own position similar to or different from Northey's view?
- If you have a supervisee who refuses to provide services on religious grounds, or any other value system, how would you address and explore the issues?
- How do you decide when or if you should reach out for consultation to other members of the system in which you work?

Reference

Caldwell, B. E. (2011). The dilemma: Can a religious therapist refuse to treat gay and lesbian couples? *Family Therapy Magazine, 10*(5), 50–52.

Acknowledgments

We wish to acknowledge Ben Caldwell's support in creating this exercise. I, TB, wish to also thank Helen Meek for her collaboration in using this exercise in a supervision course we taught together.

Summary

Supervisors and trainers use a wide variety of methods to train therapists to become culturally competent. Multiple methods are utilized to promote cultural awareness and sensitivity. These methods include case consultation, audiotapes, videotapes, live supervision, role-playing, and a variety of experiential exercises. From our perspective, experiential teaching and learning is the hallmark of training and supervision designed to promote cultural sensitivity. The exercises in this chapter provide opportunities for personal exploration and for increasing awareness and sensitivity in working with people from various cultural backgrounds.

PART IV

Tactics for Negotiating Difficult Dialogues in Supervision and Training

16

POLITICALLY INCORRECT

Sense and sensibilities for culturally astute supervision and training

Soh-Leong Lim, PhD, and Ben K. Lim, PhD

We are two overseas born Chinese (*huayi* 华艺) whose Fujianese ancestors migrated to the South Seas (*Nanyang* 南洋) and who have now made the United States our home. Our first-generation immigrant grandparents/parents fled China to the Malay peninsula (*Tanah Melayu*, now Malaysia) during periods of unrest in China. As second-generation (Ben) and third-generation (Soh-Leong) Malaysians, we were born into a pluralistic cultural milieu of British colonial rule. Growing up, we heard stories from our parents about the brutality of the Japanese who briefly occupied our country. As young children, we also remember the celebration of *Merdeka* (independence) when we gained independence from Britain on August 31, 1957. Until recently, Malaysians, whether Malays, Chinese, Indians, Indigenous, or others, lived in relative harmony with each other. We are trilingual—speaking Fujianese with our parents, English with our peers and siblings, and Malay in all governmental affairs, school, and work.

In 1995, we left Malaysia to pursue our PhDs in Marital and Family Therapy at Texas Tech University, Lubbock, Texas. September 11, 2001, was an important event in our family life. Our initial plan to return home after we completed our studies changed. In the aftermath of 9/11, with Malaysia implicated in the harboring of terrorists, travel was complicated. As a couple, we decided to stay together as a family unit, rather than leave the United States while our children stayed behind to complete their studies. Since we left Malaysia, there had also been a resurgence of Malay nationalism and increasing Islamization in our homeland. Today, there are racial tensions and a significant brain drain, as ethnic minorities feel pushed out by policies that favor the dominant Malays. The local minority population calls this *kulitfication*. *Kulit* is *skin* in Malay. *Kulitfication*, a wordplay of *qualification*, means one's skin color determines access to jobs, promotions, etc., with the Malays being privileged by virtue of their dominant Malay-Muslim culture. Just as there are racial tensions in the United States, there are also fragile race relations in Malaysia. In the United States, there is White privilege; in Malaysia, there is Malay-Muslim privilege. Oppression comes in different colors and different religious ideologies. In our experience, it can come in the form of White bias (British colonization), yellow brutality (Japanese occupation), and brown Malay-Muslim supremacy (*pertuanan Melayu*).

Privilege that comes with being people of color

After 20 years in the United States, we now describe ourselves as Malaysian Chinese Americans. We pride ourselves in our ethnic Chinese cultural heritage that emphasizes education, hard work, frugality, and filial piety. In the United States, we acquired a new identity: *people of color*. This label interestingly gives us power to call things as they are without fear, especially in training and supervising our students. On one occasion, a Latino student was unhappy with my (Soh-Leong) feedback in a supervision context. He called me a *racist*. As a *person of color* who has endured oppressions in different immigrant contexts, this label did not faze me. This is important because not being fazed means I am able to be clearheaded to hear the student out and to consider where I may have wronged him. I was able to listen non-reactively to the student and be open to his feedback. As supervisors, we are aware that we can more readily exercise our power because we do not fear the "racist" label. This is not to say that people of color cannot be racist in their actions; however, within the context of a dominant White culture, people of color have the unique privilege of calling out things as they are in ways that Whites may not have. I see this also in trainee interactions. On one occasion, students were having a heated conversation on immigration. A Guatemalan student went on a tirade against the United States. Calmly, a Colombian American student said, "If people are not happy with this country, they don't have to migrate here." The class could accept these words because it came from this particular student, who was an immigrant herself and a person of color. A White person would not have been able to say this without being perceived as bigoted. The sociocultural location of a person matters; there are privileges that come with being a person of color. We use our privilege for *fear-less* supervision even though it rides on a question-begging, socially constructed identity label: *people of color.*

Political correctness: An antithesis to authenticity and transformative growth

In our observation, political correctness, while necessary in some contexts, has stilted, or worse, robbed the clinical context of many potentially transformative supervisor-supervisee conversations. We care about meaningful learning, and in the service of such learning, we are not afraid to be politically incorrect. We let students know where we are coming from so that we are all on the same page with regard to our quest for learning. Here are some useful pointers for authentic fearless conversations.

- *We recognize Microaggression's ever-lurking presence, and when she cries foul, we do not get all bent out of shape*. Sometimes, students are afraid to ask certain questions in the classroom. "Microaggression" (Sue, 2010) becomes an ever-present, oversensitive guest in our interactions, and, for fear of offending her, students tiptoe around her and make polite conversation. Isomorphically, this translates to timidity in our supervisees' conversations with their clients. Therapy becomes boring, tepid at best. When someone gets offended, which will inevitably happen, it provides a hotbed for transformative growth for both the offended and the offender. In one of my (Ben) multicultural class discussions on gender issues, the topic of intimate partner violence (IPV) came up. A female student, who had experienced IPV, was incensed when a male student asked a question that implied the reactive role of women in IPV. His seemingly naive question and her visibly strong reaction collided—and Microaggression announced her presence. As the instructor, I noted that it takes courage to ask such questions, which could also be in the minds of other fellow learners. I also affirmed the female student for speaking passionately from her lived experience. Because both students were real about where they each were in their journey, there was authenticity in their interaction. Transformative growth happens when questions that arise in the hearts of our trainees can be asked without fear. Some questions that are genuine in the inquirer's mind may come across as microaggressions to others. We accept that this is inevitable and we work with it when it happens.
- *We relegate Oughts and Shoulds outside the circle of our conversations*. Our students come with expectations. Often they have strong ideas on what their peers ought to be or think to

be in a MFT multicultural program. Those who are vocal and passionate can unwittingly set up a learning atmosphere that is hostile or fearful. When students pick up on the Oughts and Shoulds, they freeze and learn to talk the talk of political correctness to avoid being judged. There is no conviction in the talk. It is hollow. There is no authenticity, merely a polite, sickly facade. Multicultural sensitivity involves being able to be in conversation with those who are vastly different from us. This does not mean only differences in gender, religion, race, ethnicity, age, sexual orientation, economic status, education, and disabilities—the varied dimensions covered in any multicultural class—it also applies to so-called levels of self or other appraised "multicultural competence." I (Soh-Leong) had a student who graduated in ethnic studies from a prestigious university and who walked, talked, and breathed critical race theory. While she was a brilliant student, she wanted nothing to do with those with sensibilities other than critical race theory. My challenge to her was to develop her multicultural competence to include being able to sit with those whose perspectives are different from hers, that is, those whom she thinks are so "multiculturally incompetent" as to not embrace critical race theory. What good is it that a trainee is brilliant but cannot bridge the gap between her and the other? A multicultural program necessarily reflects a diversity of views on any given issue, and we are not afraid of differences in opinion. In one of our cohorts, there was a student who was married to a border-patrol husband. Some students could not tolerate her because they saw her as antithetical to their social justice sensibilities. It is precisely these jarring discomforts that make for needed conversations. We train our students to be able to sit and have conversations with those who are different.

- *We inculcate in students the Yin and Yang (南洋) of thinking in complex issues.* When emotionally difficult issues are discussed, trainees tend to swing toward rigid and polarized thinking. In the issue of undocumented immigration, for instance, some students are passionate advocates of immigrants' rights and deem those who dare raise questions as bigoted and racist. Prefacing such potentially polarizing conversations with *both/and* thinking (Lao Tze's middle path, 中道) gives students a road map where they are more able to tolerate differing viewpoints. In legal and ethical issues for MFTs, we talk of principle and virtue ethics. These concepts are most helpful in discussing sensitive issues like immigration. Students who advocate for undocumented immigrants have valid points. On our conceptual road map, they have positioned themselves on the side of virtue ethics. They feel compassion for the plight of those who risk crossing the border for a better future. Students who question what they see as illegal immigration also have valid viewpoints. They raise their questions from the perspective of principle ethics. They see that the laws of the land must be upheld and respected. Both compassion for the undocumented and respect for the sovereignty of the nation are important. Like yin (南) and yang (洋), *both* are valid. The answer lies somewhere between, in flux, depending on the context. We validate students who are compassionate advocates of undocumented immigrants *and* we also validate students who have concerns about respecting the laws of our country, without which there could be chaos. Those who raise valid questions have their voices respected. They are not bigots.

- *We do not romanticize culture—each culture has its pride and shame issues, and we acknowledge them without fear or favor.* Culture is not our god, to be glorified and put on a pedestal. There are limits to multiculturalism (Lim & Lim, 2009). Culture has both blessings and curses. It is a blessing when it serves as the glue or provides the platform to bring people together in traditions that have shared meaning and purpose; it is a curse when it oppresses. Culture can indeed be oppressive. I (Soh-Leong) shared with my students how as a teenager, I was given the odious task of washing my grandmother's bound feet. The practice of foot-binding (纏足) was part of Chinese culture for approximately 1000 years. Culture failed women when little girls' feet were bound for the warped cultural ideal of *lotus* feet (步步生蓮), the epitome of feminine beauty being three inches of contorted feet encased in outwardly pretty embroidered shoes. In our multicultural classes, some tend to romanticize cultures, especially indigenous or Eastern ones; however, all cultures have their prides and shames. Being able to talk of culture in this manner brings about more authentic dialogues. When we acknowledge the questionable parts of culture, we are not being racist. We are discerning. We are advocates of justice, standing on the side of those who are oppressed by some aspects of their cultures.

- *We each have our values, and it is important to know how they segue with the values of others*. Multicultural sensitivity does not mean disowning one's values. When we converse with someone who has different values, we listen with an open mind. We understand and validate the other without necessarily agreeing. In our classes, students work on group projects with communities underserved in mental health. Each group forms a student-community collaborative panel where the voice of the community is heard and represented. Over the years, students have worked with the homeless; undocumented immigrants; the transgender community; refugees; the military; the polyamorous community; the BDSM (bondage, dominance, sado-masochism) community, and so on. For instance, with the polyamorous community as represented on one panel, I (Soh Leong) encouraged my students to listen with an open mind and be willing to examine their own values and assumptions on love, commitment, and attachment. Our premise is that even if trainees continue to hold on to their earlier convictions, they would be in a place of greater understanding and compassion after listening to the stories and lived experiences of the other.

- *As supervisor, we lead by example*. We believe that as supervisors, we can better manage strong emotions and heightened anxiety arising from difficult conversations when we are diligent in attending to our own self-of-therapist and family-of-origin work. We seek to lead by example. In our classes, we often first share our cultural genograms with our students before we ask them to share theirs. We want them to be unafraid to own their stories, whether they are considered pride or shame, or politically correct or not. In our cultural genogram presentations, we tell our lived stories. We share our ethnic and racial backgrounds as well as our migration story over four generations. We also share our pride and shame issues. A critical part of our cultural genogram is the role of religion and spirituality in our family stories. For both of us, faith is central to our cultural identity. This stems from our spiritual encounter as children growing up in Asia. As a 10-year-old (Ben) and as a 13-year-old (Soh-Leong), we each, in our own separate hometowns on opposite coasts of the Malay Peninsula, made a life-changing profession of faith after hearing/reading the gospel. Our families were livid and punished us; but our faith became more real in the face of suffering. For me (Ben), my father beat me up and threatened to disown me. Our faith profession was countercultural and politically incorrect in each of our ancestor-worshipping homes and in Muslim Malaysia. It was a shame issue in each of our families. This was particularly so given that my (Ben) father was the head of the Lim's Clan ancestral temple. Over time, however, many of our family members, including our parents, had their conversion experiences. What was once a shame issue became an important organizing principle in our families. My (Soh-Leong) father's late-life conversion also resulted in his being healed from chronic alcoholism, which his ten children and wife had to endure over a total period of 45 years. There were no AA or Al-Anon meetings in the town I grew up in. Neither was there any talk therapy to aid us. In desperation, my father reached out to a neighborhood Bible study group for help. That night, through the laying on of hands and prayer, my father was healed of his chronic alcoholism. In the spiritual worldview, it was a miracle. In mental health nomenclature, it was alternative healing at its best. We tell our lived stories to our students as they embark on their own cultural genogram journey. The shame issues of either alcoholism or persecution are painful, but they encourage students to acknowledge their own family stories. We tell our stories as a matter of personal lived history. Our central identity as Christians resonates with some but disconcerts others. Every student is encouraged to listen to their own reactions as they listen to our stories. The emotions that arise in each of their hearts are important. They tell each student about their own stories, of the way they have been hurt or encouraged, of their own faith journeys or lack thereof. Spirituality is an important dimension in culturally astute therapy. It is one of the difficult issues we have conversations on as a class. With these fearless conversations, we train our students to be unafraid to broach issues of spirituality or any other difficult issues in their work with clients.

- ***We accept each student where they are in their multifaceted life journey.*** Our belief is that no one person, supervisor or supervisee, is culturally competent on *all* given dimensions of multiculturalism. This understanding helps students to have realistic appraisals of themselves and greater acceptance of the other in context. It reduces judgmental attitudes, which drive students to feel the need to *appear* competent all the time.

In our case, we grew up with South Indians, Chinese of many dialects, Malays, and Eurasians, and with people of diverse spiritual practices—Hindus, Muslims, Sikhs, Buddhists, Taoists, ancestral worshippers, Animists, and so on. By virtue of our childhood environment, we were given a heritage of greater "competence" in the multicultural dimensions of race, ethnicity, and spirituality. We also grew up in multigenerational households with a high respect for age. We practiced filial piety (*xiao shun* 孝順) as another multicultural heritage. However, within our Malaysian context, sexuality was not our multicultural heritage of competence. Growing up, issues of sexual orientation, eroticism, sex, love, and affection, were barely discussed. We began our MFT training as international students "without having met" a gay man or lesbian in Malaysia. More accurately, we may have but were not cognizant of having encountered a gay man or lesbian, as it was not safe to be out in Muslim Malaysia. We had a steep learning curve on the multicultural dimension of sexuality when we first started our MFT programs in the United States. We continue to learn and grow through openness to listening to LGBTs' (lesbian, gay, bisexual, transgender) lived experiences and to give feedback on any blind spots that we may have. In sharing this example with our students, we normalize our process of multicultural development on a multidimensional level. We emphasize that there is no shame in acknowledging that we each come with areas of needed growth because of the context we each grew up in. Our growth is measured from where we first started and not in comparison with each other. I (Soh-Leong) saw the impact of laying down this premise for a better learning environment in my class. I had a gay student who felt disturbed that some of his peers did not know what he sees as "obvious" LGBT knowledge. When he grasped the concept of multicultural heritages and different starting points, he felt more comfortable and accepting of each trainee's LGBT awareness and knowledge levels. Further, he realized that while he was competent in LGBT issues, he was "behind" in other multicultural dimensions, particularly on issues of race and ethnicity. This was because he grew up in a homogeneous White culture in Europe. This realization of differing heritages and starting points led him to accept those who were not as yet on the same page as he was on LGBT advocacy. He was also humbled to know that he had a lot to learn from others on other multicultural dimensions. Each trainee has an area of cultural strength—a gift to offer the other. This is significant. An exercise we do to symbolize this is to have students greet each other in turn at the beginning and end of the semester with these solemn words: "Thank you for being my teacher on my way to become a multicultural therapist." This cultural humility (Tervalon & Murray-Garcia, 1998) must undergird the quest for cultural astuteness.

Conclusion

Growth in multicultural astuteness cannot be coerced, neither can it be hurried. If coerced or hurried, the outcome is often hollow. We respect transformative learning enough to come alongside each trainee, whatever the stage of their development is, and give them permission to show up authentically on the different dimensions of multiculturalism. Authentic learning and political correctness are not good bedfellows. We seek to have genuine multicultural dialogues with good therapeutic sense and sensibilities. Such interactions, however, carry much risk and often pain. In our teaching and supervision, we seek to facilitate the creation of a safe learning environment where our supervisees may raise any questions or voice any doubts or ambivalence that is in their hearts and minds. The classroom is an ideal place for messy and difficult conversations. When our trainees can stay with such conversations, they would have done well in the service of their clients. Our trainees become effective therapists because they do not skirt around difficult issues with their clients. The courage inherent in the supervisory triadic process is isomorphically transformative.

References

Lim, B., & Lim, S. (2009). Cultural competency: A transformative developmental journey. *American Association for Marriage and Family Therapy: California Division News, 17*(1), 1–3.

Sue, D. W. (2010). *Microaggressions in everyday life: Race, gender, and sexual orientation.* Hoboken, NJ: Wiley.

Tervalon, M., & Murray-García, J. (1998). Cultural humility versus cultural competence: A critical distinction in defining physician training outcomes in multicultural education. *Journal of Health Care for the Poor Underserved, 9*(2), 117–125. doi: 10.1353/hpu.2010.0233.

17

DIALOGUES ABOUT POWER, PRIVILEGE, AND DIFFERENCE

Toby Bobes, PhD

My core perspectives about teaching, diversity, and social justice have evolved over 36 years as a therapist, supervisor, teacher, and author. My personal experiences and cultural history inform the principles, practices, biases, and assumptions of my personal and professional life. I am continually aware of the multiple contextual influences that shape my interactions. I am a white, privileged, Jewish, heterosexual, married woman. I reflect upon how these aspects of my cultural identity influence my interactions when working with those who are culturally different from myself. Becoming culturally competent requires educators to develop an awareness of their cultural identities and to understand how aspects of their identities impact those with whom they work.

I invite you to think along with me to consider the importance of the connections between your personal cultural context and the principles and practices that influence your professional work today. In this chapter, I will introduce this perspective personally by sharing some of my early history and how cultural experiences informed my belief systems about race, gender, privilege, and difference. I am ever vigilant about these *oppressive remnants*[1] from my history that continually challenge me to give voice and to confront power inequities and injustices when I sense them, experience them, and see them. These cultural experiences contribute significantly to understanding my social location and use of self, and to facilitating culturally sensitive dialogues.

Vivid recollections of my cultural history: Lessons learned

All aspects of my cultural identity and history contribute to who I am today. I am a white privileged woman from the Deep South, Atlanta, Georgia. I grew up in a middle-class family. My white privilege and gender inequality were never acknowledged. The only aspect of my identity that was acknowledged was my Jewish religion. I was part of society's silence in keeping issues about difference invisible and unspoken—especially race and gender. Many of my experiences and images are emotionally palpable even today. As I write about this, a profound sense of shame wells up. I recall lunch counters for "Whites" and lunch counters for "Coloreds." I recall my discomfort as a young girl sitting in the front of the bus and African Americans sitting in the back. I recall public restrooms for "Whites" and restrooms for "Coloreds." Even the emergency rooms at local hospitals were racially segregated. Everywhere I turned, this dehumanization process was embedded in behaviors, interactions, language, customs, schools, public facilities, and in every aspect of our culture.

These pivotal life events defined my childhood meaning-making and belief systems and remain as vivid today as they were when I first encountered them. My early beliefs and perceptions about race and gender inequality were continually reinforced by everyone around me. We were all contributors to the unspoken invisible web of racism. These events planted the seeds for my eventual commitment to social justice and to expanding dialogues so that inclusivity becomes more real in our everyday practices of therapy, supervision, and training.

I learned early on to silence my voice to the discomfort and uneasiness I felt in witnessing and experiencing social oppressions. It has only been in recent years that I have begun to put words to my experiences of inequalities. This enabled me to open up dialogues with colleagues and friends about race, gender, privilege, and power. Most importantly, I am developing the courage to move outside my usual comfort zone so that I can raise these topics in various learning contexts.

Acknowledging my whiteness

Acknowledging my whiteness has been a real eye-opener for me. It is both a painful and jarring experience to realize that I have been in an exploitative position as beneficiary to victims of oppression. My reflexive stance of silence at the lunch counter or on the bus was a way to use victims, themselves entrapped in the invisible web of racism, to relieve my tension and anxiety. Elaine Pinderhughes (2008, p. 133) describes this process:

> When the stories of African Americans, descendants of those who were entrapped in slavery and its destructive aftermath, are listened to by those who have been "beneficiaries," the victims will really feel heard. And those who are beneficiaries must also tell their stories, examining how and why they may have been trapped in exploitative positions as beneficiaries, vulnerable to using the victims to relieve tension and reduce anxiety for themselves.

It is only when I connect to my cultural history and tell my story responsibly that I will be able to really listen and understand the lived experiences of those with whom I work. In order to authentically facilitate cross-racial and same-racial interactions in supervision and training, it is essential to acknowledge my whiteness as well as all the dimensions of my cultural being. Holding a mirror up to whiteness is critical for effective cross-racial conversations (Watson, 2016).

It is inevitable that my unconscious biases will create blind spots that emerge despite my continuing vigilance. I have found that race- and gender-based conversations in supervision and in the classroom frequently become emotionally charged and provide the greatest challenge for me with respect to moving beyond my comfort zone. Over time I have worked on developing "thick skin" by staying in difficult conversations even beyond the point where it feels comfortable to do so. Developing thick skin is a critical task of the privileged (Hardy, 2016).

I realize now that I kept my whiteness invisible to protect myself from exposure as an oppressor, in fact, as a beneficiary to victims of oppression. My cultural context has, indeed, shaped my lessons learned.

The use of self as a cultural being

The use of self as a cultural being is at the heart of enhancing cultural sensitivity in supervision and training. I have found that through cultural sharing, or telling my own story, trainees become more engaged in the conversation. They often follow my comments with their own stories. Group members experience increased connection as they begin to feel heard and understood by each other. When we honor our trainees' cultural stories, we can more readily connect to their lived experiences and more effectively validate them.

The aspects of my cultural being that I find continually challenging are being white and being privileged. I have a responsibility to be on the lookout for the effects of my privilege upon those with whom I work. As Karl Tomm says when he writes of his own privilege, "I need to…seek to see the effects of my privilege through the eyes of those who are less advantaged. This enables the awareness I need to become more coherent in promoting social justice" (Tomm, 2003, p. 31). I need to be continually mindful of my privilege, power, biases, and assumptions that are inherited from my conditioning (Sue, 2010). The effects of my white privilege are invisible, elusive, and pervasive experiences of unearned advantage (McIntosh, 2008). Hardy and McGoldrick (2008) write about the effects of our privilege upon others:

> The more privilege we have, the harder it is to think about how our own actions have affected others with less privilege or to understand the rage of powerlessness. We take our privilege for granted—our right to safety; to acknowledgement; to being heard, treated fairly, and taken care of; our right to take up available time, space, and resources; and so on. (p. 456)

I recognize that some aspects of my use of power and privilege may remain hidden and invisible due to inevitable blind spots. As a supervisor and trainer, the decisions I make; what I choose to pay attention to; the topics I emphasize, include, or exclude in conversations; and whose experiences I may overlook are all examples of blind spots that are shaped by biases, attitudes, and life experiences. I invite group members into the conversation during our work together to speak about how privilege, power, and difference affect relationships at every level of the system. Natalie Porter (2014) writes about the nuanced aspects of power and privilege in the supervisory relationship. Explicitly naming and addressing power relations is a core competency in supervision and training.

I recall an incident in a class I was teaching when a student pointed out that I had failed to validate her experience as an African American woman during an exercise in which people were sharing stories about feeling "different from." I thanked her for her valuable feedback and candor. I also apologized for overlooking her experience. I later reflected upon this conversation in order to move toward a greater understanding of my failure to acknowledge the lived experience of this student. I found it very useful to consult with a trusted colleague to expand upon my self-reflective process. The critical lesson learned is that identifying and managing emotional triggers is often facilitated by increased knowledge of self, ongoing self-reflection, and self-interrogation (Hardy, 2016).

Supervision vignette

In the following vignette, I, as the supervisor, address an intense encounter in group supervision. This group of six supervisees has been working together for 8 months and is comprised of two white women, two Latina women, one African American man, and one white man.

Dan, who is white, briefly presents to the group his recent experiences as therapist with Julio and Carmen, a Latino couple he has been working with in weekly sessions for the past six weeks.

Following Dan's presentation, Rosa, a Latina supervisee, blurts out, "Dan, I don't like the way you are working with this couple. You failed to even ask them about their immigration experience. This is such a central part of a Latino's life."

Dan angrily replies, "Here we go again. Rosa, you make such a big deal about including the immigration experience. I don't see why you are so emotional about this!"

I experience the charged atmosphere in the room. I note the tears on Rosa's face and Dan's distant facial expression. The group appears to be stunned by this interchange. Although they had been working together for a number of months, they had not previously encountered a difficult dialogue. I begin a conversation with Rosa and Dan. "I can hear the passion in each of your voices. I wonder if you, Rosa, can start by telling me what you are experiencing?" Rosa tearfully replies, "I just feel so misunderstood. Dan's comments are a wipeout of me and of the importance of my history!" I turned to Dan. "What are you feeling, Dan, as you hear Rosa speak about her experience? Do you have a sense of what she is saying?"

Dan says, "I don't really get it. I see that Rosa is crying, and I hear her anger. But I really don't understand why she is so emotional!"

Rosa and Dan appear to be at an impasse. I turn to the group and ask, "What are your views of this interchange between Rosa and Dan?" I invite other group members to speak about what is going on in order to bring everyone into the conversation.

Connie speaks first. "I had a big reaction when I heard Dan accuse Rosa of being so emotional. Whenever I hear a woman being labeled too emotional, it comes across as a sexist put-down."

Jerry says, "I agree with Connie about the point she makes regarding labeling. I believe that labels devalue a person. I have been called an angry black man just because I voiced a strong opinion. It's not fair!"

Mary joins the conversation. "I have felt misunderstood as a Latina woman many times so I identify strongly with Rosa. Some people think a woman's opinion just doesn't count. I wonder if Dan realizes the impact of his words."

Bernice adds, "As a woman, I relate to what Connie and Mary said. And it's uncomfortable for me to sit with the intense emotions I feel now. I can see that Dan is confused, but his choice of words has put him in a corner."

I address the group. "I appreciate that all of you are so open and willing to share your experiences with each other. It takes courage to sit with intense emotions. Now I would like to ask Rosa and Dan about their reactions to our comments." By now, the dialogue appeared to have diffused the tension in the room. Rosa and Dan commented that they felt heard by the group. Dan acknowledged that he came across as harsh, and the feedback helped him to begin to look at parts of himself that he previously had not seen.

I speak to the group. "As a group, we have just experienced a conversation in which strong feelings were voiced, and yet we all stayed with the intensity in the room. I appreciate your openness and courage during the difficult moments of our discussion. We can only move toward greater understanding of others when we are willing to take the risks involved in respectfully listening to different viewpoints." In a subsequent supervision session, Rosa told her story of her family's immigration experiences and why this personal history is so important to her. Rosa's story enabled Dan to experience her differently and softened his responses. Cultural storytelling softens the images people hold of each other and enables them to handle their differences and find common ground (Arora, 2016).

Later in the supervisory process, I encouraged Dan to look at the three levels of privilege he holds: as a man, as a white person, and as a citizen. Dan had been oblivious to his status as a US-born citizen and as a white privileged male. It was difficult for Dan to hear this feedback. He felt vulnerable and exposed. He wondered aloud what judgments we had about him. I took the lead and shared my story of vulnerability in acknowledging my whiteness and other dimensions of privilege that I hold. I invited group members to share their stories and reflect upon how power, privilege, and subjugation impact their lives and roles as therapists. This conversation provided an opportunity for supervisees to deepen their examination of the privileged and subjugated aspects of their identities and social locations. This was a first step for Dan in becoming accountable for his privilege.

A supervisor's culturally based triggers

It is our responsibility as supervisors to work on our personal issues that are triggered in the supervision relationship and that arise from the very first moment of contact (Watson, 2016).

In the above vignette, I became emotionally triggered the moment that Dan made his accusatory remarks to Rosa. I resonated deeply with Rosa's comment that she felt that Dan wiped out the importance of her and her history. I took a protective stance toward Rosa and to the other Latina woman in the room. My compassion for the Latina women in the group connected emotionally to my history and experience of witnessing subjugation and oppression. I am no longer the powerless young girl witnessing injustices. I continually struggle with these oppressive remnants from my cultural history. I still get caught up in the invisible web of racism and gender inequalities that persist today. The vivid recollections of my cultural history are ever-present reminders to me to actively give voice to injustices when I sense them, experience them, and see them.

Facilitating group interactions

I modeled cultural sensitivity as I empathically resonated with group members. I responded to Rosa and Dan's interaction by asking each of them about their experiences rather than focusing upon the content alone. I further facilitated the emotionally charged conversation by inviting other group members to speak about their reactions.[2] Throughout the conversation, I demonstrated my curiosity by listening respectfully to each supervisee's point of view. I listened for the possible meanings and struggles of what was being said. I was aware that in listening to group members' reactions, there were a number of comments that reflected stories of devaluation and experiences of oppression. I validated and affirmed these stories and experiences. The tension and discomfort were diffused as I responded to the emotions and reactions of each person in the room. It has been my experience that group members often join the process by validating each other.

The supervisor bears the primary responsibility for working through emotional discomfort when it inevitably arises during conversations about multicultural differences. This is an essential core competence for supervisors and trainers. These points are made by Christiansen et al. (2011, p. 109): "Dealing with cultural differences in supervision can be awkward and difficult…and can lead to misunderstanding and hurt feelings."

These conversations

> do require that supervisors and therapists to have the ability to sit with the discomfort of these feelings and to continue to be open and engaged in the supervision process by working through the discomfort…The primary responsibility for both bearing and diffusing the anxiety belongs to the supervisor (p. 118).

Model identification of social location[3]

I am privileged due to my being white, my educational background, and my power and influence as a supervisor and trainer. These aspects of my privilege and identity, both personal and professional, are disclosed at the initial supervision or training session. I invite a conversation about social location:

> I am a white, privileged, Jewish woman, heterosexual, married for 53 years, mother of three grown children, and grandmother of four. I was raised in Atlanta, Georgia. I really want this to be an open process between us so I invite you to talk about how the similarities and differences between us and how our mix of experiences may affect our work together.

I have found that trainees welcome this conversation at the initial session. Conversations become more collaborative and transparent when trainers and trainees share relevant aspects of their cultural identities. Group members of diverse backgrounds want to know where their supervisor stands with respect to social location (Porter, 2014). Natalie Porter points out the importance of this initial conversation with students of diverse backgrounds: "My addressing these issues is one way of addressing the power dynamics between us. Even students with greater social privilege appear to welcome this initial conversation" (p. 70).

My cultural context has profoundly shaped my lessons learned. The following are essential strategies that I utilize as a supervisor and trainer.

Strategies for infusing cultural differences into supervision and training dialogues

The personal experience of difference is essential to enhancing cultural sensitivity. Exploring one's attitudes about difference evokes a wide range of emotional responses and visceral reactions to the experience of difference. The ethical guidelines of our profession require that we are aware and sensitive to how one's own cultural identities, values, and beliefs affect therapeutic and supervision processes. Therefore, we need to increase awareness of our attitudes toward difference. Specifically, we need to increase sensitivity to contextual variables such as gender, race, class, sexual orientation, ethnicity, and so on. "The Difference Exercise" in Chapter 15 enhances sensitivity to cultural differences with an emphasis upon experiential learning about one's personal response to difference.

It is the responsibility of supervisors and trainers to open up conversations about cultural differences at the beginning and throughout supervision and training experiences. Whether supervisor, trainer, or learner, the primary objective is to develop "a more comprehensive view of themselves and others as cultural beings" (Hardy & McGoldrick, 2008, p. 454).

Supervisors and trainers have had insufficient education and training in addressing multicultural issues, particularly in situations that are unfamiliar and move us beyond our comfort zones (Sue, 2010; Porter, 2014; Laszloffy & Habekost, 2010). We must remain alert to our own discomforts and emotional responses that inevitably arise when addressing cultural differences. Sue (2010) writes:

> Because very few teachers can have experiences with all groups who differ from them in worldviews, they will always feel discomfort and confusion when different diversity/multicultural issues arise. These feelings are natural and should not be avoided; rather making sense of them is important. Being able to monitor them and infer meaning to feelings and emotional reactions and those of students are important in dialogues. (p. 252)

It is often helpful to turn to colleagues for support and consultation. In addition, supervisors and trainers may benefit from professional support groups in which concerns and experiences are shared. When I have felt "professionally lonely," I have found it both comforting and enlightening to know that colleagues share similar concerns.

In summary, the following strategies will equip supervisors and trainers to take a proactive role in facilitating culturally sensitive dialogues:

- **Introduce yourself culturally.** The use of self through cultural sharing is a powerful way to bring differences into the conversation, create safety, and connect to trainees' lived experiences. One way of inviting cultural sharing that I have found useful is to ask group members to "describe something you like most about your cultural background and something you find hardest to deal with" (Hardy & McGoldrick, 2008, p. 454). I share my own experience first.
- **Model identification of social location.** The trainer invites a conversation with trainees about social location and takes the lead by sharing locations he or she occupies. Trainers and

trainees dialogue about similarities and differences in their key identities such as race, gender, class, sexual orientation, and how these intersecting identities influence therapy, supervision, and training (Watts Jones, 2010). Modeling and transparency promote a climate of safety and risk-taking in dialogues about dimensions of diversity.

- **Identify and address culturally based triggers.** It is essential that supervisors and trainers identify and address culturally based triggers when they arise. Monitoring responses and making sense of one's feelings and those of trainees are important to facilitate learning (Sue, 2010).
- **Engage in ongoing self-reflection throughout the learning experience.** Cultural sensitivity is enhanced as supervisors, trainers, and trainees practice self-reflection. This "looking-within process" enables us to expand on knowledge of self to include a deeper understanding of what happens to/with one's cultural self as it interacts with the cultural selves of others (Hardy, 2016).
- **Embrace a stance of cultural humility.** Cultural competence is not just about acquiring knowledge. It is also about having the humility to say what we do not know. This means a lifelong commitment to self-reflection and self-critique as well as to redressing power imbalances (Tervalon & Murray-Garcia, 1998). Matthew Mock defines cultural humility: having the ability to acknowledge that "we can never truly know another person, her or his experiences, lives, and legacies, unless we are open to acknowledging what we do not know" (2008, p. 432). By embracing a stance of cultural humility, supervisors, trainers, and trainees demonstrate authenticity, caring, and a genuine curiosity and desire to expand understanding of the lived experiences of those with whom they work. Humility and transparency are requisite skills for promoting cultural sensitivity.
- **Promote cultural sensitivity through experiential learning.** Supervisors and trainers take a proactive role in creating educational experiences that promote cultural sensitivity. Exercises that focus upon activating the self of the trainer and self of the trainee are essential to learning deeply about ourselves.

Supervisors and trainers embrace a stance of compassion, humility, and curiosity in facilitating culturally sensitive dialogues. They demonstrate the ability to self-reflect during intense conversations and have an unrelenting commitment to remain curious—not just about "the other" but also about one's own perceptions, feelings, and reactions (Hardy, 2016).

Personal reflections

It is truly humbling to acknowledge that my blind spots, which reflect unconscious bias, will inevitably emerge. However, expressions of unconscious bias may lead to valuable teaching moments. On those occasions when I failed to recognize and validate an emotional experience of a trainee, and I later acknowledged my omission, subsequent conversations often led to repair and a larger group discussion about difference. Ongoing self-reflection and making meaning of my own personal emotional responses have been the key to learning from dialogues about difference.

As supervisors, trainers, and trainees, we reach deep within ourselves and our own humanity to more meaningfully connect and engage with those with whom we work (Aponte & Carlsen, 2009). It is through these meaningful connections that hope and change emerge. Through this process of learning deeply about ourselves and our own identities, we are enabled to more authentically affirm others' identities[4] and lived experiences.

Notes

1 John Lawless used the term *oppressive remnants* in the context of referencing his cultural history (2008, p. 195).
2 Derald Wing Sue discusses what educators must do for successful facilitation of difficult dialog. The reader is referred to pages 250–254 for suggestions about effective facilitation (Sue, 2010).
3 Monica McGoldrick describes a Social Location Exercise in which "Trainers model identification of their social location…to encourage trainees to discuss their own social locations" (Hardy and McGoldrick, 2008, p. 455).
4 B. Tatum writes about the central role of teachers in affirming identity: "Our ability to engage our students in the kind of education they need, and that our society requires, depends on this foundational concept from which all else can flow" (2007, p. 23).

References

Anderson, H. (1997). *Conversation, language, and possibilities: A postmodern approach to therapy.* New York, NY: Basic Books.

Aponte, H. J., & Carlsen, J. C. (2009). An instrument for person-of-the-therapist supervision. *Journal of Marital and Family Therapy, 35*(4), 395–405.

Arora, K. (2016). Expanding the human spirit: Pathway to promoting cultural sensitivity. In K. V. Hardy & T. Bobes (Eds.), *Culturally sensitive supervision and training: Diverse perspectives and practical applications* (pp. 94–100). New York, NY: Routledge.

Bermudez, J. M. (2011). Supervising multi-lingual/multi-cultural therapists in training: What do we need to know? *Family Therapy Magazine, 10*(6), 44–45.

Campbell, J. M. (2006). *Essentials of Clinical Supervision.* Hoboken, NJ: Wiley.

Christiansen, A. T., Thomas, V., Kafescioglu, N. et al. (2011). Multicultural supervision: Lessons learned about an ongoing struggle. *Journal of Marital and Family Therapy, 37*(1), 109–119.

Hardy, K. V. (2016). Towards the development of a multicultural relational perspective in training and supervision. In K. V. Hardy & T. Bobes (Eds.), *Culturally sensitive supervision and training: Diverse perspectives and practical applications* (pp. 3–10). New York, NY: Routledge.

Hardy, K. V., & McGoldrick, M. (2008). Re-visioning training. In M. McGoldrick & K. Hardy (Eds.), *Re-visioning family therapy: Race, culture, and gender in clinical practice* (2nd ed.) (pp. 442–460). New York, NY: Guilford Press.

Lappin, J., & Hardy, K. V. (2002). Keeping context in view: The heart of supervision. In T. C. Todd & C. L. Storm (Eds.), *The complete systemic supervisor: Context, philosophy, and pragmatics* (pp. 41–58). Lincoln, NE: Authors Choice.

Laszloffy, T., & Habekost, J. (2010). Using experiential tasks to enhance cultural sensitivity among MFT trainees. *Journal of Marital and Family Therapy, 36*(3), 333–346.

Lawless, J. J. (2008). Transforming a racist legacy. In M. McGoldrick & K. Hardy (Eds.), *Re-visioning family therapy: Race, culture, and gender in clinical practice* (2nd ed.) (pp. 191–196). New York, NY: Guilford Press.

McIntosh, P. (2008). White privilege and male privilege: A personal account. In M. McGoldrick & K. Hardy (Eds.), *Re-visioning family therapy: Race, culture, and gender in clinical practice* (2nd ed.) (pp. 238–249). New York, NY: Guilford Press.

Mock, M. R. (2008). Visioning social justice: Narratives of diversity, social location, and personal compassion. In M. McGoldrick & K. Hardy (Eds.), *Re-visioning family therapy: Race, culture, and gender in clinical practice* (2nd ed.) (pp. 425–441). New York, NY: Guilford Press.

Porter, N. (2014). Women, culture, and social justice: Supervision across the intersections. In C. A. Falender, E. P. Shafranske & C. J. Falicov (Eds.), *Multiculturalism and diversity in clinical supervision* (pp. 59–82). Washington, DC: American Psychological Association.

Sue, D. W. (2010). *Microaggressions in everyday life: Race, gender, and sexual orientation.* Hoboken, NJ: Wiley.

Tatum, B. D. (2007). *Can we talk about race? And other conversations in an era of school resegregation.* Boston, MA: Beacon Press.

Tervalon, M., & Murray-Garcia, J. (1998). Cultural humility versus cultural competence: A critical distinction in defining physician training outcomes in multicultural education. *Journal of Health Care for the Poor and Underserved, 9*(2), 117–123.

Tomm, K. (2003). Promoting social justice as an "ethical imperative." *Family Therapy Magazine, 2*(1), 30–31.

Turner, J., & Fine, M. (2002). Gender and supervision: Evolving debates. In T. C. Todd & C. L. Storm (Eds.), *The complete systemic supervisor: Context, philosophy, and pragmatics* (pp. 72–82). Lincoln, NE: Authors Choice.

Watson, M. (2016). Supervision in black and white: Navigating cross-racial interactions in the supervisory process. In K. V. Hardy & T. Bobes (Eds.), *Culturally sensitive supervision and training: Diverse perspectives and practical applications* (pp. 43–49). New York: Routledge.

Watts Jones, D. (2010). Location of self: Opening the door to dialogue on intersectionality in the therapy process. *Family Process, 49*, 405–420.

18

MASTERING CONTEXT TALK

Practical skills for effective engagement

Kenneth V. Hardy, PhD

Context talk is essentially any conversation or dialogue that involves talking about any dimension of diversity. Whether focused on religion, sexual orientation, class, race, or any of the hosts of other potential dimensions, context talk is always a daunting task. Regardless of the setting, the demographics of the participants involved, or the purpose of the conversation, context talk is seldom progressive, meaningful, or effectively executed. Earnest attempts to have fully engaged conversations are often fraught with conflict escalation, verbal withdrawal, emotional cutoff, or diversion and distraction.

Conflict escalation is a frequent and predictable outcome of most attempts to meaningfully engage in context talk. It is usually precipitated by one or several of the following: a) Participating partners usually preferring to talk *at* each other rather than *to* each other, b) one or both parties demonstrating an inability or unwillingness to listen to the other, or c) one or both participants passionately and righteously preaching or attempting to "teach" the other while also failing to listen. The inevitable conflict is often fueled and sustained by each party proclaiming to be "objective" and knowledgeable of not only their respective cultural context but also that of the person with whom they are engaged with. Voice escalation, blaming, and morally superior lecturing are common aspects of context-related conflict escalation.

Intense diversity-related conflict escalation is often preceded and/or followed by some form of emotional cutoff or disengagement. The fear and anxiety of context talk either getting out of control or creating discomfort and conflict often make it easy to avoid engagement altogether. Worries about saying something offensive or being offended or misunderstood are often chief reasons for avoiding conversations. Disengagement, whether achieved by cutoff, avoidance, or distraction, is a frequently used strategy for accomplishing the goal of not actively participating in context talk. Unfortunately, many diversity-related conversations are often quickly aborted by the lack of engagement, or they implode quickly as a result of unbridled anger. Neither of these responses renders positive and functional outcomes.

It is common for meaningful context talk to either never start in a productive and progressive way or to start and quickly spiral out of control in ways that are often hurtful, destructive, and regressive. Due to the emotionally charged nature of most attempts to engage in context talk, it is virtually impossible to do so without preparation, practice, and the acquisition of effective skills. As Hardy (2016) noted, effective conversations about race and other contextual variables require a commitment to "will" and "skill" by participants. The former refers to having the tenacity and fortitude to "stay in the conversation" even when it is potentially conflictual, stagnant, or sluggish. "Skill," on the other hand, refers to possessing the mastery to implement tactics and strategies that facilitate effective engagement and conversation. Skill also involves having a critical understanding of the importance of "timing," especially regarding when the use of a given tactic is indicated or contraindicated as dictated by circumstances. There are two interrelated skill sets that are essential to mastering context talk: *generic* and *specialized*.

Generic skills

Generic skills are those rudimentary communication skills that are needed to effectively communicate with others. Since these skills are typically difficult to effectively implement in non–emotionally charged conversations, they are certainly worth re-emphasizing in this chapter. Mastery of the following generic skills is a necessary precursor to developing the specialized skills needed to engage in effective context talk.

1. **Practice Deep Listening.** The ability to listen attentively and purposefully is critical to effective communication. Deep Listening refers to actively and acutely listening to the speaker with the expressed goal of understanding what s/he is saying (content) without interruption or distraction. The art and skill of Deep Listening positions the listener to avoid reliance on common but destructive interpersonal communication pitfalls such as interrupting, advice-giving, critiquing, negating, admonishing, or being preoccupied with preparing a rebuttal to discredit verbal claims advanced by the speaker. Deep Listening sounds simple when described in isolation; however, when emotional triggers become activated, all forms of listening are quickly abandoned.

2. **Providing skillful feedback.** Once Deep Listening has been exercised, the listener is in a much more empowered position to provide skillful feedback. The essence of this skill resides in the listener's ability to restate the message disclosed by the speaker while avoiding analysis, interpretation, accusation, or attribution. Skillful feedback is buttressed by the liberal use of "I messages" and acknowledgment of the sentiments, thoughts, and feelings expressed by the speaker. It also entails the listener-speaker freely and sensitively expressing beliefs, feelings, and/ or reactions to the information shared by the speaker-listener.

3. **Using "I messages."** These messages allow the speaker to take responsibility for personal thoughts and feelings. "I messages" eliminate the use of "You messages," which convey blame, criticism, abdication of personal responsibility, and personal attack, usually regardless of the intent of the speaker. When used liberally and consistently in conversations, I messages promote greater intensity and vulnerability in conversations and relationships.

4. **Attending to verbal and nonverbal communication.** This skill involves listening with *one's ears and eyes*. Communication is often powerfully transmitted through not only what is stated verbally but also through what is expressed nonverbally. Effective communication requires both the speaker and listener, in their respective alternating roles, to be mindful of what is being said verbally and what is potentially being conveyed nonverbally. It is important to be attentive to the *what* that is being expressed, the *how* it is stated, and the powerful messages that are communicated nonverbally by gestures, facial expressions, and so on.

5. **Developing refined meta-communication skills.** It is inevitable that efforts to communicate will get stifled, stagnant, or stuck. When this occurs, the effective use of meta-communication can be a potent lubricant for stuck communication. Meta-communication refers to the ability and willingness to "communicate about the communication." Meta-communication allows participants in a stuck conversation to pause, revisit, and examine how and why the communication is stalled. Rather than affix blame, effective meta-communication identifies how the

pattern of communication between two or more parties can be modified, purified, or adjusted to ensure a more desirable outcome. Demonstrating the ability to communicate about how one is communicating can be an effective catalyst to making movement in a stuck conversation (Bateson, 1972).

6. **Developing a communication style that imbues intimacy, intensity, congruency, transparency, and authenticity.** These five principles are central to effective communication and relationship development. "Intimacy," as the term is used in this context, refers to the ability to be vulnerable, non-defensive, and open in one's approach to communicating. Intensity, the counterpart to intimacy, is characterized by a willingness to engage in relational risk-taking and to "stretch" beyond one's normal and customary comfort zone. Congruency is measured by the degree of coherence that exists between thoughts and feelings as well as verbal and nonverbal messages. High levels of congruency make it easier to practice and master transparency, which is the demonstrated ability to show one's authentic self and the willingness to have one's authentic self be seen. And the fifth principle, authenticity, refers to the ability to embrace one's congruent thoughts and feelings and to express them in ways that honestly and genuinely convey one's character and soul. These five principles are highly interrelated and as such can really expedite or retard the development of each other. For example, if one communicates incongruently, it not only compromises one's sense of authenticity, but it also negatively affects the ability to be transparent. When transparency is disrupted, intimacy and intensity also can be as well.

7. **Effectively using expressions of acknowledgment.** It is not uncommon, especially during intense and acrimonious conversations, for *speakers to speak* and for *listeners to fail to listen*. In other words, under these circumstances there is incessant talking void of listening. Becoming adept at acknowledging what a speaker has stated is an important key to communicating effectively. Any feedback to a speaker that *acknowledges* that s/he has spoken and has been heard, and especially *understood*, plays a vital role in facilitating a more progressive and less antagonistic conversation. Expressing acknowledgment is a key element to developing the skill of providing skillful feedback.

8. **Responding therapeutically.** Verbal exchanges, expressions, or approaches to communication that essentially de-escalate conversations that are designed for escalation constitute a therapeutic response. Possessing the ability to respond therapeutically in the midst of a rapidly escalating, contentious conversation is crucial to resolving conflict and disrupting destructive patterns of communication. Responding therapeutically is *not* intended to imply responding like a therapist, whatever that might be. Instead it refers to expressing a series of noncombative, non-symmetrical, non-hierarchal responses that ultimately slows down a fast-paced interaction and paves the way for more healthy and progressive interactions.

9. **Developing proficiency in expressing thoughts and feelings and recognizing the difference between the two.** Effective interpersonal communication requires participants to openly, honestly, and congruently express relevant thoughts and feelings. Too much expression of one to the exclusion of the other can hijack a conversation. It is imperative that disclosures of feelings actually use "feeling words"; otherwise, they are disguised thoughts. For example, "I feel that you will say whatever you need to say to please me" is stated as a feeling but is really a thought. Alternatively, "I feel suspicious and anxious because I believe you will say whatever you need to say to please me" distinguishes between a thought and feelings.

10. **Allowing (emotional) space for reflection and contemplation.** This skill involves developing a level of comfort with gaps of silence in a conversation while remaining authentically connected to it. This skill is crucial because it affords both the speaker and listener an opportunity to be more thoughtful, reflective, and contemplative. When properly and effectively

implemented, it infuses "breathing room" into a conversation that prevents escalation by slowing down an interaction to a functional pace.

Developing good generic skills is a prerequisite to acquiring the more specialized ones that are critical for mastering context talk. The generic skills provide an important foundation for effective communication, but it is the skillful honing of the specialized skills that is more aptly suited for diversity-related conversations.

Specialized skills

Specialized skills are the communication competencies that are specifically germane to having meaningful and progressive conversations regarding the isms and the various dimensions of culture. Specialized skills are comprised of a mixture of conceptual and executive skills, both of which are critical for the effective execution of context talk. The following is a list and brief description of the various specialized skills that require proficiency.

1. **Develop a Multidimensional View of the Self.** In many ways the development of a Multidimensional View of the Self is one of the most significant of the specialized skills. The development of a Multidimensional View of the Self alters how we see ourselves and sensitizes us to the variety of ways in which others might see us. Instead of thinking about one's Self in a unidimensional way such as, "I am American" or "I am human," a more complex view of the Self emerges that takes into account the various cultural contexts in which we all are embedded. Thus, in addition to thinking about one's Self as "American" or "human," there is a heightened consciousness about other significant culturally based identities that comprise the Self. In this regard, one might also conclude that one's Self is also significantly defined by gender, class, race, religion, ethnicity, and so forth. The development and refinement of this skill helps us to appreciate that what we see, how we see ourselves, how we are seen, and how we believe we are seen are profoundly shaped by the cultural context in which we (and others) are embedded at any given moment. Another key factor associated with the development of this skill is the recognition that the multiple selves that we possess are either valued (privileged) or devalued (subjugated) in the broader society. The reader is referred back to Chapter 1 for a more detailed description of the "Privileged and Subjugated Selves."

2. **Know thy Selves**. Expanding the knowledge of our multiple Selves is another crucial conceptual skill. This task involves not only getting intimately acquainted with the various parts of our Selves that are shaped by the many dimensions of culture, but also with any emotional triggers that might be attached to them as well. As a result it becomes imperative to develop effective skills for identifying and managing emotional reactivity. Knowing when and how various dimensions of diversity trigger you is critical. It is equally important to know what one's behavioral tendencies are in the wake of being triggered. Effectively managing emotional triggers is often facilitated by the increased knowledge of (our) Self, combined with the use of the generic skills discussed in the previous session. The seamless integration of both sets of skills is needed to ensure maximal effectiveness in mastering context talk.

3. **Location of a Self.** The increased knowledge of one's Selves paves the way to better locate one's Self in a given relationship and conversation. It is important to be mindful of what dimension(s) of diversity is/are operating in a given conversation between two of more people. Being intentional and explicit about locating the relevant Self within the relationship and the conversation is crucial. For example, in a conversation about sexual orientation, it is vital to the conversation that I locate my heterosexual Self within the context of the conversation. By doing so I am highlighting and "notifying" the other participants that my views are shaped by

my heterosexual perspective. It may also help to provide an important piece of context to the conversation and relationship with the other participants.

4. **Perceiving, naming, and claiming the dimension**. Navigating effective context talk is often complicated, convoluted, and polluted by language and a reticence to name the issue. Context talk begins to break down when participants are reticent to clearly and overtly name the issue. Speaking in vague, nondescript generalities add an unnecessary element of ambiguity to the conversation. Naming the issue(s) helps to establish and maintain a sharper focus to the conversation. The skill that is involved here is first and foremost having the ability *to see* the contextual variables (Class, Religion, etc.) and then to "name" it, which means to be overt and explicit in labeling it, and finally claiming its relevancy to one's Self. This skill and the Location of Self are very closely aligned and reliant on each other.

5. **Speak from the location that is most germane to the (difficult) conversation at hand.** If a conversation is about religion, then speaking from that position is essential. Infusing ethnicity or some other contextual variable into a conversation about religion, for example, serves only to obscure the focus and lead to escalating conflict.

6. **Know and exercise, when appropriate, the tasks of the privilege.** Power and privilege can be misused, abused, or used responsibly. When it is used responsibly, those who have it willingly take greater responsibility for initiating context talk, and for ensuring that it is facilitative. Each of us has Privileged and Subjugated Selves. These Selves are fluid, and we can shift from one to the other as a conversation shifts. Thus having a keen knowledge of the tasks of the Privileged and Subjugated is essential for all. Having the ability to discern when which tasks are necessary and appropriate is an instrumental component of this skill.

The tasks of the Privileged

The tasks of the Privileged are applicable to any situation, circumstance, or identity where one holds a position of power and privilege that is superior to that of those with whom one currently shares a relationship. The tasks are systemic and thus gain considerable potency and poignancy from their confluence. The tasks of the Privileged are as follows:

1. **Differentiate between intentions and consequences and always start with an acknowledgment of the latter.** It is common for those in the Privileged Position to attempt to focus context talk around their "good intentions" rather than on the consequences of their (unintended but deleterious) actions regarding those in a Subjugated Position. Regardless of how misunderstood or personally attacked one in the Privileged Position might feel, it is important that the sentiments (consequences) expressed by the Subjugated are responded to with tenacity, authenticity, and congruency prior to *any* attempt to clarify, restate, or expand regarding "intentionality."

2. **Avoid the overt and covert negation of subjugated conversations and disclosures.** Conversations and disclosures that negate the views of the Subjugated are never intended to do so, yet they do and seldom inconsequentially. In conversations where the Privileged and Subjugated have obvious differences in perceptions and experiences, it is often difficult from the Privileged Position to embrace, entertain, or authentically hold the position of the Subjugated without dismissing, correcting, reinterpreting, or attempting to expand their worldview by "teaching" them. All of these seemingly benign, innocent, and benevolent acts are tools of negation. The process of negation is a rather complex and sophisticated one. It is relatively easy to negate the opinions of (Subjugated) others without the awareness that it has happened.

3. **Avoid the issuance of prescriptions.** *The issuance of prescriptions* refers to a seemingly benign but often explosive dynamic that involves the person or group in the Privileged Position

offering what is believed to be value-free, "objective," and benevolent advice to the Subjugated regarding their well-being. The underlying implication of the prescription issuance is that the person or group in the Privileged Position knows the needs of the Subjugated better than they do themselves. This dynamic reinforces extant broader societal messages regarding superiority/ inferiority and who is intelligent and who isn't. Although it clearly may not be the "intention" of the Privileged to reify such polarizing and devaluing messages, the "consequence" is almost always to the contrary.

4. **Develop thick skin.** As noted earlier, Context Talk, when fully it is engaged, can be very emotionally charged and difficult at best. The temptation for all participants to retreat from the conversation is often enormous and hard to resist. While *all* participants have a responsibility to work assiduously to prevent escalation and to stay in the conversation, the participant in the Privileged Position has the greatest responsibility. This belief is based on the old adage that "to whom much is given, much is expected" (Bill Gates, Bible Source, 2007). The operating premise here is that participants cannot genuinely have equal responsibility in a relationship when they don't share equal power and privilege. Thus, the responsible use of power and privilege requires the Privileged to assume a greater responsibility *to the relationship.* In this regard it becomes incumbent for the Privileged to develop "thick skin," which is demonstrating the ability and internal fortitude to *stay in* difficult conversations even beyond the point where it feels comfortable to do so. The development of thick skin builds over time and is strengthened by the continued immersion into challenging conversations centered on Context Talk.

5. **Distinguish between safety and comfort.** "Not feeling safe" is one of the principal reasons often cited by those in the Privileged Position for quickly retreating from a difficult conversation involving Context Talk. The lack of feeling safe is usually a by-product of being challenged, the presence of emotional intensity, not feeling unconditionally accepted, not having the power to guide what happens next, and so on. While all of these conditions create an environment of considerable intensity and discomfort, safety usually isn't at stake. The compromise of one's safety would suggest that there is an imminent threat for harm to be inflicted to someone emotionally, psychologically, and/or physically. Comfort, on the other hand, speaks to the sense of ease and relaxation that one might experience. Context Talk is uncomfortable. When seriously undertaken, it stretches most of us well beyond our normal comfort zones. The development of thick skin facilitates the process of distinguishing between comfort and safety much more easily. It is also true that more clearly distinguishing between comfort and safety facilitates the development of thick skin. With regards to Context Talk, everyone is entitled to safety and *no one*, especially one in the Privileged Position, is entitled to comfort.

6. **Know and exercise, when appropriate, the tasks of the Subjugated.** Since both the Privileged and Subjugated Positions are fluid and either can be occupied depending on the conversation, it is important for us to know which position we are in as well as the tasks associated with it. The following is a list of tasks that must be performed when in the Subjugated Position.

The tasks of the Subjugated

1. **Overcome learned voicelessness.** Whether attributable to race, class, gender, sexual orientation, or some other dimension of diversity, voicelessness is a normal and predictable outcome of being placed in a subjugated position. Voicelessness is a learned and adaptive response to domination and subjugation. When interacting with the Privileged, the "voice" of the Subjugated often gets marginalized, dismissed, even muted altogether. Expecting not to be authentically acknowledged or validated, the Subjugated "learn" the futility of attempting to speak fully, openly, and honestly when interacting with the Privileged. Hence, silence and learned voicelessness become a common adaptive strategy for the Subjugated when attempting to converse

with the Privileged. While this well-polished coping strategy serves a viable function, it is simultaneously maladaptive and perpetuates the status quo. It helps to create a zone of safety and comfort for the Privileged at the expense of the Subjugated while eliminating virtually all possibilities for meaningful and progressive conversations. Overcoming learned voicelessness requires the Subjugated to rely on intimacy, intensity, authenticity, transparency, and congruency to regain and utilize one's voice. It is important to note that exercising one's voice is not ultimately about being "heard" by the Privileged but instead about self-advocacy and empowerment for the Subjugated. Meaningful and progressive context talk cannot be properly executed when one party can't or won't listen and the other can't or refuses to speak.

2. **Regulate rage and other strong emotions.** There is a symbiotic-type relationship that exists between voicelessness and rage. The more one's voice is suppressed, the greater the degree of rage experienced. In fact, rage is the by-product of unexpressed emotions that build up over time due to voicelessness. When rage is eventually expressed, it is generally done so inappropriately and/or in (self) destructive ways. A key specialized task of the Subjugated is to develop strategies for managing and regulating rage. When rage is not suitably regulated, it tends to get expressed in precipitous, attacking, and damaging ways. The pathway to rage regulation requires the following: 1) distinguishing between anger (an immediate episodic emotion) and rage (a primitive emotion tied to degradation) (Hardy, 2016); 2) acknowledging/validating the existence of rage; 3) understanding the underlying hurt that is often disguised by rage; and 4) owning and naming both rage and hurt as a preface to expressing rage. The following vignette provides a wonderful illustration of a rage-regulated response:

The case of affirmative action in action

Heather, a White 32-year-old supervisee, stated in group supervision: "I know this is very small-minded and prejudicial of me, but I have this terrible habit of thinking whenever I see professional black people that they got to where they are because of affirmative action." Before she could finish her statement, I noticed that Sylvia, an African American supervisee, was immediately triggered. Instead of responding instantaneously and reactively to Heather as she might have done a year ago, she instead sat still, obviously attempting to relax and center herself. After a few seconds, Sylvia turned to Heather and stated firmly, respectfully, and with a stream of tears, "I want to thank you for your honesty even though what you said *really* hurt, it *really* hurt me because of how hard I know I have worked to get to this place and *yes*, I am pissed…furious…that you would think such a thing. Your comment and belief about black people is what makes it hard for me to trust white people."

Sylvia used the opportunity to embrace and express both her rage and hurt. She expressed her feelings in a way that allowed for a more meaningful, albeit difficult, conversation to take place. More importantly, the extensive effort that she had devoted to understanding and regulating her rage throughout the year was noticeable.

3. **De-center "the Privileged."** The Privileged play a central role in the life of the Subjugated. How the Subjugated is perceived by the Privileged is a major organizing principle for the former. It is standard protocol for the Subjugated to know and understand what is important to the Privileged. However, the reverse is generally not true. Moreover, whatever is important to the Privileged must de facto be important to the Subjugated. The survival of the Subjugated is predicated on knowing and understanding what is important to the Privileged. This dynamic

is one of the many privileges of privilege: possessing the power and privilege to define/shape others' experiences. If the Subjugated is to earnestly and honestly participate in progressive context talk, a de-centering of the Privileged is vital. As long as the Subjugated is preoccupied with receiving the approval of the Privileged or how one will be perceived, honest and authentic conversation will be virtually impossible. In the previous vignette, Sylvia was hurt and devastated by Heather's Affirmative Action comment because at some level, "whiteness" (the Privileged) was still at least partially central in her life. If it were not, it is questionable whether Heather's perception of black people would have penetrated and hurt Sylvia so deeply. On the other hand, the fact that Sylvia did acknowledge and express her rage was an excellent sign. It demonstrated that "whiteness," to some extent, has been de-centered in her life because she was no longer concerned about how the expression of her rage would be framed or perceived by Heather. To successfully master this task, not only does the Privileged have to be de-centered, but the positioning of the Subjugated also has to be realigned from "margin to center" (hooks, 2001).

4. **Engage in a process of exhaling.** There are many negative and toxic messages that are systematically promulgated by the Privileged about the Subjugated. Many of these messages are transmitted in the form of stereotypes and innuendo. Unfortunately, many of these same messages become firmly etched within the psyche of the Subjugated even when they are overtly repudiated. These internalized messages are often a major obstacle to the Subjugated fully participating in Context Talk. If one has internalized a toxic dominant contextual narrative such as one is "not smart enough," "too emotional," "too angry," or "too anxious," it can be difficult to block these messages out during the midst of an intense conversation even if/when they have been overtly rejected by the Subjugated. Furthermore, there is always the worry that even though the messages have been rejected by the Subjugated, they may not have been by the Privileged. As in the case of Heather and Sylvia, how the Privileged views the Subjugated tends to matter. The process of exhaling involves a three-step process: 1) identification, validation, and repudiation of all toxic and debilitating internalized messages; 2) de-centering the Privileged; and 3) Speaking Up! When these steps are accomplished, the internalized messages lose their power to sabotage the voice and self-empowerment of the Subjugated.

5. **Use the VCR Approach efficiently.** The VCR Approach (Hardy and Laszloffy, 2002) is a strengths-based model for conducting and sustaining difficult conversations. According to Hardy and Laszloffy (2002), the VCR approach is both a worldview and a strategy. As a worldview it is based on the belief that all behavior and ultimately all human beings possess redeemable parts that can be observed if we simply look for them. The aspect of the approach that constitutes a strategy centers on the ability to effectively validate, challenge, and make relevant requests. The core principles associated with the VCR Approach are 1) all verbal exchanges should commence with a Validating response; 2) Validation is not synonymous with agreement; 3) Validation must always precede a challenging comment; 4) the behavior/trait that is being **V**alidated should also be the focal point of the **C**hallenge message as well as the **R**equest message; and 5) since the VCR promotes *both/and thinking*, the word "*and*" should always be used to replace the word "*but*." No matter how volatile the comment, the initial response of the recipient must begin with a validating comment. If we return to the conversation between Heather and Sylvia regarding blacks and Affirmative Action, if Sylvia were skilled in using the VCR she would have stated the following:

Validation: "Heather, I really appreciate your honesty and openness in sharing your unwanted thoughts about blacks and Affirmative Action with me."

Challenge: "And on the other hand, I felt really hurt by your comment, *really* hurt *and* I was pissed really pissed because it wasn't clear to me that you thought about how hurtful your honest comment might be to me as the only black person in our group."

Request: So I want you to continue to be honest and open with me about all of your private racial beliefs—both good and bad—*and* I would love for you to take a few minutes to think about how I, as the only black in the group, might feel in the process. Can you continue to be honest and open with me *and* think about me as well?"

Sylvia's feedback to Heather starts with a Validation and stays focused on the same theme through the *V*, *C*, and the *R*. Sylvia obviously strongly disagreed with Heather's assertion about blacks and Affirmative Action, yet it should not deter her from validating Heather from the outset of the interaction.

The VCR is a very useful tool for de-escalating conflict, promoting intimacy in conversations, and confronting difficult behavior in a humane and respectful manner.

6. **Disclose the motivation for participating and engaging in Context Talk**. It is important to be transparent about the motivation for participating in Context Talk because it helps to set the tone for the ensuing conversation. This is another form of location of Self. It conveys to all involved parties the level of significance that is/will be attached to the conversation and what one's level of investment is in both the conversation and the outcome.
7. **Explore and disclose what your desired outcome is for the conversation.** It is often difficult if not impossible to reach consensus, establish a positive outcome, or have a progressive conversation regarding contentious, intense, diversity-related conversations when the desired outcome has neither been overtly discussed, acknowledged, or negotiated. The type of disclosure that is recommended here and in point 9 above requires adeptness in the five generic skills of intimacy, intensity, authenticity, transparency, and congruency. An attempted conversation about motivations and outcomes void of the aforementioned attributes will undoubtedly unravel quickly.

Both in and outside of therapy, we have reached a critical juncture in our society where having the ability to engage in meaningful conversations across an ever-widening *gulf of divide* is no longer an area of casual interest but an ethical imperative. The next generation of clinicians and those of us who supervise them must be ready to meet the challenge of a rapidly changing demographic where the discovery of common ground is increasingly elusive. Fortunately, there is tremendous healing and transformative potential in dialogue and conversation, especially when we can engage in it thoughtfully and respectfully. As the hues of our society continue to shift, the definition of marriage and gender become more fluid, the income gap between the rich and poor broadens, and the borders of the United States are traversed from virtually every corner, our need to understand and be in relationship with the so-called *other* is not just a way of life but a necessity of life. Having the ability to communicate effectively and master context talk is not just a mere matter of clinical convenience but a life skill.

Summary

This chapter has outlined a series of generic and specialized skills necessary for altering the course of our much-maligned efforts to have meaningful and progressive conversations about the various dimensions of diversity. The term "Context Talk" was introduced as an all-encompassing reference to any dialogue or conversation that has any dimension of diversity at its focal point. A major premise of mastering Context Talk is based on the notion that power and privilege are exceedingly influential forces dictating the course of the conversation and must be deliberately taken into consideration. Accordingly, it is argued that there are certain prescribed tasks that participants should adhere to, based on the relative privilege or subjugation that has been assigned to the dimension of diversity that is central to their conversation.

References

Bateson, G. (1972). *Steps to an ecology of mind*. Chicago, IL: University of Chicago Press.

Gates, B. (2007). Graduation speech to Harvard University graduates. www.onphilanthropy.com (accessed March 24, 2016).

Hardy, K. V. (2016). Anti-racist approaches for shaping theoretical and practice paradigms. In A. J. Carten, M. Pender-Greene, & A. Siskin (Eds.), *Anti-racist strategies for the health and human services* (pp. 189–211). Oxford, UK: Oxford University Press.

Hardy, K. V., & Laszloffy, T. A. (2002). Couple therapy using a multicultural perspective. In A. S. Gurman & N. S. Jacobson (Eds.), *Clinical handbook of couple therapy* (3rd ed.) (pp. 569–593). New York, NY: HarperCollins.

hooks, b. (2001) *All about love*. New York, NY: HarperCollins.

INDEX